Julian of Norwich and the Ecological Crisis

This book presents ecological insights drawn from a reading of Julian of Norwich, considering how effectively she can help us in our current plight. The argument is that to address the ecological crisis with the mindset that created it will only cause more problems, and that to really undo the harm humanity has done and continues to do will take a transformation of selfhood and hence of perception, from the *Gestell*, technological self that is the child of the Enlightenment to the porous self that we truly are, underneath our buffered, separated, controlling and lonely exterior. The author suggests Julian of Norwich's text *Revelations of Divine Love* has the power to effect this transformation if we can learn to read it as disciples, not masters, just as Julian received and responded to her revelations as a performative, porous, receptive disciple. The chapters describe the technological mindset and its causal relationship with the ecological crisis, and articulate in detail how, if they are to transform us, we must read the Julian texts, taking first steps away from our technological selves as we do so. The book then takes significant passages from Julian and reads them in the performative, porous way that has been recommended. It will be of particular interest to scholars of theology and ecology, as well as medieval mysticism.

Claire Gilbert is an author and visiting fellow of Jesus College, Cambridge. She is founder of Westminster Abbey Institute.

Routledge Science and Religion Series
Series editors:
Michael S. Burdett, University of Nottingham, UK
Mark Harris, University of Edinburgh, UK

Science and religion have often been thought to be at loggerheads but much contemporary work in this flourishing interdisciplinary field suggests this is far from the case. The Science and Religion Series presents exciting new work to advance interdisciplinary study, research and debate across key themes in science and religion. Contemporary issues in philosophy and theology are debated, as are prevailing cultural assumptions. The series enables leading international authors from a range of different disciplinary perspectives to apply the insights of the various sciences, theology, philosophy and history in order to look at the relations between the different disciplines and the connections that can be made between them. These accessible, stimulating new contributions to key topics across science and religion will appeal particularly to individual academics and researchers, graduates, postgraduates and upper-undergraduate students.

Conjunctive Explanations in Science and Religion
*edited by Diarmid A. Finnegan, David H. Glass,
Mikael Leidenhag and David N. Livingstone*

**The Philosophical and Theological Relevance of
Evolutionary Anthropology**
Engagements with Michael Tomasello
Edited by Martin Breul and Caroline Helmus

God and the Book of Nature
Experiments in Theology of Science
Edited by Mark Harris

Julian of Norwich and the Ecological Crisis
Restoring Porosity
Claire Gilbert

For more information and a full list of titles in the series, please visit: https://www.routledge.com/religion/series/ASCIREL

Julian of Norwich and the Ecological Crisis
Restoring Porosity

Claire Gilbert

LONDON AND NEW YORK

First published 2025
by Routledge
4 Park Square, Milton Park, Abingdon, Oxon OX14 4RN

and by Routledge
605 Third Avenue, New York, NY 10158

Routledge is an imprint of the Taylor & Francis Group, an informa business

© 2025 Claire Gilbert

The right of Claire Gilbert to be identified as author of this work has been asserted in accordance with sections 77 and 78 of the Copyright, Designs and Patents Act 1988.

All rights reserved. No part of this book may be reprinted or reproduced or utilised in any form or by any electronic, mechanical, or other means, now known or hereafter invented, including photocopying and recording, or in any information storage or retrieval system, without permission in writing from the publishers.

Trademark notice: Product or corporate names may be trademarks or registered trademarks, and are used only for identification and explanation without intent to infringe.

British Library Cataloguing-in-Publication Data
A catalogue record for this book is available from the British Library

ISBN: 9781032593340 (hbk)
ISBN: 9781032623931 (pbk)
ISBN: 9781032623948 (ebk)

DOI: 10.4324/9781032623948

Typeset in Sabon
by KnowledgeWorks Global Ltd.

Contents

Acknowledgements vi

Introduction 1

1 Defining the Ecological Challenge as Our Buffered, *Gestell* Subjectivity 8

2 Developing a Post-Ricoeurian Hermeneutical Approach 29

3 Julian's Wounds 60

4 The Eighth Revelation 96

5 The Fourteenth Revelation 128

Conclusion: Julian's Porosity as a Basis for a New Ecological Niche 152

Appendix: Addressing the Historical and Manuscript Challenges of Julian of Norwich: A Case for My Methodological Approach 161
Bibliography 171
Index 179

Acknowledgements

Sincere thanks are due to

Michael Burdett, Ellen Davies, Oliver Davies, R Yuga Harini, Mark Harris, Joy Hillyer, Hannah Lucas, Seán Moore, Katherine Ong, Kavitha Sathish, Lydia Schumacher, Nicholas Watson and Vernon White.

Introduction

This book seeks to answer the question: can the Julian of Norwich texts be read today in such a way that they can help address the 21st-century ecological crisis? I argue that they can. They do so by transforming our 'buffered' subjectivity into the 'porous' subjectivity Julian brought to and learnt from her revelations. The question and its answer are predicated upon an argument that the human destruction of habitat is a symptom of a subjectivity that is *Gestell*, a 'buffered' seeing of all of nature and ultimately itself as objective, functional and expendable. For our destructive behaviour towards the planet to change, the subjectivity of humanity has to change and become 'porous'. I develop a hermeneutical approach to reading the Julian texts, which emphasises the porous nature of the interaction of the Julian of the text with her revelations, and the reader's porous interaction with the text, arguing that porosity is an originary state to which the reader can be restored, rather than a new state as such. I then study extracts from the Julian texts using the hermeneutical approach I have developed. Through this means, I uncover the text's power to communicate the immediacy of Julian's experience, effecting a responsive, subjectivity-changing porosity in her readers. With restored porosity comes the possibility of an attitude of relationality and interdependence with nature, giving hope for the changed behaviour towards it that is needed now. Some observations about the implications of a Julian-effected porosity for our attitude and behaviour towards nature are explored at the close of each of the chapters that study the Julian texts and in the conclusion. Thus, although my argument draws upon philosophy and modern inter-disciplinary science, I maintain a theological register throughout, which is focussed (and limited) by Julian's theology.

Before diving into a close reading of the Julian texts, then, two tasks have to be undertaken. The first is to substantiate my claim that the *Gestell* self is the cause of the ecological crisis. The second is to develop the hermeneutical approach that will unlock Julian's potential to address this cause. I begin the first task by describing *Gestell*, as defined by Martin Heidegger, as a mindset that sees everything as an object able to be critiqued, manipulated and controlled by the transcendent subject, and who ends up treating the subject itself in the same way. This diagnosis of *Gestell* subjectivity is supported by

2 Introduction

Hannah Arendt, who describes human beings as having become *homo faber*, we who make rather than discover truth, and who find ourselves caught up in a world where everything, including us, has become process without end. I also draw upon others who have given a similar account, including Pope Francis who writes about the technological paradigm, which has humanity treating the other, nature or person, as an adversarial object with whom one has to enter into a contractual, not a loving or trusting, relationship, and Iain McGilchrist who identifies the objectifying, organising self with the left brain hemisphere. He and Martin Buber, who calls this persona *It* as opposed to *Thou*, see that the less definable right brain or *Thou* is easily eclipsed by the organising left brain or *It*, *homo faber*, *Gestell*, who cannot appreciate the softer, non-adversarial *Thou*. I also explore Charles Taylor's historical account of a similar turn: the medieval 'porous' self who has been imprisoned by a 'buffered' self over the period between the 16th and the 21st centuries, finding its supreme expression in Descartes' *cogito* self.

I then show how the ecological harm that is being done by humanity can be understood as an expression, often with the best of intentions, of *Gestell* subjectivity, looking at each of the spheres of the planet – atmosphere, hydrosphere, lithosphere, pedosphere and biosphere – in turn. For example, harm to the pedosphere is caused by farming that sees the land as a means of production, stripping it of its natural ecological richness by forcing a pace and rate of agrarian production its natural state cannot sustain. Harm to the atmosphere takes place by treating it like a gigantic aerial dustbin for greenhouse gases to the point where it is unable to process them naturally, not least because of a pedosphere denuded of trees. These are examples of humanity forcing nature to operate at our speeded-up pace to meet our ever-growing demand, without noticing what nature needs for its own survival and flourishing. These intrinsic needs are not relevant to the *Gestell* mindset because they are not, in any obvious way, needed by humanity. But *Gestell* is infectious: as it treats nature, it ends up treating other humans, who become valuable only insofar as they are useful to the project of production itself. Everything becomes a means, not an end.

I explore how solutions, which are in common currency today, arise from a *Gestell* mindset, such as utilitarianly calculated technological solutions, drastically reducing population size or creating an artificial world that does not depend on Earth's[1] ecological health. Such solutions, which have an internal logic and force, nevertheless do not work. They resemble earlier solutions to other problems, such as feeding a rapidly growing population by invasive and damaging agri-techniques or ridding an area of pests – solutions whose unforeseen and unintended consequences caused yet more problems. Even attractive solutions that turn to renewable energy sources are flawed if they seek to reduce the wind or the sun to 'standing reserve', likely to precipitate further unintended harm to nature. The mindset itself, I suggest, with Heidegger, has to change so that humanity's way of being with and in the world does not have to play catch-up with processes set in motion by *Gestell* perceptions of problems and their solutions, however well-intentioned. The stresses on the planet have reached such a level that we no longer have time for such expensive mistakes.

Having defined the ecological challenge as the need to change human subjectivity by escaping from its enslavement to *Gestell*, I argue, as Heidegger does not, that what is needed is a restored porosity of selfhood. Humanity has to cease its arrogant attitude of control and return to an attitude of service, an intentional porosity that is characterised by humility. Heidegger writes of salvation from *Gestell* by means of a phenomenological process of returning to the Being that exists at the point where the *Gestell* mindset arises. But this Being of beings is an ahistorical and transcendent subject, resembling Descartes' *cogito* self, which, by Descartes' own account, thinks it is able to arrogate the powers of nature to itself, not a relational and porous self that knows its dependence upon others. Heidegger's solution implies that a transcendent being, having freed itself, is then able to 'choose' a different subjectivity from *Gestell*; as if nature, in this case human nature, were still apparently at its command. Paul Ricoeur, in critiquing phenomenology with hermeneutics, undermines the *cogito* self itself by acknowledging the fallibility of the reader, who is summoned and changed by poetic texts in particular. Oliver Davies argues that medieval mystical texts like Julian's have the capacity to effect a change in the subjectivity of the reading self through their power to communicate the transformation of the original encounter, which in Julian's case was with her revelations. For Julian, as I will argue, it is the 'intimately communicated', to use Davies' term, porosity she brings to and learns from her revelations that is of particular importance to my argument. My definition of 'porosity' has begun at this point.

Turning to the Julian texts requires that some significant manuscript challenges be addressed. There is no conclusive evidence that links the extant manuscripts, which all post-date Julian, with the 14th–15th century Julian of Norwich, whom we know existed from independent historical evidence of bequests and a meeting described by her contemporary Margery Kempe. Moreover, the manuscripts have numerous, if minor, disagreements with each other. The ground has to be cleared of these challenges, and, as this is familiar territory to many Julian scholars, I have placed the discussion in an appendix. I have retained it for reference because it helps make the case for my approach to reading the Julian texts. I use the uncertainty about the historical Julian as a reason to confine my analysis to the text itself and not draw conclusions that depend upon the Julian of the text being identified with the Julian of history.

The case made in the Appendix explains why the base text we are going to read will be Bibliothèque Nationale MS Fonds anglais 40, known as 'Paris', as published by Colledge and Walsh in 1978 (page references will come from there, as ST or LT, giving the page numbers and lines on the page). Colledge and Walsh's edition show alternate readings from Sloane (British Library MS Sloane 2499 and British Library MS Sloane 3705), Westminster (Westminster

Cathedral Treasury MS 4 fols. 72-112), Cressy (1670) and Upholland (a 17th-century manuscript including extracts from the Julian texts), so if there are important differences, we can look at them, but for the most part, they do not change the force of our understanding: the transformative power of the text is as present in Paris as it is in Sloane, so we will not disappear down a scholarly rabbit hole of pedantry to show small changes. Most of the readings come from the Long Text; there are also readings from the Short Text but no conclusions will be drawn that depend upon their chronological order.

My hermeneutical approach is then developed by taking important principles from Paul Ricoeur and building on them. Ricoeur's argument for the independence of the text from its author, original audience and original setting is the basis upon which I can read the text as I have received it, without having to discern the intentions of its original, unknown author. It frees me to attend to the Julian of the text, who mediates by example and language the remarkable subjectivity-changing experience of her revelations. I adopt Ricoeur's notion of the hermeneut being *in medias res*, in a long line of interpreters, without the last word, and in this role, I take advice from Ben Quash to bring, intentionally, my own question from my own time to the text, in this case my question of how to escape from the mindset that is harming the planet. I accept Ricoeur's concept of the power of the poetic text to transform the reader's subjectivity and his account of the summoning of the reader to the text.

Ricoeur's insights thus establish readers as selves summoned to an independent poetic text that will change us. On this stable foundation, I build a three-pillared hermeneutical structure, which emphasises the transformative effect of the encounter of the reader with the text. I use examples from the Julian texts to illustrate the approach and as an initial demonstration of its ability to unlock their transformative effect on the reader. The first part of the structure is the understanding that making sense of a text involves 'performative engagement' with it. To help explain what I mean, I draw upon the insights of the enactivists, an interdisciplinary group of scientists and philosophers influenced by phenomenology, who articulate through their research the way in which, in order to make sense, subjects have to enter into relationships with that which they are trying to understand, not just view it from a distance. They have to step forwards and enter the frame, reaching through the text to what lies beyond it and enacting it in real time. This performative engagement offers an adequate account of how Julian responds to her revelations and also establishes the 'summoned' attitude readers must embody as we approach the text. The enactment of performative meaning-making also both requires and brings about porosity of self. 'Porosity of encounter' is the second pillar built on Ricoeurian foundations, already implied by Ricoeur's summoned self. Performatively reading a text like Julian's, in which Julian is herself porously and performatively responding to her revelations, both demands porosity from her readers and also brings porosity about. It is this above all that is Julian's gift to our 21st century subjectivity: through the communicative power of her language, she can spring the trap of *Gestell* enslavement by wounding our *cogito* selves and making us porous again. I define 'porosity' more fully at this point, therefore. The porosity to which Julian can restore us is both ancient: indicated by Taylor in his historical account of the porous medieval self that is prior to the post-Reformation and Enlightenment buffered self, and it is also originary: deep within us, indicated by enactivist neuroscientists Leonard Schilbach and colleagues, who detect a 'dark', pre-linguistic relationality in the human brain.

The third pillar of the post-Ricoeurian triad identifies the world that is brought to the text by the subjectivity of the reading selves, and also the world that is created by our changed subjectivity; these I call 'niches' in recognition of their significance as homes, habitats, and the promise that if a changed subjectivity will lead to a different world, then our restored porous subjectivity will make possible a world in which we can live interdependently and relationally in alignment with nature and the planet, not adversarially and harmfully.

With the foregoing, necessary preparatory work completed, I bring the three-pillared, post-Ricoeurian hermeneutical approach to the Julian texts, seeking to demonstrate their ability to communicate and bring about porosity (thereby further defined in practice) in the reader. I first look at passages that relate to the three wounds for which she asked in her early life: 'contricion' (contrition), compassion and a longing to God. Under the heading of the wound of 'contrition' I look at Julian's own subjectivity and the way in which she refuses any label for herself. Insisting that the revelations she receives are not for her alone but for all, she calls on the reader to attend not to her but to the revelations. Her subjectivity is thus established as porous from the start, but she is not invisible; it is *her* way of porously and performatively interacting with her revelations that is such a powerful example for her readers. I look at Julian's loyalty to 'holy chyrch', the one fixed aspect of her subjectivity that she does not surrender, and show how her determined retention of its teaching alongside incompatible revelations brings about a porosity of the holy church itself without any intention of heresy. I also study Julian's sustained porous attitude of 'reuerente drede', which ensures a continuous openness to the subjectivity-changing surprises and paradoxes of the revelations. Under the heading of the wound of 'compassion' I look again at Julian's porous subjectivity, this time in relation to the people in her sickroom who play critical roles in the unfolding of her revelations and who become representative of all Julian's 'evyn cristen' (fellow Christians). I look at Julian's identity with her 'evyn cristen' and show how even this category is porous so that it becomes difficult to confine it to just one group of people; ultimately, Julian is identified as everyman. The niche of her revelations itself is also porous, as it expands to include all creation, heaven and hell. Under the heading of her wound of 'longing to God', I study the recurring use of vocabulary related to 'seeing' and 'looking' as the porous means to understanding and coming closer to God. I also study Julian's transformative account of prayer as 'beseeching' and 'beseking'. From these studies, I draw some concluding indications of how, freed by Julian from *Gestell* and restored to porosity, our subjectivity might then express a new 'wounded' ecological consciousness.

Next, I study the eighth revelation narratively, highlighting the profound porosity of Julian to Christ in her encounter with him at the time of his Passion. The encounter is so close that Julian herself suffers the pains of the Passion, which go beyond anything she could have imagined or that she had experienced before. Her porous and performative encounter with pain means that as she understands that the pain is born of love, so love infuses the niche of the Passion revelation, and these two, in turn, are transformed by, but do not disappear into, the joy of the Resurrection, which Julian also experiences as taking place on the Cross itself, of the same bloody, tortured body of Christ. At the end of this study, I draw out some observations of an ecological consciousness emerging from the porosity Julian embodied in her identification with the Passion: one that will identify with the suffering of the Earth and give birth to greater love and service, not defensive fear.

Finally, I look at the 14th revelation, a metaphorical account of the fall of Adam and its identity with the Incarnation as Christ 'falls' into Mary's womb. The revelation enacts this identity through the character of a servant, who, as both Adam and Christ, shows none of the expected aspects of a fallen man: he is not disobedient, he is not proud, and he never stops loving his lord, who brings about his fall by sending him on a mission he is only too eager to fulfil. The pain and loss of the fall are due to the literal falling of the servant, as he runs in his eagerness to do the will of the lord, which leaves his body sore and bruised and his head turned in such a way that he cannot see the lord anymore, and in particular cannot see that the lord continues to hold a steadfast loving gaze upon him. This paradoxical account is so 'marvellous' to Julian that she returns to it again and again over many years, her method being to look ever more closely at the details of the revelation. It is her performative interaction with the detail that draws her, and her reader, porously into the story as a means to awaken to the meaning of that which seems to make no sense. The detail is inspected and re-inspected until she and her readers experience transformed understanding and hence subjectivity: if we, as Adam or everyman, are being enacted by the character of the servant, then we are also enclosed in Christ's porous subjectivity, and we are thereby included in the Trinity's porous subjectivity. Ecological consciousness that emerges from the porosity of the 14th revelation sees the gifts of the Earth as the face of Christ expressing God's love; the tilling and keeping of the Earth as a porous participation in the salvific work of the Incarnation; and the desecration of the Earth as a denial of the Incarnation.

I conclude that the Julian texts are indeed capable of helping the 21st-century challenge of the ecological crisis by addressing its cause: that of a *Gestell* mindset only capable of seeing the other as a utilitarian standing reserve. Julian can release her readers from captivity to *Gestell* by restoring our porosity. Such porosity brings about a new world or niche in which the Earth is no longer an object to be used but a performative participant with intrinsic value, porous interaction with which brings about learning from it, tuning into it, and living non-harmfully within it. My conclusion acknowledges that choosing the Julian texts as a route to freedom from enslavement engenders a recognition of the sacred in creation.

Note

1 Following Flannery (2007), I capitalise Earth to equate it with other planets who enjoy initial capitals: Mars, Venus, etc.

1 Defining the Ecological Challenge as Our Buffered, *Gestell* Subjectivity

Introduction

In order to help address the damage that is being done to the planet, humanity has first to address its own 'damaged' subjectivity. That is to say, our behaviour will change to avoid harm to the planet when our subjectivity changes, and not otherwise. It is our subjectivity that makes us see the world as something to be exploited; it follows that if our subjectivity were to change we would no longer see the world that way, and our behaviour would change. To help explain what I mean, I will use Martin Heidegger's account of human subjectivity's enslavement to a perspective he calls *Gestell*, 'enframed', the 'essence of technology'. Heidegger's arguments resonate with a number of other philosophers and theologians who see that humanity is entrapped by a technological mindset that brings about harmful behaviour and, worse still, prevents the possibility of seeing other perspectives out of which different behaviour might emerge. That is the task of the first part of this chapter: to demonstrate our enslavement. In the following sections, I will explore examples of how *Gestell* subjectivity harms the planet and of current, unsatisfactory *Gestell* solutions to the harm. I will end in agreement with Heidegger's diagnosis of the problem, but not with his solution, which leaves our selfhood intact, 'transcendent'. I will propose in its place a hermeneutical approach, which draws and builds upon Paul Ricoeur's insight: that poetic texts have the power to summon and change the (only apparently) transcendent self. The Julian of Norwich texts are such poetic texts. Herein lies our salvation.

Enslaved to Heidegger's *Gestell* subjectivity

Martin Heidegger argues that humanity is threatened not by technology itself, but by its 'essence', which makes us see both the world and ourselves as *Gestell*, 'enframed'. *Gestell* brings about a way of thinking that renders everything, including humanity, as utilitarian 'standing reserve', affecting the way we behave towards each other and towards the planet. There is no escape from *Gestell* subjectivity, argues Heidegger, unless we can return to the place from which it springs and see there are other ways of being and thinking.

Heidegger explores *Gestell* in his essay 'The Question Concerning Technology' (1949/1977), which is part two of a four-part lecture series he delivered in Bremen in 1949 (1949/2012). We should note in passing that Heidegger famously and notoriously was seen as an intellectual leader within Nazism (eg Blitz 2014 p 66). This is Heidegger's first public address after the Second World War, raising the question of whether the lectures represent an attempt to understand how he came to hold in himself such morally outrageous views. The essay proposes that the danger of technology is not the lethal weaponry it can produce but the way it makes man[1] look at the world and himself. This is *Gestell*, or 'the essence of technology'.

Gestell is hard to translate; in the version I use Lovitt calls it 'enframed'; others have called it 'positionality'. Neither term quite does justice to the concept, as Blitz has observed (2014 p 73), and so I am going to retain the word *Gestell*. *Gestell* subjectivity determines not just a framework for seeing but also an inner core: a bookcase and also a skeleton, as Heidegger puts it. He says that, like a mountain chain that unfolds the mountains into mountain ranges, *Gestell* is a disposition that unfolds the way we have feelings (1949/1977 p 9). It thus has an all-enveloping effect, both as a concept that determines selfhood and as a way of seeing and making sense of the world. We are prone, mistakenly, to look at technology as the cause of our problems, or the solution to our problems, or as a neutral force to be used by us for good or ill. All these perspectives are wrong, argues Heidegger, because they flow from the technological way of thinking that sits behind the technology that we see, which has turned all of nature and ultimately ourselves into things to be used. The 'things to be used' are in 'standing reserve', so everything is either being used or waiting to be used. Thus *Gestell* is to be understood as the 'enframing that sets everything in standing reserve'. Nothing and no one is there for it in its own intrinsic value and existence. Like the interchangeable parts of a machine, nature and humanity have become interchangeable parts to be used or discarded in the same way. We see nature as enframed, but we ourselves are also enframed.

Heidegger regards *Gestell* as beginning its 'reign' when modern natural science was born. But it was not brought to birth by modern science, he says, rather it was *Gestell* that determined the birth. The question might reasonably be asked, What then did give rise to the *Gestell* perspective? Heidegger does not answer the question but others seek to, as I will briefly explore. They do not agree with each other! For Heidegger, the *Gestell* perspective was in place before the eighteenth century when natural science became a recognised discipline and modern technology began significantly to change the landscape. *Gestell* subjectivity was what challenged nature to unlock its forces and changed our behaviour towards it and ourselves as a result. Nature became something to control, count, store and use as a result of *Gestell* subjectivity. Before he became enslaved to a *Gestell* perspective, man's relationship to nature was benign, peaceful and even reverent. Nature was left to its own determination, while man worked with it using his simple agricultural tools of the horse-drawn plough and the hammer. A windmill represents this earlier approach to nature, while a hydroelectric dam, which turns the Rhine into standing reserve, is the result of *Gestell* thinking. The difference between the two approaches to energy is that the former works only when the wind blows and leaves the wind unaffected. The latter creates an artificial force in the water that is constant, not contingent upon the natural flow of the river, allowing energy to be gathered without a break and to be stored; and the river is affected so that those downstream have a denuded supply and flow of water. The river has become something that serves (some) men's ends.

There was no golden age of humanity living in harmony with nature, argues environmental historian JR McNeill (2000). Humans have always used the things of the Earth for their own ends. We are vulnerable to our environment: we do not have fur to keep us warm; a shell to protect us; developed senses of smell or sight or hearing to alert us to danger; speed to flee from that danger or the strength to fight it. We had to use our brains to find ways of sheltering ourselves, of putting ourselves at the top of the food chain, and of staying there. This developed into a highly sophisticated ability to make the environment adapt to our needs, rather than adapt ourselves to the environment, and under this regimen, not least because forming communities and working with each other was essential to its success, humanity flourished. Our brains expanded measurably as tool creation and use involved intense social engagement, social anthropologist and historian Agustin Fuentes points out (2015 p 307).

Our relationship has always been adversarial and always, according to evolutionary biologist EO Wilson, detrimental to nature (2001 p 241). In serving our own needs, humans have never attended to the ecological preservation of a planet that seemed to go on forever. He writes:

> As the human wave rolled over the last of the virgin lands like a smothering blanket, Paleo-Indians throughout America, Polynesians across the Pacific, Indonesians into Madagascar, Dutch sailors ashore on Mauritius (to meet and extirpate the dodo), they were constrained by neither knowledge of endemicity nor any ethic of conservation. For them the world must have seemed to stretch forever beyond the horizon. If fruit pigeons and giant tortoises disappear from this island, they will surely be found on the next one. What counts is food today, a healthy family, and tribute for the chief, victory celebrations, rites of passage, feasts. As the Mexican truck driver said who shot one of the last two imperial woodpeckers, largest of all the world's woodpeckers, "It was a great piece of meat."
>
> (Wilson 2001 p 241)

Defining the Ecological Challenge as Our Buffered, Gestell Self

His views are not without their detractors, he admits (2001 pp 235ff), and there are plenty of examples of human communities that do seem to have managed to live in harmony with their environments for thousands of years. But it is also notable that their way of life is not sought after by the majority of humanity, and has itself been severely disrupted by the onslaught of industrialisation. Not least, as sociologist Margot Jeffries pointed out to me in a private conversation, because some indigenous peoples themselves succumb to the desire for the benefits industrialised societies seem to confer.

Industrialisation, which Heidegger would say, was caused by the *Gestell* perspective, and both EO Wilson and JR McNeill would say was a continuation of the same destructive urge to survive, just a more powerful one, nevertheless brought about a distinctive change in humanity's relationship with nature. In 1712, Thomas Newcomen invented and built the first steam engine that could pump water continuously from a coal mine at Dudley Castle in Staffordshire and this, as James Lovelock puts it, heralded the 'Anthropocene era', the era of human domination (2014 p 4). From that time humanity's power to use and adapt nature to serve its own ends increased exponentially, and harm to the planet increased exponentially as well. From then on humanity could, as it seemed, exercise control over nature, command it and store its power so that it was always available for human use. Humans felt they were no longer subject to the exigencies of nature.

In Wilson's and McNeill's views, technology exists, and always has done, to serve human ends. If we now find that through technology we are harming the planet, we think that we simply need to use it differently to heal the planet. Technological solutions should deal with the ecological crisis as they seem to have dealt with everything else, and that is what our minds should bend towards, now we know how much damage we have done. Ecologist and explorer Tim Flannery has suggested that this is a possible direction of travel (2015 pp 151ff), citing a number of excellent examples of technology turned towards saving, not destroying the planet. But he is not so hubristic as to think that humanity will save the planet by its technological brilliance alone (2015 eg pp 187, 213). Heidegger would say that in fact *Gestell* subjectivity is using humans as much as it is using technology, and the appearance that technology is serving humans is only that: an appearance, so we should be wary of 'solutions' arising from the same subjectivity.

The perspective that turns everything into 'standing reserve'

The *Gestell* perspective 'sets upon nature, challenging it to yield what man requires' (Heidegger 1949/1977 p 6). It makes nature look as though it is at our command. So, for example, we build a hydroelectric dam on the Rhine, turning the river from a work of natural art into power. Nature becomes merely potential, on standby, not of intrinsic value but something that is waiting to be used, in 'standing reserve' (p 7). But humans too find themselves caught up in this way of seeing: as soon as nature is of concern only as standing reserve, quantifiable and available for use, humanity becomes nothing but the 'orderer of the standing reserve' (p 14). We too become merely something available for use. We drive technology forward, but we do not do so freely: we do it because we, like nature, are challenged to. From this *Gestell* way of seeing, humans encounter only the world we have created, which is a world in which everything, including ourselves, is for use.

If everything becomes available for use, then everything is calculable. 'Correct' determining can follow from this way of seeing, but the correct is not necessarily the true. For example, a utilitarian calculation that works out the maximum productivity of a herd of cows may be a correct calculation, but the cows *qua* cows have become hidden behind their function as repositories of milk or meat. The truth 'withdraw[s]' (p 13). Two kinds of danger emerge from this. First, as soon as nature concerns man only inasmuch as it is available for use ('standing reserve') and humans are nothing but the 'orderers of the standing reserve' (p 14), encountering everything as our own construct, as we ourselves become no more than standing reserve, we all the while nevertheless *feel* as though we are lords of the universe. Thus would the hubristic commander of technology that turns the Rhine into a constant supply of energy feel: masterly. JR McNeill writes that in 1908, Churchill stood before Lake Victoria, watching the waters of the world's second-largest lake flow over Owen Falls into the world's longest river, the Nile. He later recorded his thoughts:

> So much power running to waste [...] such a lever to control the natural forces of Africa ungripped, cannot but vex and stimulate the imagination. And what fun to make the immemorial Nile begin its journey by diving into a turbine!
> (McNeill 2000 p 149)

Second, it appears as though humans everywhere only encounter themselves because we make our own world using technology. In fact, we never encounter ourselves, our essence, because we are in attendance on the perception of everything being for use, not perceiving that that is happening. This perception banishes humanity into 'revealing as ordering': what emerges does so only to be used. This conceals other kinds of revealing, in particular revealing what Heidegger calls 'presences', the true being of things. *Gestell*-bound people do not see the river: we see a potential supply of electricity. So the way of seeing and ordering and objectifying that is *Gestell*, the essence of technology, prevents true revelation. 'Enframing blocks the shining-forth and holding-sway of truth', says Heidegger (p 14). He argues that science, by detaching itself from our everyday experience, thus restricts our perspective, because it closes off pathways to depth that our ordinary use of things opens up. Science takes itself away from experience, which might have taught a different way of seeing, into a controlled environment.

Other philosophers and theologians concur with Heidegger's diagnosis of a false world created by *Gestell*. His former student Hannah Arendt argues that, with the science of Galileo, *homo faber* emerged: man who 'makes' truth. From the time of Galileo, scientists discovered the truth by doing, not by thinking, and depended upon technology, not on philosophy (Arendt 1958/1998 pp 293ff). We turned ourselves and our actions into mere utility when history became 'making things' and, grammatically, 'for the sake of' and 'in order to' lost their distinction (1954/2006 p 78). She writes:

> The danger of transforming the unknown and unknowable 'higher aims' into planned and willed intentions was that meaning and meaningfulness were transformed into ends – which is what happened when Marx took the Hegelian meaning of all history – the progressive unfolding and actualisation of the idea of Freedom – to be an end of human action, and when he furthermore, in accordance with tradition, viewed the ultimate 'end' as the end product of the manufacturing process. But neither freedom nor any other meaning can ever be the product of a human activity in the sense in which the table is clearly the end-product of the carpenter's activity [...]. The growing meaninglessness of the modern world is perhaps nowhere more clearly foreshadowed than in this identification of meaning and end.
>
> (Arendt 1954/2006 p 78)

Arendt sees that *homo faber*, the one who makes or fabricates, does not survive the process of fabrication. Although we have found undreamed of ways of producing things and measuring the infinitely small and the infinitely large, like the *Gestell* subject we see ourselves as merely part of the processes of nature and history. The technological way of seeing, presenting a false world, then blinds us to any other way of seeing. *Homo faber* may believe he is in charge, but he has no other purpose than the process itself, becoming indistinguishable from *animal laborans*, for whom 'only the distinction between productive and unproductive labor [...] matters' (1958/1998 pp 85ff). He descends into 'redoubled activity or despair' (p 293). Richard Sennett writes that such a one is a 'drudge condemned to routine' (2008 p 6). Sennett critiques Arendt's account of *animal laborans* to raise his status to that of the craftsman who discovers creativity in the very act of making, an important redemptive route out of 'despair' to which I will briefly return at the end of the book.

We have become 'one dimensional', as Paul Ricoeur puts it, serving an industrial system that is given over to 'growth without limit or end beyond itself' (1995 p 65). Deep ecologist Arne Naess writes of the developer's mindset who sees a forest not as an entity with a heart and its own intrinsic value, but only as potential economic gain (2016 p 77). JR McNeill argues that it is the idea of economic growth that has now enslaved humanity, and this is what has brought about the exponential acceleration of technological power and damage to the Earth in the twentieth century (2000 p 355).

Martin Buber writes of the individual who becomes *It* not *Thou* by having no '[g]enuine subjectivity' (1923/2013 p 44). He echoes Heidegger's account of enframing: in the fierce blaze of technology, '*Thou* cannot resist the electric light of *It*' (p 45). And Iain McGilchrist (2009), after conducting a meta-analysis of research into left and right brain hemisphere perception, offers a historical account of humanity coming under the sway of the left hemisphere that coheres with Buber, Arendt and Heidegger. The left brain, which is organised, mathematical, rigorous and binary, suits our technological age. If it is in charge, it will not listen to the right brain, which is open to the unknown, poetic, simple, chaotic and empathetic. The left brain will silence and outflank its gentler other half, creating its own version of external reality through technology; the right brain cannot withstand the left. To illustrate his argument (and to provide the title for his book) McGilchrist recounts the Nietzschean story of the master who was benevolent, wise and nonviolent, who ruled a realm that grew and flourished so much that he had to appoint emissaries. These he sent out, knowing that he had to let them rule in his name and not be closely overseen by him. One of the emissaries took the master's benevolent non-intervention as weakness, became contemptuous of his master, usurped him, duped the people, became a tyrant and the dominion collapsed in ruins (McGilchrist 2009 p 24). In the analogy, the master is the right brain hemisphere and the emissary is the left brain hemisphere. The point is that the left should serve the right, which is open to the unknown, to beauty, to the value of incommensurable things, but it does not; just as for Buber, *It* should serve *Thou*, but does not.

Paul Ricoeur writes of a 'desacralised' modern world, in which nature 'is no longer a store of signs'. The universe is objectified as science becomes not just a form of knowledge but a way of looking (1995 p 61). The utilitarian world is one which signifies nothing other than use, and is thus a world without divinity. Olivier Clément describes 'the technical universe' as having the power to 'weaken the heart-spirit' and thus change what we see:

> If we are not careful, the technical universe, left to its own devices, will damage human nature in its very depths. The abnormal growth of purely cerebral calculation; the sensual refusal, in our leisure time, to do any real thinking; the increasing difficulty, while working, of 'thinking with one's hands'; the coldness of metal, the abstraction of synthetic materials, the constant noise, the invasion of images that appeal to our sniggering instincts, all conduce to a weakening of the unifying powers of the 'heart-spirit'. Today, these powers must be renewed, if humanity and its cosmic environment are not to be destroyed.
> (Clément 2000 p 122)

Charles Taylor argues that a shift from a 'porous' to a 'buffered' self came about between 1500 and 2000. The character of Taylor's buffered self emerges as the Reformation, reacting to corruption within the Church, 'flattened' all orders of holiness: priests and religious were no longer the guardians of the sacred, and all people had to be equally holy (2007 p 80). The post-Reformation mindset, which should have resulted in a world where God was not only in some special holy places but also everywhere, in fact made it possible for God to be 'lopped off' altogether (p 86), and the age of secularism commenced, with only ourselves and the structures we might create anew on rational principles to rely upon. Out of this, argues Taylor, came a move to human-imposed discipline, within a person and within society. The sacred was expelled, and things that might have been magical became instrumental in building order: enchantment was driven out. 'In consequence the subject as porous fades more and more away' (p 85). The buffered self, says Taylor, finds its 'complete definition in René Descartes' *cogito* self who:

> knowing the force and action of fire, water, air, the stars, heavens and all other bodies that environ us [...] can in the same way *employ them* in all those uses to which they are adapted, and thus render ourselves the *masters and possessors of nature*.
>
> (Descartes 1637/1970, my italics)

With Descartes' ideas come the closing off of intimacy and connectedness with each other, says Taylor (2007 p 133).

Pope Francis sees humanity falling prey to the 'technological paradigm' as 'rapidification' has speeded up human activity to a pace far faster than nature (Francis 2015 p 15), in the process turning all the elements of creation, including ourselves, into commodities (p 23). Technology becomes the key to the meaning of existence and 'our lives surrender to its conditioning' (p 83).

These scholars give different accounts of how the 'buffering' of the human self happened and use different language to describe it, but they are all notably similar in their diagnosis that at some point before the industrial revolution humanity took on a controlling, adversarial subjectivity in relation to nature and ourselves, and we are now enslaved by it.

How *Gestell* brings about ecological damage

The damaging effect of *Gestell* subjectivity comes about through the way it makes humanity perceive and thus behave towards nature. We see everything as 'standing reserve', and the machines we invent are intended to ever increase and improve our use of nature. Modern machines have this quality, thinks Heidegger. They are in a different category from old machines such as spinning wheels or wind and water mills, which work and flow at the pace of nature. Turning nature into standing reserve, waiting to serve humans: the energy of nature is unlocked and transformed, stored, distributed and switched about (1949/1977 p 7). *Gestell* subjectivity 'puts to nature the unreasonable demand that it supply energy that can be extracted and stored as such' (p 6). This is different from windmills whose sails are entirely dependent upon the wind blowing, and water mills, which are turned by the river's flow. Windmills do not unlock energy and store it, whereas *Gestell* thinking 'sets upon' nature, challenging it to yield what man requires (p 6) so man, enslaved to this way of thinking, creates a hydroelectric plant on the Rhine which turns the river itself into standing reserve (p 7). But it is *Gestell* thinking which 'uses' man to treat nature in this way. If man has brought about this exploiting of nature because he is challenged by his *Gestell* subjectivity, then he too is being used as 'standing reserve'. Heidegger gives an example of the forester (it could be any modern operative in any number of contexts, including digital) who is 'challenged' to meet the requirements of the lumber yard. Like the rest of the operation, he becomes an interchangeable piece of machinery: he is 'subordinate to the orderability of cellulose, which is challenged forth by the need for paper' (p 8). The use to which man is put by his *Gestell* perspective is to drive technology forward (p 8). When he 'ensnares nature', he has already been claimed by *Gestell* subjectivity as he is challenged to approach nature as an object of research (p 9).

Heidegger uses the *Gestell* perspective to explain how it is that agriculture becomes the same as corpses in gas chambers, blockading and starving countries and the production of hydrogen bombs, and Martin Blitz is appalled by this (2014 p 70). He is clear that there is a moral difference between these activities, and that we can choose between them, regardless of the dominance of the *Gestell* perspective. I think he may be missing the point. Heidegger is perhaps trying to understand how it was that he himself could have supported Nazism, how *Gestell* can indeed lead to hitherto unthinkable behaviour. *Gestell* thinking treats *everything* as standing reserve. Modern technological approaches to agriculture turn the animals, the land and its produce into things that can be used. Once they have lost their intrinsic value, they no longer need to be treated with respect or reverence. If man too is caught in standing reserve in the same way by his *Gestell* subjectivity, then man too can be treated as a thing without respect or reverence, and any action towards him becomes possible if it can be utilitarianly justified.

The *Gestell* perspective dehumanises us, makes us slaves to process, and that slavish process is destroying the planet. JR McNeill gives an account of the damage by working through each of the spheres of the planet: the atmosphere, the hydrosphere, the lithosphere, the pedosphere and the biosphere. Drawing extensively on his poetic description, I will describe humanity's effects on each of these spheres to demonstrate the bondage of *Gestell* thinking: with good intentions great harm is done. McNeill's account avoids the danger of only telling part of the story: just climate change, for example, or just biodiversity loss. James Lovelock notices how the stress on the planet is seen according to the scientific discipline of the investigation. Like specialist doctors who only see one illness in their patients, they miss the whole, far more devastating picture. Lovelock argues for taking the approach of the general practitioner who will see in general the state of a person's body

Defining the Ecological Challenge as Our Buffered, Gestell Self 17

(1988 p xvii). This is the basis for Lovelock's Gaia hypothesis, which attracted ire from both scientists and theologians, because he seemed to be turning the planet into a god. At the suggestion of his friend, the novelist William Golding, he adopted the Earth goddess Gaia as the name for his holistic approach to the challenges of the planet in order to make his readers see them as parts of a whole and the planet itself as a single living organism, like a human body (2001 p 3). The categories of the five spheres of the planet demonstrate rather than undermine the interconnectedness of every part of the planet. They present a comprehensive view of what amounts to our wholesale destruction of habitat, of Earth as home.

The atmosphere

The atmosphere is the thin, gaseous envelope that surrounds the Earth. Tim Flannery calls it our 'great aerial ocean' (2007 p 19). It is about 100 kilometres thick, although the outer boundary is arbitrary as it shades off gradually into outer space. Air contains thousands of gases, but two predominate: nitrogen (78%) and oxygen (21%). In the long term the chemistry of the atmosphere has changed. In the very early days of Earth many low-density gases were lost to outer space, and before there were plants on Earth there was not much oxygen. Now there are many cycles of motion of gases, created by changes of temperature in the outer regions of the atmosphere known as the stratosphere, and at the lowest altitudes by exchanges of heat, moisture and gases with soil, water and living things. The outermost regions of the atmosphere receive and reflect the all-important sun's rays. The gases in the atmosphere maintain a balance between them to make life possible, supported by the reception of the sun's rays on the outer edge and by photosynthesis and other activities of the Earth's surface on the inner edge. If such a balance were not maintained, Earth could be more like Mars, whose average temperature is minus 23°C, or it could resemble Venus, where temperatures are above the boiling point of water. Lovelock sees the state of Venus as Earth's destiny if the plant life that creates breathable air were to be extinguished (Lovelock 2014 p 158). Not much needs to be done to the gases to alter conditions on Earth fundamentally; as Flannery points out, gases such as carbon dioxide and methane are trace gases so that only tiny changes in their concentration trigger vast changes in the atmosphere (Flannery 2007 p 42).

The acceleration of carbon dioxide emissions into the atmosphere from 1800 onwards, together with other greenhouse gases following industrialisation, meant that heat from the sun was more effectively trapped. This was not understood. Soot and dust injected into what seemed like infinite space slightly lowered the amount of solar energy reaching the Earth's surface and meant that the increase in the warmth of the Earth, now known to be due to greenhouse gases, was reduced. But the Earth is warming more quickly now. In each successive report from the Inter-governmental Panel on Climate

Change the statements about the warming of Earth have become more assertive, more extreme and more urgent. The Panel's 2014 Assessment Report stated:

> Each of the last three decades has been successively warmer at the Earth's surface than any preceding decade since 1850. The period from 1983 to 2012 was *likely*[2] the warmest 30-year period of the last 1400 years in the Northern Hemisphere.
> (IPCC 2014 p 2, authors' italics)

In 2022:

> Global warming, reaching 1.5° C in the near-term, would cause unavoidable increases in multiple climate hazards and present multiple risks to ecosystems and humans (*very high confidence*).[3]
> (IPCC 2022 p 15, authors' italics)

The heating of the atmosphere and its consequent dramatic shifts in weather patterns mean that species, including humans, are forced to abandon their habitats and seek new homes elsewhere, when 'elsewhere' is inexorably dwindling in size. But even as attempts are made to reduce carbon dioxide and other greenhouse gas emissions, the causes of those emissions, fossil fuels, are *still* being prospected for. What is the point of seeking to reduce fossil fuel emissions while still mining for them? We are trying to close off one end of the pipeline while still pumping oil into the other end (George Marshall 2014 p 162).

The hydrosphere

There is so much water in the Earth – 1.4 billion cubic kilometres – that some call it the 'blue planet'. More than 97% of Earth's water is in the oceans. Every year, the sun gathers up about half a million cubic kilometres, which falls back on to the Earth as rain and snow. This is the source of all the world's stock of fresh water. Two-thirds of it is currently frozen in ice caps and glaciers, almost all of that in Antarctica. Nearly all of that which is left is underground in currently inaccessible depths. Only about one-quarter of 1% of the world's fresh water (approximately 90,000 cubic kilometres) is in lakes and rivers where it is accessible. Of this, about a quarter is in Lake Baikal in Siberia, though the water volume is steadily shrinking and increasingly threatened by pollution. Water is also found in the atmosphere, in permafrost (sub-soil which remains freezing throughout the year), and in living organisms (McNeill 2000 p 119).

We need water as much as we need oxygen. For a very long time, we only needed water to drink. But in the last few thousand years we have also relied upon water to irrigate our crops, carry our waste, wash our bodies and our possessions, and much more recently to power our mills and machines. We have used cheap labour and then modern technology to move and control water on vast scales. As our attitude to water has changed and the power we have available to control it increases, so its use, waste and pollution have increased. So has the replumbing of the planet through dams, influencing water courses on a massive scale and affecting life downstream (McNeill 2000 pp 120ff). Additionally, warming and eutrophication (an excessive amount of nutrients in the water giving rise to algae blooms that suffocate aquatic biodiversity) of the oceans means that what were methane sinks and home to underwater biodiversity are set not only to become uninhabitable but also to emit the greenhouse gas methane on an imaginably vast scale (IPCC 2014 p 4), forcing global temperatures to rise even more.

Without intending harm, but with an approach to policy-making out of a *Gestell* subjectivity that can only think in utilitarian terms, the Earth's hydrosphere has been damaged perhaps beyond repair. The treatment of Lake Victoria during the twentieth century, cited by the UN Environment Panel, is an example of *Gestell* solutions to human need, imposed with the best of intentions, that only gave rise to worse problems. Lake Victoria has provided food and livelihoods for those living around it, human and other creatures, for centuries. The fish in the Lake ate algae and snails that host the larvae of Schistosomes that cause bilharzia in humans. With the introduction of gill nets by European settlers at the beginning of the twentieth century, indigenous fish species began to decline. With no algae-eating fish, the lake started to eutrophicate and the people were exposed to more disease. Other fish species were introduced to boost stocks, but they were non-native and harmed the indigenous fish still further. Nile perch were introduced in the 1960s for commercial fisheries, and the local people suffered as their livelihoods were threatened. They began to experience malnutrition, having previously gained all their food needs from the Lake. Wetlands around the Lake were converted to grow cotton, rice and sugarcane and their role as filters for silt and nutrients was lost so that run-off went straight into the Lake, increasing eutrophication. The cloudy waters became ideal for Nile perch and deathly for indigenous species who preferred clear waters. Sewage in particular encouraged the growth of water hyacinth, originally introduced for aesthetic reasons. The water hyacinth is one of the world's most invasive plants. Its spread on the Lake hampered small fishing boats. The dense cover in turn encouraged weed growth, an ideal habitat for snails and mosquitoes, increasing the threat of bilharzia and malaria (UNEP 2002 p 305). The process of destroying the life of the Lake was immensely exacerbated when it became a closed water system. Churchill's dream of making the Nile serve humanity was finally realised in 1946 when construction began on the Owen Falls Dam. In 1954, the Nile waters at last dived into turbines. Uganda and eastern Kenya got 150,000 kilowatts of electrical capacity, but Lake Victoria became a reservoir (McNeill 2000 p 149). The latest UNEP report remains gloomy (2012 p 126).

The lithosphere

The lithosphere is the outer crust of Earth, some 120 km thick, made of rock which floats on molten rock. The rocks have eroded, deposited on ocean floors as sediment, consolidated into rock again, and been thrust up above sea level again, only a few times in the history of Earth (McNeill 2000 p 22). By contrast, human impact has been minuscule until the industrial age. From the twentieth century humans have moved enough soil and rock to rival natural disturbances for the first time. By the end of the century, mining and soil cultivation moved 42 billion tons of rock and soil. This is comparable to natural movements such as, for example, the 30 billion tonnes moved per annum by oceanic volcanoes, or 4.3 billion tonnes per annum by glacier movement (McNeill 2000 p 30). Mining for fossil fuels destroys habitats, and is further evidence of the dominance of *Gestell* thinking even when it makes no sense: as observed above, we are still seeking to fill oil and gas pipelines at one end while trying to reduce our use of what comes out at the other end.

The pedosphere

The pedosphere is the soil that lies on top of the lithosphere like skin on flesh, on average about half a metre thick, made of sand, clay, silt and organic matter, acting as a cleansing and protecting membrane between the lithosphere and the atmosphere. Changes to the pedosphere take place continually by means of water and wind. Humans have affected the pedosphere through the cultivation of the land as they settled on it. The first wave of human expansion and settlement took place in the Middle East, India and China, when agriculture spread from the river valleys to forest lands, between 2000 BC and 1000 AD. As forests were cut or burned to make way for crops and animals, the erosion of soil resulted, though this stabilised as farms developed (McNeill 2000 p 35ff). More significant and potentially damaging effects to the pedosphere took place as Europe expanded, beginning with the Americas in 1492, and inappropriate farming methods were applied to new landscapes. Northern European farmers were used to mild rainfall, low slopes and heavy soils resistant to erosion. Their hoofed animals and sowing methods desertified the more fragile landscapes of the Americas, South Africa, Australasia and Inner Asia, and the power of the European conquerors to shunt native populations around meant that marginal lands came under the plough and the digging stick (McNeill 2000 pp 39ff).

Together with mass deforestation, the cultivation of the topsoil has deprived Earth of the ability to deal with carbon dioxide in the atmosphere, thus multiplying the damaging effects. Farming, which brought about settled homes for humans, scaled up for productivity to feed growing populations but also for profit, has unsettled the habitats of other species, destroying the bio-diversity that ensures a healthy soil and ultimately undermining the habitats of humans too (eg Tudge 2004 pp 185ff).

The biosphere

The biosphere is the sum of all the habitats in which species live. It includes every home in every part of the world, from the 'bubbling seafloor vents teeming with bacteria' to 'glaciers at dizzy heights where the occasional beetle may be found' and everywhere in between (McNeill 2000 p 192). The biosphere is the home of the biota, which is the name for all living things, including humans. It is the diversity of species, not individual species, that ensures a balance of life on Earth, creating and sustaining the habitats in which life flourishes, including human life. In a thimbleful of earth can be found algae, fungi, nematodes, mites, springtails, enchytraeid worms and thousands of species of bacteria (Wilson 2001 p 328). This is a tiny fragment of one ecosystem, showing in microcosm the interdependence of species that is replicated throughout the planet. McNeill shows that by the end of the twentieth century, for the richer third of the world, the human species was able to dominate all the other species as never before. This was due to its ability to feed itself and treat diseases that had hitherto been fatal. For species other than human, the chances of survival depended on their ability to live within a human-dominated biosphere. There were those organisms that met human needs and were capable of being domesticated, such as cattle, rice and eucalyptus, and they fared well. There were those that found niches within the biosphere, such as rats, crab-grass and tuberculosis bacillus, and these too survived well. Creatures that humans found useful but incapable of domestication, such as blue whales and bison, and those that could not adjust to a human-dominated biosphere, such as gorillas and the smallpox virus, faced extinction. Their survival depended upon whether humans suffered them or not.

This human domination is only apparent. The changes for which humans have been responsible have for the most part been inadvertent: humans have not intended to wipe out species (apart from some disease-bearing viruses and bacteria), but that is what has happened (McNeill 2000 pp 265ff).

The five spheres of Earth all show considerable and interconnected signs of distress, which can be attributed to *Gestell* human interventions that did not intend harm: the atmosphere with its increase in greenhouse gases that makes it act like a blanket thrown over an already warming Earth; the hydrosphere replumbed and polluted and emitting into the atmosphere gases it once stored; the lithosphere mined and plundered for fossil fuels that also emit greenhouse gases; the pedosphere stripped of its protecting green cover so that Earth cannot cool itself by transforming carbon dioxide through photosynthesis; and the biosphere so reduced in diversity of species as to threaten all life. Each sphere seems enormous to the individual human perspective, and yet we have managed to dominate and change them all.

The failure of current approaches to solve the ecological crisis

The implication of Heidegger's argument is that the only way to address the ecological crisis is to be 'saved' from *Gestell* subjectivity. But is it the only way? Many efforts to solve the problem are being made already: do we have to agree to such a fundamental transformation of our very selfhood? For example, are technological responses really not sufficient? Would a utilitarian approach work? Do we need to ensure wealth creation before we can properly address the ecological crisis? Will some tremendous disaster make us realise our responsibility and change our behaviour?

An artificial world?

Renewable sources of energy are an attractive, indeed essential, alternative to the use of fossil fuels. But adopted with a *Gestell* mindset, they are being harnessed on industrial scales with the unchanged intention of providing energy for humans as much and as reliably as hitherto. We do not want to harm it, but we *still* think of nature as a machine-like servant of our voracious needs. Sir Chris Llewelyn Smith of the Oxford Energy Network pointed out that a sunny area the size of the British Isles covered with solar panels would be enough to meet all the world's energy needs (Highfield 2017 p 39), but the impracticality of such a solution is not the only reason why it would fail. Thousands of miles of fields covered by solar panels may harness quantities of sunlight but they themselves and the infrastructure they demand in order to store and transport the energy will inflict other kinds of damage on wildlife habitats. And they are not beautiful. Sara Maitland, who spent a long time searching for and then finding a wild enough landscape for her home, was devastated with grief as wind turbines were built there on an industrial scale, invading not just the landscape but also the soundscape of her beloved Galloway (2012). The essay is a moving description of her attempts to find the turbines beautiful. She believes they are just, given the threat of climate change particularly to the poorest communities in the world. It is not the technology itself that is the problem here. It is the *Gestell* mindset that uses it on industrial scales and cannot see how else to do so.

As alternative sources of energy fail to solve the problem in the way *Gestell* thinking believes it has to, the same way of thinking has us looking beyond the natural resources of Earth to a fully technological solution: an artificial world. We thought Earth was infinite; now we think space is infinite, so let us colonise other planets. EO Wilson writes:

> It is [...] possible for some to dream that people will go on living comfortably in a biologically impoverished world. They suppose that a prosthetic environment is within the power of technology, that human life can still flourish in a completely humanised world, where medicines would all be synthesised from chemicals off the shelf, food grown from a few dozen

domestic crop species, the atmosphere and climate regulated by computer-driven fusion energy, and the earth made over until it becomes a literal spaceship rather than a metaphorical one, with people reading displays and touching buttons on the bridge. Such is the terminus of the philosophy of exemptionalism: do not weep for the past, humanity is a new order of life, let species die if they block progress, scientific and technological genius will find another way. Look up and see the stars awaiting us.

(Wilson 2001 p 332)

Of course technological enhancements offer huge benefits: they have transformed the lives of those suffering from physical disabilities, for example. Humans are swift to adapt to their use, from a stick to help with walking to an electronic aid to help with seeing, as Andy Clark points out (2011 pp 34, 37). Such devices become part of our functioning selves: the tip of the stick can feel sensitive as though it were a living extension of the hand that wields it.

The proposal that humanity could adapt to and thrive in a wholly artificial world, however, is of a different order. Suppose we could create a human-life-supporting capsule that could go on doing so indefinitely? Although it is not possible to prove beforehand that we would be unable to adapt to and thrive within it, the evidence indicates otherwise. 'Humanity co-evolved with the rest of life on this particular planet; other worlds are not in our genes' says EO Wilson (2001 p 330), and Hannah Arendt agrees: 'the earth is the very quintessence of the human condition, and earthly nature, for all we know, may be unique in the universe in providing human beings with the habitat in which they can move and breathe without effort and without artifice' (1958/1998 p 2). Earth is humanity's home. Most humans choose to connect with nature, given sufficient leisure, finding it restful, a tendency which EO Wilson calls 'biophilia': 'the connection that human beings subconsciously seek with the rest of life' (2001 p 334). Michael McCarthy, environmental journalist, calls this connection 'joy'. He cites a study of patients who recovered from the same operation a great deal faster when they awoke to a window view of greenery as opposed to a view of a brick wall (2015 p 60f). The research is evidence of some deep-seated restorative power of nature on humans. Research commissioned by Natural England showed significant benefits of nature-based interventions for mental health care (Bragg and Atkins 2016). Natural beauty is not a luxury: it meets a fundamental need, says former Director General of the National Trust Fiona Reynolds (2016).

On these accounts, we would be unlikely to thrive in an artificial environment, even were we to succeed in creating one. It would instate the Eremezoic Era, the 'age of loneliness', declares EO Wilson (2006 p 91). Our culture, who we are physically and emotionally, evolved through two million years, across thousands of generations, during which we have been profoundly influenced by our co-evolution with all the other creatures of Earth, and Earth itself. 'Only in the last moment of human history has the delusion arisen that people can flourish apart from the living world', he writes (2001 p 331).

Calculate our way out of the problem?

The utilitarian approach to moral thinking and policy making, articulated in the late eighteenth century by Jeremy Bentham, has dominated responses to many of the challenges humans have faced since then, including the ecological crisis. Bentham argues that law-making and the morality that underlies it are, simply, a matter of mathematical calculation. He proposes that an action is good if more people are benefitted than harmed, and not good if more are harmed than benefitted (1789/1962). The 'benefit-cost ratio' is an explicitly acknowledged basis for policy-making in the United Kingdom, for example, in a number of Government Departments, an approach which has been debated in seminars at Westminster Abbey Institute since 2014.

But the ecological challenge cannot be solved in this way. The challenge faces the entire planet, and the entire human family, so it confounds the principle of benefitting greater numbers and sacrificing fewer. If only some communities or countries take the necessary measures (whatever they are) to ameliorate the damage, they may well be penalised economically and neither they nor those who take no action will be helped, because if everyone does not participate, the measures will have no effect. The atmosphere cannot be carved up and handed out only to some people.

The challenge can be understood by analogy with the Prisoners' Dilemma, which was devised by Flood and Dresher in 1950 and poses the following: two prisoners, A and B, interrogated separately, are both offered choices between testifying against the other or remaining silent. If A testifies against B and B remains silent, A will be let off and B will receive ten years' imprisonment, and *vice versa*. If both A and B testify against each other, both will receive two years' imprisonment. If both remain silent, both will receive six months' imprisonment, the maximum sentence the court can give in the absence of evidence (related in, eg McGilchrist 2009 p 145). *Gestell* mindsets (and the digital codes they write) will work through the numerous permutations algorithmically to try and calculate the best possible choice for A or B, as they would do in climate change negotiations. But we only gain if we all work together, not: I will if you will, but: I will because I believe you will too; and that requires 'an act of trust in my right or capacity to act and give' (Williams 2000 p 72). Our *Gestell* selves cannot see how that could possibly happen.

Another analogy that makes the point that calculation cannot address the kind of challenge that the ecological crisis presents is offered by Amartya Sen (2010). Anne, Bob and Carla quarrel over one flute which each of them wants. Anne is the only one who can play the flute (the others do not dispute this) so thinks she should have the flute. If we only knew this argument we would probably want to give Anne the flute. Bob is the poorest and has no other toys whereas Anne and Carla, as both agree, have plenty of other toys. If we only knew Bob's argument we would want to give the flute to him. Carla made the flute, over several weeks and with great care; again this is not disputed by the others and again, if this was the only argument we heard, we would say Carla should have the flute (Sen 2010 p 12). Justice cannot be meted out if only part of the story is known. But nor can it be meted out algorithmically if all three are known. If 'flute' stands for 'habitat', how can any solution be right that does not find a way of granting the flute to all three children? As with the Prisoners' Dilemma, something else will have to intervene to resolve the matter, but for the *Gestell* self, one narrative has to be favoured over the others, or nothing at all can be done. The *Gestell* self cannot see how else to resolve the question, thinking it has to accept that those whose narratives are denied are themselves denied. It leads inexorably to the brutalist solution in which some humans retreat and survive on a few islands kept cool by surrounding water, while everyone else burns up, an outcome predicted by Lovelock (2006 p 60).

Get rich first, then mend the planet?

Addressing environmental concerns can only happen after a certain level of development has taken place, suggest many governments, either explicitly or by their policies which put the goal of economic growth before everything else. Environmentally friendly living is a luxury that many societies cannot afford, goes the argument: goodness is expensive and can only be paid for by the rich. For EF Schumacher this is a continuation, which he rightly rejects, of the Keynesian view that 'avarice and usury and precaution must be our gods for a little longer still' (Schumacher 1975 p 40). We have seen that the rich cannot be relied upon to lead in environmentally sustainable life styles, as large wealthy nations squabble self-interestedly, abstain or withdraw altogether from international agreements to reduce carbon dioxide emissions, and the greatest *per capita* ecological footprints are consistently generated by the nations with the highest incomes (eg WWF 2014 p 37). It is the mindset that is the problem, not the lack of money. As Arne Naess observes: 'it is an embarrassing scandal that the rich industrial nations do not use the urgency of work to be done to overcome the global ecological crisis as a basis for the significant reduction of unemployment. The jobs in this area are clearly more labour intensive than jobs in industry' (2016 p 101). The scandal *is* embarrassing, so why are we so incapable of addressing it? What capricious god has the economy become, that we cannot make it serve our need for meaningful work but rather forces us into the jobs it greedily demands that we (and only some of us) do? Our helplessness in the face of this realisation is a demonstration of our enslavement to a *Gestell* perspective.

When things get really bad, humans will change

George Marshall (2014), who has studied and engaged with numerous environmental organisations and their campaigns, understands that our failure to respond comes out of the way we are and think. He suggests that we have a default mechanism in us to avoid the anxiety that prefigures the changes that the ecological crisis requires in us and of us. With other major threats, there are 'clear markers that would normally lead our brains to overrule our short-term interests' (for example, Hitler invading Czechoslovakia in 1939 which tipped Britain into declaring war) but these do not happen with climate change, rather 'we actively conspire with each other, and mobilise our own biases, to keep it perpetually in the background' (pp 228ff). If only, think some environmental campaigners, a sufficiently devastating natural event clearly caused by climate change would happen. Then governments and people would wake up and policies would change, as they had to on the eve of war, as more recently they had to in the face of the Covid-19 pandemic. (What a terrible thing to wish for.) But when weather disasters hit, as they are with increasing frequency, even if climate change can be named as a cause, it is never straightforwardly so. And such disasters turn out, as Marshall notices (p 9) to be precisely not the time to talk about bigger causes. People are too busy recovering and restoring their nests, discovering new neighbourliness in the face of adversity, attending to their very real and present local needs, to be concerned about global climate change.

We will not change even if things become really bad, says Marshall, because we are in the wrong story. In his book *The Myth Gap* (2017) former UN adviser Alex Evans agrees. We make sense of data through narratives, and the narrative that has forced fundamental change and galvanised collective responses hitherto has been the enemy narrative, appropriate for war. It is a narrative with which the technological paradigm fits best, as *Gestell* selves make common cause with others against a common enemy. But we cannot turn the ecological disaster into a foe to be conquered. The enemy narrative will not make sense of the data because the 'enemy' is all of us, collectively and unwittingly causing the harm that gives rise to disaster. 'If there is an enemy, it is really our 'shadow' – our greedy internal child whom we don't wish to acknowledge or recognise and who compels us to project our own unacceptable attributes onto others' (Marshall 2014 p 43).

Salvation from *Gestell*, the limitations of phenomenology and the porous self

The need to seek salvation from *Gestell* subjectivity is not to be avoided. It is a harder and more radical task: nevertheless it offers the potential not only to cease the harm to the planet's distressed spheres but also save humanity from its own 'redoubled activity or despair' (Arendt 1958/1998 p 293).

But how? Heidegger writes that we have to take heed of the 'place or time of the arising of the technological point of view' (1949/1977 p 17). We have to return to the place whence the *Gestell* perspective arises, he says, which means entering a phenomenological process whereby we 'cease to stare at the technological' (p 17) and catch sight of the coming into being of that way of seeing. It is an inward movement, a meditative process which gives us the opportunity to think differently. But this process retains a self, the one undertaking the meditation, who is itself not open to transformation. Terry Eagleton is scornful: 'all Heidegger does [...] is to set up a different kind of metaphysical entity [...] His work represents a flight from history as much as an encounter with it; and the same can be said of the fascism with which he flirted' (quoted in Jeanrond 1991 p 109). The undoing of *Gestell* subjectivity will not happen through a self, caught up in one way of thinking, 'deciding' to take up a different way of thinking. Heidegger's self is too resonant with Descartes *cogito* self which believes that it is 'master and possessor of nature' (1637/1970 p 119). No: the self itself must be undone, otherwise the belief that nature (in this case, human nature) can be controlled will not be challenged.

The transformation of the self will come about, I propose, by means of its 'wounding' that both creates but also restores porosity. The term 'porous' comes, as we saw, from Charles Taylor, who places it in the historical context of a medieval world. Taylor shows the distinction between the porous selves we were and the buffered – *Gestell* – selves that we have become. Illustrating what he means, he writes of the change in our notion of what is inside us and what is outside ourselves: we have boundaries now that were not there 500 years ago. Today, we think of making meaning of the world by which we are surrounded, outside ourselves. Five hundred years ago, the meaning was visited upon us by the spirits of the world and beyond, to which we were subject. Today, we are still affected by what goes on outside ourselves, but we can objectify and make sense of it, for example, we think of 'catching' a cold from outside, diagnose it and prescribe medicine for it. We can observe outside things and take a view on them. Then, we were affected in a third way, over which we had less or no control, because the thing that had power, the object or agent, could bring us within its forcefield and impose quite alien things upon us. Hence the medieval notion of 'being possessed' (Taylor 2007 pp 32f).

Taylor's buffered self, which the porous self becomes over this 500-year period, is resonant with Heidegger's *Gestell* self, and certainly part of the task of undoing *Gestell* involves reaching behind it to a time and place when it did not dominate human subjectivity. But the task is not that of restoring an earlier age: we would not easily return to a language of 'being possessed', and in any case, as JR McNeill and EO Wilson and others suggest, our pre-industrial subjectivity was not intentionally benign towards nature. The task, rather, involves finding a way of piercing the buffered, *Gestell* self itself and finding its porosity now, in our twenty-first-century world, albeit a porosity that will be resonant with the pre-industrial self.

In this, we are helped by modern neuroscience which has detected a pre-cognitive relationality in our selfhood, research to which I will return as I explore porosity more deeply in the next chapter. Porosity is not intended to imply that that self disappears altogether, rather that its fundamental connectivity is asserted, which I will show is both ancient and originary. Porosity's restoration opens up the possibility for new ways of being in the world that are predicated upon relationship, respect, and even reverence for the intrinsic value of nature and humanity.

Hence, salvation from *Gestell* subjectivity is to be found in that which restores porosity. My task is to show that the writing of Julian of Norwich can help. Julian's encounter with Christ in her revelations transforms her subjectivity, and the 'world' that is created out of the encounter, that is to say her writing, is capable of transforming the subjectivity of its reader in turn. Julian was an anchoress (hermit) who lived in Norwich in the second half of the fourteenth century and the beginning of the fifteenth, at a time when Taylor says human subjectivity was porous. Although the medieval context is relevant, it is not merely Julian's historical place that makes her valuable to us today. Moreover there are numerous difficulties that stand in the way of identifying the Julian of history with the Julian in the writing, so her value cannot depend upon her being a medieval person, or her readers becoming medieval in order to be transformed by what she says. I have examined these difficulties, familiar to Julian scholars, in the Appendix. They are important because they help make the case for my reading of Julian. I aim to show that, regardless of when it was written, the text retains the power to draw its readers into the transformative encounter. The text does the work: Julian makes herself the means within the text for its readers to undergo what she did. The text does what it speaks of: with disarming language that has the communicative power to soften and then pierce the *Gestell* self, a transformation of perception takes place. This is the wounding the *Gestell* self needs in order to become porous and to be saved from the technological paradigm by which it is bound.

Heidegger acknowledges that the 'fine arts' can by 'poetic revealing' foster the growth of the 'saving power' that is needed to escape from *Gestell* subjectivity (1949/1977 p 19). But it takes the hermeneutics of Paul Ricoeur, who critiques the phenomenological process advocated by Heidegger, to see how 'poetic' texts have the power to summon and change the apparently transcendent self. The reading of Julian that I recommend is guided by and builds upon Ricoeur, therefore, and so the next chapter proposes my post-Ricoeurian hermeneutical approach. It will use preliminary examples from the Julian texts but undertake an in-depth reading once the approach has been established.

Notes

1 Here and elsewhere if the writer has used the masculine form I retain it.
2 'Likely' in IPCC reports means 66%–100% likely.
3 It is going to happen.

2 Developing a Post-Ricoeurian Hermeneutical Approach

Introduction

In Chapter 1, I characterised the ecological challenge as the need for humanity to be 'saved' from its nature-damaging *Gestell* subjectivity by means of a restored porosity. For the *Gestell* self everything, not just nature but also humanity, is in 'standing reserve', being used or waiting to be used and has no intrinsic but only utilitarian value. I concluded that while Heidegger's diagnosis of enslavement to *Gestell* was right, his solution was not: a phenomenological return to an essential self which then decides to see differently will not spring the trap. The self that thinks it can decide to change its nature is too akin to the Cartesian *cogito* self who believes it is the master of nature. It still thinks it is in charge. Instead I turn to Paul Ricoeur, who recognises that the self itself is to be transformed, and it can do so by means of hermeneutics, by reading. Texts can change us in a way that we cannot change ourselves. In particular, poetic texts have the power to 'wound' the self, undermining its buffered subjectivity and opening it up to the possibility of a restored porosity. Reading the Julian texts with the help of Ricoeur will have this effect.

This important preliminary chapter will develop the hermeneutical approach that will release the texts' transformative power. I will start by laying four initial foundations from Paul Ricoeur's hermeneutics: first, texts once written are independent of their author and original audiences; second, readers' interpretation are always *in medias res*, one among many; third, the particular effect of poetic texts and fourth, the reading self is summoned and changed by poetic texts. On these initial Ricoeurian foundations I will then build a three-pillared post-Ricoeurian hermeneutical approach that emphasises the reader's and the text's porosity and the new ways of seeing and being that can ensue. I will use examples from the Julian texts in this chapter but the deep, transformative reading will begin properly in the following chapters, once the hermeneutical approach has been established.

DOI: 10.4324/9781032623948-3

Initial Ricoeurian foundations

The independence of the text

Historical and manuscript challenges, addressed in the Appendix, mean that we cannot assume the context of a 14th–15th-century anchoress in Norwich for the Julian texts. This absence of context is recognised in hermeneutical theory to be a danger because it removes any historical reference point to guard the hermeneut, the reader, from straying into fanciful waters. Paul Ricoeur addresses this difficulty when he suggests that the text, once written, becomes independent of its author, its *sitz im leben* or situation of its being written and its first audience (1977 p 22). The issue of the text, that which it is about, can go further than ('burst') the author and the author's world. He uses the example of biblical texts, which are given a spurious and fixed authority by readers in historical time taking upon themselves the for-all-time understanding of the Bible and a magisterium, also operating in historical time, imposing a body of doctrines for all time. Praying, he says, is mistakenly conflated with believing. The differences between biblical discourses – narrative, hymnic, prophetic, prescriptive and sapiental – show how impossible it is to fix a meaning on these texts. In particular, Ricoeur questions the notion of 'revelation' that asserts that God spoke to the writers of the sacred texts in the same way as just one type of biblical narrative, prophecy, claims. Prophets speak as God speaking through them, directly: God told me to say this and I am saying this. The prescriptive writings of the law, for example are not couched in these direct, dictated terms and nor are the psalms. By reference to such examples and the different ways in which they must be considered, Ricoeur shows how inappropriate a single interpretation is and how the text must be available to be studied and considered and re-interpreted in order to reveal itself anew. The text must be allowed to speak into the present.

So the reader can approach the text afresh, without the burden of discovering the original intention of the author. The historical difficulties of linking the Julian whom we know from the bequests of the 14th and 15th centuries to the author of the extant 16th- and 17th-century manuscripts are, on this understanding, not a confounding issue. The Julian that is found in the text, however, refers to herself as the author, and Julian-as-author in the text is important. The Julian of the text makes explicit that she does not want to be seen or known (eg LT pp 320.34ff), but it is her way of receiving her revelations and communicating their self-transforming power to her readers that is the basis of my argument for her contribution to addressing the ecological challenge. This will become evident repeatedly when we read the text in Chapters 3–5. And although Ricoeur has loosened the ties of the text's historical setting, and therefore the reader from the burden of having to adopt the mantle of the historian, the 14th century in which the

Julian of the Short and Long Texts says, *in the text*, that she had her revelations is significant:

> This reuelation was made to a symple creature vnlettyrde leving in deadly flesh, the yer of our lord a thousande and three hundered and lxxiij, the xiij [or, in Sloane, viij] daie of May.
>
> (LT p 285.2ff)

The Julian of the text writes not in a chronological vacuum but in a medieval paradigm that is not *Gestell*, as Taylor shows.

Our hermeneutical approach, then, will adopt the Ricoeurian argument that the Julian texts can be treated independently, which frees us to take every word of them seriously, and accept them on their own terms, without having to try to make sense of them only by connecting them to a historical author. However, the person of Julian who emerges in the text will turn out to be critical for our reading, as she shows herself to be an example of a porous, non-*Gestell* self, whose way of writing is capable of transforming the *Gestell* self of her readers by, in turn, restoring our porosity.

The hermeneut always stands in medias res

Ricoeur writes that the 'world of the text can burst the world of the author', which means the text is set free from its author. It also means that 'whoever receives the text' is also free: not bound by 'the finite horizon' of the text's original audience (1977 p 22). Thus any of us can come to the text and make our own interpretation. Each of us is, though, making it as one among many people and cultures. We can never be the final interpreter, giving the last word on a text. We are always *in medias res* (Ricoeur 1975 p 91). This emphasises that the text has already passed through many interpretative hands. It holds the stamp of its earliest author(s) and scribes, and carries the thoughts of previous interpreters, who cast their shadows more or less strongly. So although we are free to make our own interpretation, we are also in a historical line, joining a community of interpreters, on some of whom we will draw as we read the Julian texts.

We readers bring our own worlds to the text from our own historical setting whether we like it or not. Ben Quash helpfully suggests that we make a virtue of this: we can intentionally bring important and deep questions from our own times. In this way, we can add positively and creatively to the meanings a text can offer. Shakespeare's plays have been interpreted anew repeatedly over the centuries since they were first written, deepening our understanding, bringing fresh insights for our own times from his words. The same is true of sacred texts. Quash uses the example of Carpaccio's painting of Job to illustrate his point. Carpaccio's own situation made him rediscover and redefine the story of Job, including in his painting aspects of the story that are not emphasised in the biblical text from which he would have worked. We in turn, because of our situation, see things in Carpaccio's painting he may not have consciously intended (2013 pp 142ff). Our encounter with the Julian texts comes from a desire to ask a question from our own time about our response to the ecological challenge, believing that her writing, which was clearly not for an audience worried about the state of the planet in the same way, will nevertheless address the underlying cause of *Gestell* subjectivity. In so doing, aspects and characteristics of the text will become evident that will have hitherto remained hidden.

The effect of the poetic text

The biblical revelation narrative, writes Ricoeur, is 'generative poetics': its poetic language generates a change in the reader (1977 p 15). It does so by bringing us to a place of communion where we no longer see things as objects. He writes '[m]y deepest conviction is that poetic language alone restores to us that participation in or belonging-to an order of things which precedes our capacity to oppose ourselves to things taken as objects opposed to a subject' (1977 p 24). Poetry saves us from turning things into 'standing reserve' but it does more than return us to Heidegger's 'place or time of the arising of the technological point of view' (1977 p 17). The 'order of things', which precedes our objectifying, is participative, not a solitary *cogito* self but a prior state of 'belonging-to'. 'Being' is relational, or in Charles Taylor's terms, porous, and poetry, according to Ricoeur, has the power to restore it.

Poetic texts, unlike scientific texts, do not demonstrate truth through adequation, equivalence, proof or rational argument, but by manifesting it, by being it through imitation of real life. Biblical texts are poetic texts, argues Ricoeur because they do not seek to prove God by argument; rather, God is that to which the hymnic, sapiental, narrative, prescriptive and supplicative texts refer. The meaning of God circulates among these different references, manifest in them but never fully, and often, intriguingly, only as that which remains hidden.

Poetic texts create new possibilities, even worlds. Readers open to the text will be exposed to its poetry and changed by it, rather than being exposed to an argument and working out whether to agree with it or not. In his later writings, Ricoeur describes the reading self experiencing a 'paroxysmic homology' (1995 p 263) in encountering a poetic text: it calls us into response and we involuntarily and suddenly move into communion with its meaning. The poetic texts he is writing about here are the calls to the prophets in the Hebrew Scriptures. The prophets-to-be are called to something far beyond anything they believe they can reach (p 265) and the call succeeds: despite themselves, the prophets are radically displaced from their familiar world. Their autonomy 'explodes' (p 61), and so by extension does mine when I encounter poetry. There follows a tussle between my autonomous conscience which has to work things out for itself, and cannot see how to address the challenge the text is presenting me, and the obedience of faith; for the prophets, faith in God as they are called to a seemingly impossible task. The obedience is not, however, blind heteronomy, blind obedience to something outside ourselves. It is a heartfelt response to the manifestation of truth through the poetic form. This is a vulnerable place for the reader to be, but if the reader is bound in *Gestell* then it is also a means of salvation. I the reader must let go of my seemingly transcendent, *cogito* subjectivity and allow the poetry to have its effect, which is to restore me to my originary relational state that precedes the subject-object divide.

Poetic texts thus have an effect rather than make an argument, and their effect is to undo the objective perspective of the reading self. The category 'poetic' works for the Julian texts because in the same way as the Julian of the text is changed by the revelations she received, so, I will seek to show, her text has the 'poetic' potential to change us as we receive them, even to call us into an entirely new way of being. If I am right to include the Julian texts in Ricoeur's category of poetic language that has the power to restore 'belonging-to' in the reader, we will experience their effect as such when we come to read them.

The reading self is summoned and changed

Ricoeur argues that the reading self is restored by the poetic text to its 'originary' state of 'belonging-to'. The *cogito* self is undermined by this process. Ricoeur's critique of the self itself began in his essay 'Phenomenology and Hermeneutics' (1975) where he opposes the idealism if not the method of phenomenology. The idealism of phenomenology, asserted by Heidegger, retains the transcendent self, and this limits its capacity to free us from *Gestell*. Werner Jeanrond explicitly brings Heidegger and Ricoeur into dialogue, contrasting Heidegger's phenomenological self with Ricoeur's hermeneutics, which are radically suspicious of the self itself and must always involve a process of self-reflection (Jeanrond 1991 pp 109ff). Phenomenology critiqued by hermeneutics ensures the apparently transcendent self is undermined. As Merold Westphal puts it, the turn to hermeneutics meant that 'finitude' (the creatureliness of the reader) and 'suspicion' (the fallibility of the reader) are able to be acknowledged as the material change effected upon the reader by a text (2009 p 273).

The turn in phenomenology to hermeneutics began with Hans-Georg Gadamer, for whom hermeneutics meant having our experience of the world changed by the text (1966/1976 p 15). The subject is not found prior to the text, as one who makes use of the text as a *Gestell* self. The subject is found by means of the text. Ricoeur says the poetic text 'completes' the subjectivity of the reader (1975 p 94). He distinguishes between the *idem* self, which is recognisably the same over time, and the *ipse* self, which changes over time. The answer to the question 'who am I?' must take the long route through the 'vast laboratory of thought experiments available to him in cultural stories and symbols' (1990 p 148). The subjectivity of the reader is the end of the hermeneutical endeavour, not the beginning of it. We are not transcendent, *cogito* selves, we are *ipse*, porous, changing all the time in the narrative of our journey through the encounters with poetic text. This Ricoeurian reader is a disciple of the text, 'summoned' and open to being changed by it (1995 pp 262ff). We appropriate the meaning of the text by disappropriating ourselves. 'Then I exchange the *me, master* of myself, for the *self, disciple* of the text' (1975 p 95, author's italics). The summoning is asymmetric because the call of the text is to a greater subjectivity: the text's meaning is greater than we are. This is the 'paroxysmic homology', the ego radically decentred by the text, despite itself.

Concluding summary

The initial foundations for my hermeneutical approach have been laid, thanks primarily to Paul Ricoeur. I have established the independence of the Julian texts so that we can take every word of them seriously, as we will receive them, without worrying about what the original author meant by them or knowing the detail (or indeed anything, conclusively) about the *sitz im leben* of the original text and its audience. I have placed us *in medias res*, one interpreter among many. This gives us permission both to receive previous interpretations and to consciously bring our own deeply felt question about the 21st-century ecological challenge to the Julian texts, without the burden of having to have the last word on them. I have introduced the concept of the poetic text, which has the power to effect a change on us as readers, calling us out of our known world, and I have said the Julian texts belong in this category. And I have introduced the insight that as readers to be transformed, we must become disciples of the text, not its masters. We have to be summoned by an asymmetric call from something greater than we are that opens us to change. Our *ipse* self is the result of our long journey into encounter with the text.

Ricoeur's critique of the self and the text offer the beginning of a response to our enslavement to *Gestell*. The approach can be developed much further, however, in ways that will release the great potential of the Julian texts to contribute to our salvation by making us porous again. The next sections will build a three-pillared hermeneutical approach on these invaluable Ricoeurian initial foundations.

Developing Ricoeur: reading is performative

Introductory: Ricoeurian foundation

Ricoeur's exposition of the *ipse* self on its long journey of encounter with the text, with no short cuts, implies that the experience of encounter is 'performative', because readers actively participate in it: we embark upon a journey. In the text, Julian is called into performative interaction with the Christ whom she encounters in her revelations. She is a wholly involved participant. Her text, emerging from her encounters as a continuing expression of them, in turn calls her readers into performative and interactive response. Julian dissolves her own and her readers' *Gestell* distance by placing herself among us, her 'evyn Cristen', so that we encounter as she does, and are changed by the encounter. She teaches by example that, like her, we are not transcendent selves interpreting a text from a distance. This approach means that 'reading' the texts involves active participation by the reading subject: a performative interaction with the text, not a critique of it. Julian wants her readers to understand and learn from what has happened to her:

> Alle that I say of me I mene in person of alle my evyn cristen, for I am lernyd in the gostely shewyng of our lord god that he meneth so. And therfore I pray yow alle for gods sake, and counceyle yow for yowre awne profyght, that ye leue the beholdyng of a wrech that it was schewde to, and myghtely, wysely and mekely behold in god, that of his curteyse loue and endlesse goodnesse wolld shew it generally in comfort of vs alle. For it is goddes wylle that *ye take it* with a grete ioy and lykyng, as Jhesu hath shewde it *to yow*.
>
> (LT pp 319.33ff, my italics)

Julian calls her writing of the text a performative act to be continued in its reception by her readers:

> This boke is begonne by goddys gyfte and his grace, but it is nott yett *performyd*, as to my syght [...] for [god] wyll haue [his meaning] knowyn more than it is.
>
> (LT pp 731.3ff, my italics)

Our hermeneutical approach will seek to do justice to this call by developing Ricoeur's account of the reader who is on a journey into the notion of 'performative participation': the understanding that meaning is made by the performative engagement of the reader *at the time* of the encounter, not worked out afterwards (or assumed beforehand). I will use theological and philosophical material to help build this hermeneutical pillar, and also turn to a collection of research by what are known as 'enactivist' scientists.

Performative philosophy and theology

A number of philosophers and theologians help to define this sense of real-time performance in encounter. For example, Julia Kristeva writes: 'poetic language cannot be understood unless it is being *carried out*' (1984 p 103, my italics). Denys Turner likewise writes that music's meaning is discovered as it is *performed* (2004 p 115). On these accounts the reader or listener may not remain passive if meaning is to be found. The reader must reach behind what Kristeva calls the 'phenotext' to the 'genotext'. The genotext embodies the hidden drives, language's 'underlying foundation' (1984 p 87), a space where the subject is not yet generated, but will be. The phenotext is what we see, making the hidden content conceptually explicit in the transfer of ideas, obeying rules of grammar and pronunciation. In the participative interaction, the reader of a poem enters into its production. Through music, Turner suggests, we experience emotion that is not ours, nor someone else's: it transcends subject and object, and we are performatively engaged with the meaning that is made. 'Music is, as it were, the body in the condition of ecstasy' (2004 p 115). He explicitly aligns this performative understanding with medieval *excessus*, a term Oliver Davies uses for Julian's revelations (Davies 1992).

Paul Janz's account of revelation could be characterised as performative. Revelation is not a conceptual communication, he writes, but a gift which has reality only when it is '*enacted* in life, made real in life' (2009 p 179, my italics). The Resurrection of Christ, as understood by Alain Badiou, is also a demonstration of performative meaning-making. The event of the Resurrection calls the self into faithful response; the Resurrection's meaning or revelation *is* the active, participative, faithful response: there is no interpretative gap between the event of the Resurrection and the Christian's belief in it (2003 pp 77f). Stanislas Breton writes of the Church as a community which expresses itself and finds its reality in its performative participation in Christ: dying *with*, suffering *with*, living *in*, etc. The actions 'recuperate the fervour of an origin (Christ) to which they are closely related' (2011 p 126, author's italics).

The material reality of performative interaction is attested by feminist theologians in particular. The theological anthropology of Shawn Copeland foregrounds the materiality of the divine revelation, arguing that the (by implication performative, interactive) *body* is the site for it (2010 p 2). Elizabeth Johnson places the feminine Holy Spirit as the performative animator that (quoting Jay G Williams) 'is God in the world, moving, stirring up, revealing, interceding' (1992 p 85), and she interprets the Incarnation as the creation of a world in which God can communicate, as the 'Whither' of our self-transcendence, the 'divine self to the other who is not divine' (2007 pp 35, 40, quoting Karl Rahner). These theologians convey the present aliveness and interactive engagement of encounter with God: the 'not divine' must participate in the performance of communication or revelation for it to happen.

Turning to the enactivists

Although these performative theologians and philosophers (if I may call them that) articulate the active engagement of the subject that is necessary for encounter to make meaning, I need to make the definition of 'performance' work harder if I am to do justice to the effect the Julian texts can have. I propose that her texts can have a visceral, material effect that call their readers into a performative response. The participative act makes meaning that transforms her readers' subjectivity; this in turn changes the way they see and live, and this addresses the ecological crisis. It is Julian's method that will help our 21st-century ecological challenge. In her text, Julian does not step away from and critique her revelations and their effect on her from a distance. She actively relives them in her years of reflection and in her writing, and this active Julian-consciousness, which is present for her readers as we encounter the texts, is what gives them their power to summon us into a performative response today. But if the meaning I seek to make of the Julian texts is to effect a change in our subjectivity, it has to find a way of retaining or rekindling the active Julian-consciousness as *I* write. To retain this 'in-the-moment' aliveness of encounter, which is the remarkable and distinguishing feature of the Julian texts, I turn to the enactivists, an interdisciplinary group of scholars of social cognition including psychology, psychiatry, philosophy, sociology and neuroscience. Their work seeks to capture without killing the embodied and embedded nature of human interaction. I draw on this material to put the definition of 'performative' to work. Davies would approve of this move: he sees in Julian's text the capacity to communicate to a reader today what it is to be a created being in a created world, through the reader's necessarily 'fully open and active consciousness' (2017 p 26).

The irony of turning to scientific research in order to 'make real' my interpretation of Julian is not lost on me. For Heidegger, all scientific research is *Gestell* because it separates subject and object in order to investigate 'object' and in so doing loses the truth of the observed object. However, the enactivists' science, emerging in the 21st century, is precisely not *Gestell*: in it one can detect a struggle to be free from *Gestell* seeing, as the enactivists try to embed their research methods in experience, not at a distance from it. Their inspiration comes from the phenomenology of Husserl, and the philosophies of Heidegger and Maurice Merleau-Ponty. In contrast to the *Gestell* science, which brings nature into a controlled and false environment in order to turn it into something useful, these researchers, wanting to understand social cognition, recognise that they *cannot* do it from a third person perspective:

> Our social lives are populated by different kinds of cognitive and affective phenomena that are related to but not exhausted by the question of how we figure out other minds. These phenomena include acting and perceiving together, verbal and non-verbal engagement, experiences of (dis-)connection, management of relations in a group, joint meaning-making, intimacy, trust, conflict, negotiation, asymmetric relations, material mediation of social interaction, collective action, contextual engagement with socio-cultural norms, structures and roles, etc.

These phenomena are often characterized by a strong participation by the cognitive agent *in contrast with the spectatorial stance* typical of social cognition research. We use the broader notion of embodied intersubjectivity to refer to this wider set of phenomena.

(Di Paolo and De Jaegher 2015 p 3, my italics)

The Julian of the text experiences powerful subjectivity-changing revelations whose meaning emerges as she participates in them *and* as she writes about them. In turn her readers can experience a changed subjectivity if we enter into performative, interactive encounter with the text, not as a spectator but as a participant. These are real-time, material acts of meaning-making, and the enactivists' research helps to make sense of them.

Enactive insights in performative encounter

One of the enactivists, Czech philosopher Alice Koubova, argues that our hidden depth, and that of others, is 'a performative aspect of our existence' (2015 p 62), using an experiment to explain what she means. Her research is a material demonstration of the Julian approach of transformative, performative encounter, because it illustrates how hidden depth, like Kristeva's genotext and the meaning of the Julian texts, can only be accessed and understood performatively. The experiment was inspired by Merleau-Ponty, who observes that we are invisible to each other corporeally because, paradoxically, our bodies are non-transparent. Our perception stops at the outer layer where material 'thickness' impedes further exploration of what lies beneath (1964 pp 166f). We are, further, invisible to each other cognitively as our presentation of, say, ideas, hides what lies behind them (1968 p 63). There is a vast mysterious store behind what we show each other and are aware of ourselves. Finding this hidden depth cannot happen theoretically but only through engaged participative performance. The experiment illustrates how our 'invisible store' is revealed by participative performance and not by cognitive reasoning. The experiment also illustrates that this hidden store is what makes further, more creative and unexpected performance possible. Since we will use these insights extensively to help understand the Julian texts when we come to read them, I will give a detailed account of the experiment, showing how each of the points it illuminates compare with words from the Julian texts.

The experiment required, in turn, each one of a group of students to enter a space with an audience made up of the other students, whom they were not to contact visually or physically. They themselves were given nothing to do. Each would remain in the space for up to five minutes. The audience was to support the actor with 'favourable attention' (Koubova 2015 p 65). The experiment took place over a year, with the students returning to the same space repeatedly. In the final part of the study, they entered the space in pairs.

The initial experience was terrifying as the students stood alone in the space with all 'stabilised normative systems of communication' removed (p 65). The first point to be illuminated by the experiment is that performative engagement is a step into the unknown, away from *Gestell* subjectivity, an act of bravery based on trust. The 'act of trust' is articulated well by Rowan Williams:

> If I know that no human dependence can serve here, only two options remain: that constantly fearful and cautious negotiation of my identity, building up what is constructive in my relation to my environment, and vigilantly looking out for the danger represented by the 'cultural' power of others; or an act of trust in my right or capacity to act and give.
> (Williams 2000 p 72)

The self so acting is Ricoeurianly 'summoned'. Julian was summoned to participate in the Passion of Christ in a comparable act of brave trust. Having fallen ill and believing she is at the point of death, she writes:

> Then cam sodenly to my mynd that I should desyer [...] that my bodie might be fulfilled with mynd and feeling of his blessed Passion [...] for I would that his paynes were my paynes [...] With him I desyred to suffer, liuying in my deadly bodie.
> (LT pp 292.43ff)

Julian's step into the unknown is a step away from her ordinary world, which is bound by her own set of subjective certainties, most of all those determined by 'holy chyrch', as we shall discover in Chapter 3.

As the experiment continued, the students began to find inner resources, such as stability: 'I felt like a rock or statue, full of meaning suddenly' (Koubova 2015 p 65); and materiality: 'I realised I was there as a body' (p 65). The second point to be illuminated is that 'inner resource' emerges materially, in performance, *after* the summoned self has responded as an act of trust. This cannot be anticipated and therefore it cannot be understood theoretically. Following immediately on from Julian's step into the unknown, her first revelation commences:

> And in this sodenly I saw the reed bloud rynnyng downe from vnder the garlande, hote and freyshely, plentuously and liuely [...] Right so, both god and man, the same that suffered for me, I conceived truly and mightly that it was him selfe that shewed it me without anie meane.
> (LT p 294.3ff)

The response to Julian's step into the unknown is a direct, unmediated ('without anie meane') showing to her of the dying Christ, who had hitherto been 'hidden' in her imagination and thoughts, not seen clearly and materially as he was now.

The students each began to explore creative play, becoming, for example, a flower or a scary crying voice. The third point thus to be illustrated is that the 'inner resource' is creatively new and unexpected. When Julian's request to experience the pains of Christ's Passion is materially answered in the eighth revelation, she suffers so much she regrets ever having asked for them:

> I felte no peyne, but for Cristes paynes; than thought me I knew fulle lytylle what payne it was that I askyd, and as a wrech I repentyd me, thyngkyng if I had wyste what it had be, loth me had been to haue preyde it.
> (LT p 364.53ff)

The desire for the pains of the Passion conceived in her youth (LT pp 285.4ff) could not prepare Julian for the actual pain, now performatively experienced.

Over time, as they repeatedly returned to the performance space, the students started to find a hidden, back-stage self: one student described over and over again coming to a point of finding and stopping at a secret shameful self she had always hidden, and deciding in one session finally to be that hidden self. She curled up on the stage like a foetus, but then quite quickly became bored, stood up and 'was born' (Koubova 2015 p 66). The self she had hidden became another actor on the stage, increasing her performative possibilities. The fourth point is that the inner self, which ordinarily remains deeply hidden, took time to be born and that required the constancy of the student in returning to the performance. But when she was finally born, she unfussedly became part of the performance: far from being exposed for the fraud she thought this secret self truly was, the student found her to be a further source of creativity. Julian's performative engagement with her revelations is powerfully enacted by her through her eyes, which are fastened on the crucifix held before them by her curate. The revelations take place on the crucifix and her constancy of gaze is critical to their meaning. So when a voice tempts her to look away and up to heaven rather than at the Cross, which is the source of such great pain, which she herself is experiencing, she refuses:

> Here me behovyd to loke vppe or elles to answere. I answeryd inwardly with alle the myght of my soule, and sayd: Nay I may nott, for thou art my heven. Thys I seyde for I wolde nott; for I had levyr a bene in that payne tylle domys day than haue come to hevyn other wyse than by hym.
> (LT pp 370.9ff)

Julian's constancy is rewarded by a deeper understanding of the nature of the Passion when she is shown the same painful, bloody, dying Christ on the Cross 'in blessydfulle chere' (LT p 379.7) as the 'hidden depths' of the pain of Christ are revealed to be love and joy. The eighth revelation, from which this example comes, will be explored in greater detail in Chapter 4.

Then the Koubova actors began to enjoy the experiment, following events rather than thinking about themselves. For example, one student found she was swaying slightly, and became aware that she was behaving as though balancing, so then she was balancing on a ship, and her fingers fluttered. These became a waving hand and she called to those to whom she was waving goodbye and 'goodbye, my hero' called imaginary others from the dock. Then she realised she was in the middle of the ocean and had no one to wave to, so now her hand, which was waving uselessly, became a sea monster that tried to bite her, she bit back and so on. The audience reported her and others' performance as fully alive and unexpected. The fifth point is that no one, neither the performer nor the engaged and attentive audience, knew what was going to happen next in the performance. It was an entirely new act that arose from the participative encounter. 'Invisible excess' is brought into play when there is relaxed curiosity and playfulness, and the audience approves, describing a certain power that moves them. An example from Julian of this 'invisible excess' is the 14th revelation, which is an 'example' or parable of a lord and a servant, a most unexpected, controversial and personal response that arose out of her urgent call to understand sin (LT pp 513.2ff), explored in detail in Chapter 5.

The final stage of the year-long experiment involved placing a second person with the actor so that there were now two people from the group on the stage. They reported a patient allowing of the other in a state of attentive playfulness, waiting to see what would happen, responding to slight moves but not worriedly. The sixth point is that at this final, relaxed and attentive point, the students are able to access and make sense of each others' hidden stores, performatively engaging with them and also drawing performance out of them. After Julian has spent 'xv yere after and mor' in participative interaction with her revelations, reflecting on what she saw, returning again and again to their detail, she is able to make sense of the 'hidden stores' of God's meaning:

> What, woldest thou wytt thy lordes menyng in this thyng? Wytt it wele, loue was his menyng. Who shewyth it the? Loue. What shewid he the? Love. Wherfore shewyth he it the? For loue. Holde the therin, thou shalt wytt more in the same.
> (LT pp 732.15ff)

The Koubova experiment thus illuminates key characteristics which will emerge in our reading of the Julian texts: of trustful stepping into the unknown; of the consequent release of creativity; of the novel nature of what is created; of the performative power of hidden depths that emerge over time; of the unanticipable nature of the performance; and of attentive responsiveness to the other which produces new creative acts. These characteristics are communicated by this enactivist experiment truthfully in the Heideggerian sense, that is not from a distance, not as *Gestell*.

42 *Developing a Post-Ricoeurian Hermeneutical Approach*

Performative encounter as enactive 'conversation'

Julian's performative engagement with her revelations means that they are not simply pageants passively observed. Her response to them, her interrogation of the God she meets in them and her musings about them are all active ingredients in what the revelations are, and in what the text we now read is. So much so, that at times it seems that the revelations are turned inside out, as Julian's understanding of and writing about them are intermingled with what happened in them. Nicholas Watson notices this (1993), as does Barry Windeatt, who observes that Julian does not disentangle the revelation from her illumination and inspiration, and does not think she needs to: they are both revealed by the same Spirit (2015 pp xlivff).

A helpful way of understanding Julian's performative engagement with her revelations, suggested by enactivism, is that she is in conversation with them. One piece of enactivist research reflects on the collective sense-making' that is conversation (Raczaszek-Leonardi, Debska, and Sochanowicz 2015). When each of two people speaking to each other is only trying to make themselves understood, then the conversation is merely representative, and each speaker bears the burden of meaning-making. Each is simply speaking and waiting to speak without listening to the other. When the conversation is directed towards coordination, then each is participating in a 'joint project' (p 353), in which they are performatively engaged in creating something new with their conversation partner, a new meaning emerging from the interaction. Fred Cummins writes of the mutuality in sense-making that is conversation creating 'a new kind of subject pole' (2015 p 335).

These enactivists offer ways of understanding how Julian's encounters in her revelations, including the sense she makes of them as she muses over them, convey such creative freshness. For example, Julian's interactions over the place and teaching of holy church, especially when it does not seem to concur with what she is being shown in her revelations, have the quality of a conversation that is seeking a new understanding. New meaning emerges with Julian's performative engagement in conversation with the revelations:

> The hygher dome god shewed hym selfe in the same tyme, and therfore me behovyd nedys to take it. And the lower dome was lernyd me before tyme in holy chyrche, and therfore I myght nott by no weye leue the lower dome.
>
> (LT p 488.23ff)

Julian presses the point: how true in God's sight is the 'dome' of holy church? New and unexpected revelations about holy church and its teachings emerge out of the 'joint project' of her participative questioning, born of her strong desire to understand, which will be explored in Chapters 3 and 5.

Another enactivist, Yanne Popova, helps us to understand how we readers, in turn, engage as performatively with the Julian texts as Julian has with her revelations, showing how fresh meaning emerges from this encounter, by viewing the narrator as a conversational partner, whom readers construct as they read. Thus written language is invested with life by the reader. We create a path as we read and the path is our own. We bring forth a reality through performative enaction. 'A meaningful encounter with a story is thus a participatory act of performance' (2015 p 325). The meaning of the text emerges moment by moment in the participative act, which becomes our own only when we enact it, as we read. In the case of our reading of the Julian texts, the Julian who emerges from our performative engagement with her is strangely elusive: she refuses any title such as teacher or narrator and she does not want to be looked at: 'leue the beholdyng of a wrech that it was schewde to' (LT p 320.36f). This elusive quality only engages our interest more and thus our interactivity: we look more closely for her in the text and find she herself is an example *par excellence* of the porous self willing to be transformed by her encounter. We will explore Julian's elusive subjectivity in Chapter 3.

The first hermeneutic pillar is built: that the encounter between the reader and the text is performative. Now, with the second, pillar, we reach into the heart of our endeavour in this book: to show how the Julian texts can restore our porosity.

Developing Ricoeur: reading is porous

Introductory: Ricoeurian foundation

The second pillar of the hermeneutical triad is concerned with the subjectivity of the reading self and how it is made porous by its encounter with the text. The restoration of porous subjectivity is of critical importance in our reading of the Julian texts because it reaches to the heart of the ecological challenge: that it is our subjectivity, bound to *Gestell*, that is the cause of the crisis of harm to the planet, and its restoration to porosity will therefore significantly contribute to addressing the crisis. Julian's help with this depends upon her ability to restore her readers' porosity. The suggestion here is that, first, we are already porous, already selves-in-relation, but second, that our porosity has to be rediscovered and third, made manifest. I will explain each of these assertions in turn.

The self is a priori relational

Ricoeur writes that the reading self is 'already a self in relation' (1995 p 262). This *a priori* state could be characterised as a state of 'woundedness' in that it implies an openness to that which is outside of or other than the self. At the beginning of her account of her revelations, Julian introduces herself as one who asks to be wounded:

> I harde a man telle of halye kyrke of the storye of saynte Cecylle, in the whilke schewynge I vndyrstode that sche hadde thre wonndys with a swerde in the nekke, with the whilke sche pynede to the dede. By the styrrynge of this I conseyvede a myghty desyre, prayande oure lorde god that he wolde grawnte me thre wonndys in my lyfe tyme, that es to saye the wonnde of contricyoun, the wonnde of compassyoun and the wonnde of wylfulle langgynge to god.
> (ST pp 204.46ff)

For Julian, the early wounds were a preparation for her revelations: readying her psychologically to receive and make sense of their powerful effect on her subjectivity. The preparedness of the self for encounter is articulated by Merleau-Ponty when he writes that perception is a 'perpetual parturition' that exists between the self and that which it perceives (1968 p 115). The predicative being is wounded as 'a sort of dehiscence opens my body in two [...] things pass into us as well as we pass into things' (p 123). For Kristeva, reaching behind the phenotext to the genotext to produce meaning calls for a decentring of the transcendent ego, 'cutting through it and opening it to a dialectic', as quoted by Graham Hughes (2003 p 106). Badiou also recognises the need for 'subjective weakness' if the truth is to continue to be deployed, because the truth 'traverses' the self (2003 p 54).

Julian's wounds of desire 'dwellid contynually' (LT p 288.46), ensuring that her subjectivity retained its porousness against the day when her revelations took place, and also, we might suggest, 'summoning' the revelations into existence. When they do happen, Julian 'marvels' and 'wonders' at them and continues to do so in the years of reflection on them thereafter. A connection between 'wound' and 'wonder' is made by Mary-Jane Rubenstein who proposes an etymological link:

> The word wonder derives from the Old English *wundor*, which some etymologists suggest might be cognate not only with the German *Wunder*, but also with *Wunde*: cut, gash, wound. While the OED does not recognise this derivation of wonder (appropriately, its origin is said to be 'unknown'), the OED does support a possible shared ancestry between wonder and wounding in the entry's 'obsolete' listings.'
> (Rubenstein 2008 p 9)

My attention was drawn to the link by anthropologist Michael Scott (2014), who notes that, for the Arosi people whom he studied, the land was their source of strength, but it only made its strength available to them by means of their 'wonder' at it. As soon as they lost their sense of wonder, they lost their strength. On this account, it is wonder that wounds, while the wounds of porous subjectivity in turn keep the wonder alive. For his own part, Scott worries that anthropology itself is committing 'wondercide' (2013 p 859) as its objectifying *Gestell*-like approach kills amazement at what is being studied.

In contrast to the *Gestell* habit of objectification, the enactivists' approach recognises that the reality of social interaction is that people are always already emotionally engaged with and hence porous to each other, so if we want to know about someone, we do not stand at a distance and watch them, at least not for long and not to any helpful end. Arne Naess, founding father of the 'deep ecology' movement, gives the example of someone witnessing two people conducting x-rays, not knowing anything of the culture and civilisation in which the x-ray is taking place. One of the clinicians is left-handed, the other right-handed and so conducts the x-ray differently. Without engaging with the clinicians, the observer will not know that this is irrelevant to the x-ray itself; they may think that they are watching two different operations. One of the clinicians may be smoking or singing; again, without knowledge of the culture and context the observer may think that this is relevant to the taking of the x-ray (Naess 2016 p 181). By contrast, the enactivists interact with them: move towards them, ask them questions and watch their facial and other bodily movements as they respond.

The enactivists draw extensively on empirical evidence from the 'second person' neuroscientific research of Leonard Schilbach and colleagues to demonstrate that we are first of all social selves. The research confounds the *Gestell* self, as it is designed to reflect the embodied and embedded nature of human intersubjective interaction (Schilbach et al 2013 p 395). Using fMRI scanning, Schilbach and colleagues measure what happens neurologically as subjects interact with each other. The research demonstrates the significance of 'joint attention', that is, doing things together, both for the enjoyment of the adult subjects and also, for younger subjects, as an important precursor of social cognitive abilities, long before they pass the 'false belief test'. This test, cited by Schilbach (p 404), is sometimes called the Sally-Anne task. The subject sees Sally put a marble in a particular place, then leave. Anne comes in, seen by the subject but not by Sally, and moves the marble to another place. The test subject is then asked, where would Sally look for the marble when she came back to retrieve it? Subjects do not usually 'pass' this test until aged four or thereabouts. As it happens this test has itself been undermined by a second-person approach, which involves not asking the subjects but watching their behaviour in response. They then appear to 'pass' the test between nine and 30 months of age (Brincker 2015).

The brain activation in the case of 'looking together' is that which is associated with seeking to grasp the mental state of the other, what the other's communicative intentions are and how to contextualise those (Schilbach et al 2013 p 403). Schilbach's research has found that there are automatic reactions in our social encounters *before* we have time to respond consciously.

The pre-conscious, pre-linguistic state, arising when we come face to face with the other, is common ground in the encounter, and is not possible to control or modify (p 403). The fMRI scan can identify the place of pre-conscious common ground, but it remains opaque: Schilbach calls it 'dark matter' (p 394). Neural activity can be seen, but not this social self itself, and yet, like dark matter, it clearly exerts profound influence. The 'dark matter' generated by the face to face encounter is a highly complex set of interactive physical responses or reflexes, which are so intense in their activity that they support higher level functions, including language (p 403). As interlocutors seek to understand each other they use conversation, but the pre-conscious common ground is already present, and other ways of communicating, such as body language, play their part. 'Interlocutors produce and monitor paralinguistic cues and one another's instrumental behaviour to ensure that they, indeed, understand one another' (p 412). The *a priori* relational self, then, is present in the face to face encounter; it arises there, it can be seen through fMRI scanning to be there. What we see and experience as two people getting to know each other is more accurately described as confirming what we already have: common ground. Our bodies, says Davies, commenting on the Schilbach findings, are fine-tuned to get to know each other interactively through self-organising mutual exchanges that are too rapid to enter consciousness. They happen before we are conscious of them. Rather, one might suggest that our sociality calls our consciousness into wakefulness. Bodies interact materially at 'a point prior to our ability to see the world as a knowing subject' (2015 p 12).

Davies explicitly connects Schilbach's modern account of second-person neuroscientific research to the effect of the language of the Julian texts (2017), arcing back over the centuries of *Gestell* thinking to Taylor's porous self. In her texts, one powerful example of *a priori* porous subjectivity is given in the 14th revelation, where the character of the servant is both Adam, who himself stands for everyman, and Christ:

> In the servant is comprehendyd the seconde person of the trynyte, and in the seruannt is comprehendyd Adam, that is to sey all men [...] When Adam felle godes sonne fell; for the ryght onyng whych was made in hevyn, goddys sonne myght nott be seperath from Adam, for by Adam I vnderstond alle man.
>
> (LT pp 532.211ff)

Less dramatically, but with no less import because in saying this she emphasises her porosity with her readers, Julian identifies herself with everyman: 'by me aloone is vnderstonde alle' (LT p 442.6f); and 'I saw that his menyng was for the generalle man, that is to sey alle man [...] of whych man I am a membre' (LT p 702.5ff). We could say that our consciousness is 'called into wakefulness' by Julian's seeing which she puts into language (Davies 2015 pp 12f); we realise our woundedness and become open to direct encounter with the Christ of her revelations as she writes of our *a priori* porous subjective identity with her.

Enactivist Miriam Kyselo raises the question that, if our subjectivity is fundamentally social, it must be unembodied, because all bodies have definition. The self, she argues, is a social self, created by the back and forth of 'social distinction and participation processes' (2015 p 78), but it is not embodied: the body 'plays an important but rather enabling role' (p 81). The body is thus not the self, but its mediator. Kyselo's logic is persuasive, if we have been regarding 'body' as the physical entity we walk around in, whose edge stops at the edge of our skin. But Andy Clark, whose work is also drawn upon by the enactivists, removes the problem of edges by removing the edges of our bodies altogether. The pencil we use for writing, or the stick for walking, or the smartphone for connecting with others or gathering information, all become a 'kind of unmediated arena for bodily action' (2011, p 10). For Clark, our subjectivity is the ever-changing product of numerous encounters or interfaces: within the brain, for example with the various parts of the brain bringing information to the hippocampus to assist its cognition; between the brain and the central nervous system; between the sensory impressions on the skin, through the eyes, ears, nose and taste in the mouth and the central nervous system; and complex cognitive and emotional interfaces with other people. He does not differentiate between encounters that take place within and outside the body.

Julian's understanding of 'body' is porous, for example:

> oure good lorde lokyd in to hys syde and behelde with joy, and with hys swete lokyng he led forth the vnderstandyng of hys creature by the same wound in to hys syd with in; and ther he shewyd a feyer and delectable place, and large jnow for alle mankynde [...] And ther with he brought to mynde hys dere worthy blode and hys precious water whych he lett poure out for loue.
>
> (LT pp 394.3ff)

We will read further of the material porosity of Christ in Chapter 3.

The first aspect of porous subjectivity, that the self is *a priori* relational, is recognised as the 'cut' woundedness of the self by Kristeva and Merleau-Ponty, and confirmed in the second-person neuroscientific research of Schilbach. This in turn informs the work of the enactivists, who are so convinced of our ontological relationality that they conclude that solitary confinement is a far crueller punishment than has been assumed, as it denies the self that is 'hard-wired to be other oriented', as Sean Gallagher puts it (2015 p 407). It is a worrying indicator of longer term problems emerging from the extensive isolation of the pandemic years of 2020–2022. Julian calls herself wounded and acknowledges the material porosity not only of herself but also of the

Christ she encounters in her revelations. But the *a priori* relationality has both to be rediscovered and restored. Reading the Julian texts can do this. We will look at rediscovery and restoration in turn.

Encounter with the text makes evident our porosity

Ricoeur articulates the experience of hermeneutics as 'belonging-to'; that is 'a relationship of inclusion which unites the allegedly autonomous subject and the allegedly adverse object' (1975 p 89). We are *a priori* relational, but it is in encounter that we discover ourselves to be so. This insight can be developed further by reference to the enactivists as the experience of a self that feels itself to be *changing* in its porous interactive engagement with the other. We saw how enactivists Popova, Raczaszek-Leonardi and Cummins showed, respectively, that reading a text, entering into a conversation, or just speaking even only to oneself, continuously produce in real time the self that knows itself as porous. For Popova, reading is an enactive performance of 'intersubjective sense-making': as we act with the aim of being understood, so we write with the aim of being understood by our readers (2015 p 316). Raczaszek-Leonardi sees conversation as a 'joint project' enacted between contributors porous to each other and to the task of collective meaning-making (2015 p 353). Cummins thinks voice gives rise to 'a transient subjecthood' (2015 p 329), its employment in different circumstances generating porous subjectivity, such as synchronous speaking or chanting, where if one speaker stumbles the other is likely to as well. Such subjective 'entanglements' (p 353) happen not just linguistically but also in gaze, posture, gestures and blinks, and neurologically. The mutuality in sense-making through voice gives rise to a new kind of 'subject pole', which is 'not co-extensive with the individual person' (p 336).

Two observations about the Julian texts show the relevance of these studies for my hermeneutical approach to reading them. First, Julian explicitly states that her writing of her own encounters with her revelations is for the purpose of drawing its readers into our own, direct encounter with God, that by implication will change us as it has changed her:

> leue the beholdyng of a wrech that it was schewde to, and myghtely, wysely and mekely behold in god.
>
> (LT p 320.36f)

Julian is not a mystical 'other' whose transformation we witness, but rather a doorway through which we readers step into direct 'beholding', and have *our* subjectivity transformed. Second, the porous subjectivity of the 'joint project' of a conversation occurs continuously as Julian engages throughout the text in dialogue with Christ and God, including her subjective 'entanglement' with the changing conditions of his face as he draws close to death in the eighth revelation, to which she pays such close attention.

For example, as Christ passes from the terrible pain of the Passion into the 'blessydfulle chere' of the Resurrection, Julian writes:

> Then brought oure lorde meryly to my mynd: Wher is now any poynt of thy payne or of thy anguysse? And I was fulle mery.
> (LT p 379.9f)

In 'conversation' with Christ Julian's subjectivity is changed: in the moment of his speaking to her she experiences in herself the shift from the profound pain of the Passion to the 'mery' Resurrection.

Our *a priori* porous subjectivity is thus rediscovered and experienced in its encounter of with text. It is actively restored by reading.

Encounter with text restores the porosity of the reader and also the text

Thirdly, and finally, we can explore how encounter restores porosity. Not only the porosity of the reading subject but also, learning from Ricoeur, the porosity of the text itself. Encounter restores porosity on both sides. Ricoeur writes that poetic language 'restores' our 'participation-in or belonging-to' (1977 p 24). But the 'restoration' reveals a greater potential in the reading subject than had hitherto been realised: the enactivists show that the porous interactive encounter has the effect of producing new, creative selves, for example the Koubova students realised the greater potential of their subjectivity as they became porous to it in themselves and in each other. As Koubova puts it: 'to make sense means not to insist on some fixed identity and closure, but rather to take the situational counterpart as one's own potential' (2015 p 67).

The porous and creative subjectivity of other kinds of entities than people or texts can also be realised by means of porous encounter. I offer the following example because it demonstrates how science can be in slavery to *Gestell* subjectivity, but in the hands of a really great scientist, can also be freed from it. Charles Darwin had found a tropical fossil near the surface of the ground in the middle of England, and observed how dismayed his companion was, because the finding, if it was what it seemed, 'would be the greatest misfortune to geology, as it would overthrow all that we know about the superficial deposits of the midland counties' (1887/1958 p 69). The 'subjectivity' of geology, from which its assumptions and inferences about data emerged, was being summoned to change because of this encounter. By virtue of the encounter with the unexpected or unknown, that which did *not* fit with the hypothesis accepted by scientists, geology was transformed. The *Gestell* tendency in science is to see only those data which support the current hypothesis. Good scientists, aware of this inner tendency, must always seek to disprove their hypotheses, as Karl Popper insisted (1959). In Darwin's day, geologists were labouring under the assumption that the upper layer of sediment in the midland counties was formed by a particular set of geological movements that Darwin's finding did not demonstrate. Darwin made geology a great deal more interesting and his companion should have rejoiced instead of fearing change. Julian would have: rather like the scientists whose fixed notions are brought into question, that which Julian had understood and believed and defined herself by, for example in the teaching of 'holy chyrch' on hell and damnation, is brought into question by what she cannot deny God has shown her in her revelations (LT pp 427.2ff). By denying neither holy church itself nor the evidence of her eyes in her revelations, Julian makes possible a porosity in the subjectivity of holy church itself, an intriguing move we will discover in Chapter 3.

As with the subjectivity of geology, so Julian's subjectivity (and that of her readers) emerges from her encounters as an expanded, greater self, like the prophets summoned to greater things (Ricoeur 1995 p 265), for example in the culmination of prayer:

and than shall we alle come in to oure lorde, oure selfe clerely knowyng and god fulsomly hauyng, and we endlesly be alle hyd in god, verely seyeng and fulsomly felyng, and hym gostely heryng, and hym delectably smellyng, and hym swetly swelwyng.

(LT p 481.49ff)

The subjectivity of Julian's self in encounter is transformed, and her cognition is transformed too. She sees, knows, has, feels, hears, smells and tastes what had hitherto been hidden from her. The transformed subjectivity changes everything for the subject.

The text is also realised as porous. Julian's wounds that 'dwellid contynually' (LT p 288.46) were expressions of desire which created an asymmetry that 'summoned' her revelations into being. The subjectivity is porous on both sides of the encounter and the asymmetric calling that transforms subjectivity is likewise on both sides. It is not just the subjectivity of the reading self that is realised as porous, but also the 'text': as we saw in the example, Darwin's subjectivity as a geologist was changed, and so was the geology he encountered in the form of the unexpected location of the fossil. His openness to enquiry called out a different response from the terrain he was exploring. The point is not that there was some sort of magical material change in the Earth; but rather that in response to his looking openly, the Earth became more porous, revealing new and unexpected things about itself *to him* (and not, for example, to his companion, whose looking was closed, nonporous). Julian's revelations and the God she encounters in them reveal new and unexpected things about themselves under her enquiring and open gaze. The porosity of the Julian texts has been noted by Watson and Windeatt (see above, p 42, and also below, pp 64), reflecting Julian's ongoing open enquiry. In our reading that follows, we will see many examples of the creative porosity of the revelations born of Julian's desire to 'see'.

My first hermeneutical pillar established the active, participative, performative nature of reading producing meaning as a joint endeavour in real time. This second pillar shows that reading makes evident our originary porosity and, in the performative participation of encounter, restores it. Not only the reader but also the text becomes porous in the act of reading. Now there is a final, stabilising third pillar to be built: that of the new world that is created out of this lively encounter.

Developing Ricoeur: reading is creative of niche

Introductory: Ricoeurian foundation

Ricoeur provides a foundation for this third pillar of my hermeneutical triad when he writes: 'what is to be interpreted in a text is the projection of a world which I could inhabit' (1975 p 93). He also writes of the world of the text as 'the new being that is displayed' (1995 p 44), opening up possibilities for the reading subject that it could not anticipate or make for itself. The world that preceded the one issuing from the text is the world of the reading subject in which the encounter with the text takes place, which is then transformed by the encounter. The third hermeneutical pillar, which I am calling 'niche construction', goes beyond this Ricoeurian foundation by including both the 'niche' of the encounter of reader with text and the 'niche' that is created by it. By 'niche' I mean all the particular features of location, including physical space, things, other people and also prevailing ideas and beliefs which determine the worlds of Julian in the text and our own worlds, we who are readers of her text. The 'existing' niche is constructed as it is by virtue of the subjectivity of each of us: each occupies a niche defined by who we are. This existing niche then interacts dynamically with the performative, porous encounter of Julian with her revelations, and of the reading self with the text; the 'ensuing niche' is the creation of the performative, porous encounter of the self with revelation or text. To put it more succinctly: as the subjectivity of the self is changed by its encounter with revelation or text, so its world is, too.

The word 'niche' is apt, because the world (niche) that is, and the world (niche) that emerges from the encounter, are particular and specific to the self. Julian's encounter with her revelations take place in a particular world (as described in the text) of: her illness; her sick room; the people who are in her sick room; the crucifix, which has religious significance for Julian, held before her eyes upon which the revelations take place; Julian's prevailing beliefs about the teaching of holy church; her state of 'wounded' porosity to what she is shown; and her beliefs about her 'evyn cristen' and her identification with them. These inner and outer features of her niche play their part in influencing Julian's encounter. In turn, her encounter with her revelations produces new niches which, as Chapters 3–5 will show, become cosmic in proportion and in what is included in them. As Julian's subjectivity changes, so does her niche. The Julian texts themselves are a niche constructed out of Julian's revelations, emerging from them and embodying them. The readers of the Julian texts bring their niches to her reading. These are *Gestell*, niches in which everything is utilitarianly in 'standing reserve', determined by our 'buffered' subjectivity. The porosity that is realised by the performative reading of the texts constructs a new niche that is not bound to *Gestell*. As Oliver Davies argues: '[t]hrough such texts, we may receive communicatively a mode of being human in the world which we could not ourselves produce' (2017 p 16).

Source of the phrase 'niche construction'

Oliver Davies has applied 'niche construction' to the study of the medieval mystical texts (Davies 2017), borrowing it from its origin within a recent iteration of evolutionary theory called 'extended evolutionary synthesis' (Laland et al. 2015). Niche construction is the name given to the dynamic interaction between organisms and environment out of which habitats form, which influence and change the organisms, and also have an effect on the wider environment. The fact that seeing a particular kind of nest can tell us exactly what species of creature lives there, without having to see the creature, is evidence of niche construction (Laland and Sterelny 2006 p 1755), as creatures inherit the same nest type from previous generations. The inheritance is not genetic: nest types are inherited phenotypic, rather than genotypic, variations (Pigliucci and Müller 2010). Phenotypic, as we saw with its use, analogously, by Kristeva, is to do with what shows, such as habitat, rather than with underlying genetic structure. We inherit appearance and behaviour by other means than genetic, including how we build our nests. This is relevant to the ecological challenge, as it indicates that behaviour change (for the better, eg building human habitats that do not harm the Earth) would also be passed on to future generations.

The nest or niche of a creature in turn affects the creature's behaviour. For example, humans are lactose intolerant except those humans who live near dairy herds (p 1756). The niche construction of earthworms affects the wider environment as they burrow into the soil to make it act as external kidneys and extensively change the structure and chemistry of the soil (p 1759). 'Even the inadvertent production of by-products by simple organisms, such as the manufacture of derivative chemicals by photosynthesising cyanobacteria, are consistent, reliable, directed sets of metabolic actions that affect a change in the environment (here, an increase in atmospheric oxygen)' (p 1755). The increase in atmospheric oxygen is critical for life for some organisms, such as humans, and not others. Niche construction interacts with its environment, affecting and being affected by others.

Niches thus emerge or are constructed from the porous encounter between the self and its environment, and Erwin Straus, an evolutionary biologist writing in the 1950s, identified this porous interdependence explicitly when he noticed that different perspectives create different niches, even when the niches are the same space. Humans stand upright, he wrote, and that means their world is very different from other creatures on all fours. Straus saw that each organism creates its own world by selecting from its environment some things and not others, depending upon what it needs (Straus 1952/1966). He recognised the dynamic two-way influence of organism and place before the term 'niche construction' was coined.

Charles Darwin himself had noticed the influence of place. In his autobiography he wrote: 'Th[e] problem [to make sense of] is the tendency in organic beings descended from the same stock to diverge in character as they become modified. That they have diverged greatly is obvious from the manner in which species of all kinds can be classed under genera, genera under families, families under sub-orders and so forth; and *I can remember the very spot in the road*, whilst in my carriage, when to my joy the solution occurred to me [...] The solution, as I believe, is that the modified offspring of all dominant and increasing forms tend to become adapted to many and highly diversified *places* in the economy of nature' (1887/1958 pp 120f, my italics). It is consistent with the concept of niche construction that Darwin has such a precise memory of where it was that he solved the problem.

These early insights into the role of place in evolution have led some biologists to question the special attention given to niche construction now. E. Mayr had already written about 'soft inheritance' (1982), and Dickens and Rahman, in their review article taking issue with the special 'extended' status that has been conferred on niche construction (2012), point out that Julian Huxley had already included competition, selection and random mutation in his 'modern synthesis' (Huxley 1942). Edmund Brodie is similarly unimpressed with the suggestion that niche construction is offering anything new to evolutionary theory (2005), but its familiarity only serves to embed niche construction within evolutionary theory more securely. As Vandermeer points out, the proponents of niche construction see their work as a culmination of what others have studied, not a novel intervention (2004).

Uses of the concept that contribute to our hermeneutical approach

The concept of niche construction has been used, not least by the enactivists, in ways that are valuable to a hermeneutical approach that foregrounds the text's material effect on the subjectivity of the reader. These are first, the development of the idea of 'affordances' which is what other things become for us when they are in our niches; second, social aspects of niche construction; third, the recognition that niche construction is not only the place of performative and porous interaction but also embodies it as the creative and material expression of it; and fourth, the way in which niche construction settles into habitat and thus habit. I will look at each of these developments of niche construction in turn, showing their relevance to my hermeneutical approach to Julian by giving examples from her texts.

'Affordances' in niche construction

Human niche construction involves the use of material tools, which the enactivists have termed 'affordances'. Affordances are those things in the world that, as we seek to make sense of ourselves and our surroundings, we engage with interactively and performatively. As affordances are drawn into the interactive performance, so they become instrumental in niche construction. A cup affords us the act of grasping it in order to drink; or a mountain for climbing; or a hat for placing on our head. Anthropologist Agustin Fuentes (2015) notes that humans modify material elements to extend their motor capabilities and this enhances their ability to interact with and change ecologies. This characterisation of use of things in the environment sounds like Heidegger's 'standing reserve'. But here the relationship between the person and the thing is porous and interactive, not utilitarian: affordances are things that we 'realise' by their use, and are ourselves changed by (Laroche, Berardi, and Brangier 2015). We work out how to use a cup or a path, coordinating ourselves with the thing and making it an affordance thereby. Our ongoing activity is an interaction with the world around us, so cognition is not transcendent knowledge from a distance but sense-making through performance, 'realised interactively' in the mix of things (p 41). This 'different seeing' of the things around us shows how our response to the world emerges from our subjectivity, which is why our response to the ecological challenge has to start with our subjectivity. Rather than dominating and controlling things, we learn to 'dance' with them. Marek McGann, who has a similar account of affordances, calls our interactive performance an 'achievement' (2015 p 20).

We see this performative interaction with things in the Julian texts, the most important of which is the crucifix her curate holds before her eyes as she lies close to death in her sickroom (LT p 291.22ff). The crucifix is an 'affordance' on these terms: Julian's 'sense-making' of her revelations involves her performative and porous interaction with it. McGann notes that light is the medium in which the dynamic encounter of agent and affordance takes place as our eyes inspect our environment and we coordinate our movements with the things around us (2015 p 21). Julian describes her crucifix as self-effulgent (LT pp 290.20ff) as the space around it grew dim, changing her niche from a quotidian sickroom to the place where her mystical revelations can happen.

Social niche construction

Our interaction with location is mediated and influenced by the group, argues Fuentes: 'actual people almost never engage with evolutionarily relevant challenges (be they nutritional, social, ecological, economic, political etc) by themselves, outside of a social (cultural) network, or even outside of spatial proximity, or without reference, to other humans' (2015 p 303). The fact that humans begin, as it were, with social relationships and shared knowledge means that these factors are critical to evolution and niche construction: they are where we start, not as one plus one plus one, each one separately seeking food, mates and an environment to live in, but straightaway socially and behaviourally acting as a group, and the social and behavioural interactions are multi-faceted:

> Heightened social and behavioural density and concomitant social complexity is a widespread, and potentially ancient, primate pattern, and the social networks of many primates are multidimensional and not best modelled as sequences of dyadic exchanges at either the individual or group level.
> (Fuentes 2015 p 304)

Humans create niches socially. Learning and teaching also have their place in niche construction, because they are developmental and evolutionary drivers for humans (Sterelny 2012). Julian's interaction with other people is critical to the niche she is in as well as the niche that is created by her revelations. These people include those who populated her sickroom, for example her mother who tried to close her eyes, thus potentially cutting off Julian from her revelations (ST p 234.29ff). When Julian later dismisses her revelations as ravings, the seriousness of the response from the religious person to whom she speaks changes her perspective (her subjectivity) and she reviews all that has happened (LT pp 632.16ff). The new niche of the text emerges out of this encounter, because (one presumes) she would not have reflected upon the revelations and then written about them if she had continued to think of them as ravings. The people in Julian's sickroom represent and become the means to reach all (LT p 319.22ff). We will read of the porous interactions with Julian's sickroom companions in Chapter 3, where we will also study Julian's psychological niche that formed out of her interaction with holy church and her 'evyn cristen' with whom she identifies. This niche later expands in the eighth revelation to include all creatures and heaven as well, as our reading in Chapter 4 will show.

Niche construction embodies performative and porous encounter

Niche construction takes place *as* we interact with other humans, the landscape, items in the landscape, use language, create symbols and signs, learn and teach. It is a dynamic activity that turns 'space' into 'place' (Davies 2016 p 92), that is both a result of interaction but also causal of it. Space is turned into creative place for enactivists Fantasia and colleagues who see how two people, meeting in a corridor, will dance to one side and then the other, unconsciously mirroring each other, evincing pre-cognitive relationality and creating a place, for a moment, in which they interact performatively and porously, before uncoupling and making space to move past each other (2015). The authors suggest that interaction opens up new domains, or niches, of sense-making that would not happen were they alone. For Julian, space becomes place as she porously and performatively interacts with Christ in her revelations, a niche whose edges are formed by the surrounding darkness and whose interior is lit by the self-effulgent crucifix. In that place, new worlds are created which ultimately include all of creation and heaven, as we will see in Chapter 4.

The created/creative nature of niche construction also shows itself in the Koubova experiment in which the students find, over time, new porous selves in the performance space created by the supportive attention of their fellow students who also created the material space by where they sat, configuring a place for their performing student colleague. Just so, Julian's sickroom attendees penetrate the gloom that surrounds the niche of her encounter with Christ on the self-effulgent crucifix, with important interactive and porous functions individually, such as her mother's arm reaching to close Julian's eyes, and also twice collectively, when their interaction brings into the niche of the revelations all 'them that shuld lyue' (including the reader), for whom, Julian realises, the 'avysion was schewde' (LT p 319.32); and later, when her sickroom companions laugh with her, they bring into the niche of Julian's revelations all her 'evyn cristen' (again, including the reader) (LT p 348.24ff).

For Raczaszek-Leonardi and colleagues, a conversation between people that is directed towards coordination makes language and the people using it creative and performative, and the participants may be said to be 'pooling the ground' (2015 p 362). The ground itself becomes creative as something more happens than the sum of the contributions to the conversation by the participants. Cummins saw that voice, in creating subjectivity, connects the subject speaking with world 'in real time' (2015 p 330): we create new niches as we speak. And as readers interact porously with the narrator whom they bring into being as they read, they also bring forth a new reality, a 'world that until then is not my own, but becomes my own when I enact it' (Popova 2015 p 326). So in turn Julian's readers, interacting porously with the text, find a new niche is being constructed as our subjectivity changes.

Enactivists John McGraw and colleagues describe the emergence of artifacts from encounter in their research. Their study was of groups of people designing cars out of LEGO. From the 'encounter' of working together on a task, an object emerged like imagination embodied. McGraw takes this process to be paradigmatic of cultural evolution: 'cognitive and cultural schemas find material realisation – are embodied – in the artifacts of material cultures' (2015 p 367), in the way they are used and embedded in action and interaction. Roman Catholicism without Bibles, incense, wafers, crucifixes and tombs is not easily recognisable as Roman Catholicism, he suggests. In times of persecution it would have had to be itself without these things, but precious things were squirrelled away in order to be kept safe for easier times, thus proving the case. In the same way, Julian's text may be said to have been 'pressed', to use a term from Andy Clark (2011 p 60), from her encounter with her revelations as an embodiment of the porous interactions they involved.

The body of Christ, with which Julian so powerfully interacts, especially in the eighth revelation, can itself be characterised as a niche because it is the *place* where our encounter with God becomes possible. Elizabeth Johnson writes of the Incarnation as the creative outcome of God's wish to communicate with creatures (2007 p 40). Stanislas Breton's account of Paul trying to mediate Christ to the nascent Church is a description of the creation of a porous niche that can, paradoxically, accommodate that which has burst all known bounds, which he describes as a 'passage from the most high to the most low, from the most universal to the most particular […] from divine transcendence to the earth of our works and days' (2011 p 106). In the eighth revelation of the dying of Christ, the stable platform of the crucifix Julian's curate held before her dimly seeing eyes (LT p 291.21), a seeming externality on which the revelations take place, provides the location for the revelatory encounter and is also creative within the encounter, as Julian's niche becomes cosmic. Even more creatively, the 14th revelation of the 'example' of the lord and the servant gives birth to a niche or world that is so novel that Julian has to return to it and re-enact the performative encounter again and again, over decades, in order to make sense of what she saw (LT pp 519.66ff).

Niche construction forms habitat and thus habit

One feature of niche construction is that it creates a place where activity can come to rest. For organisms, habitats are places where they can feel safe and habitual action, such as reproduction, becomes possible. After the 'action' of perception, as enactivist McGann (2015) puts it, out of which new possibilities arise, comes a period of habit-forming as organisms become used to new ways of doing things, often quite quickly. Thus, an unforeseen outcome of the McGraw experiment was the way that the first LEGO model swiftly became a design template for future models. The first models emerged out of the interaction of the team, technological restraints and other unanticipable contingent events in the niche. But then, 'relatively arbitrary forms' (2015 p 372) were settled upon by the teams, and despite their arbitrariness they became authoritative for later models, over time increasingly so. The pattern that emerged was of rapid conventionalisation and path dependency. The authors point to the enduring use of the QWERTY keyboard despite the fact that the technological constraint that led to that layout (typewriter key-hammer clashing) has long since disappeared. Once it has found its place to be, the creativity of encounter quickly settles into habit which in turn influences behaviours (for example, how we learn to touch-type). Habits are resistant to change, as we saw in the example of Darwin's fossil and the assumptions within geology that it did not substantiate.

But porosity can become a habit too. Clare Carlisle might have had Julian in mind when she writes of the way in which, through habitual practice, the 'less ordinary' habit of philosophy becomes a contemplative practice that 'knowing by acquaintance, turns the soul slowly towards wisdom' (2014 p 147). For Julian, habits described in the text that she had formed from her earliest youth, such as her attentive loyalty to holy church, her wounds of contrition, compassion and longing to God, and her deep knowledge and experience of prayer, formed her own steadfastly porous niche which was a creative place in which the revelations could take place and from where she could performatively participate. In turn, the revelations formed new niches and new habits, undermining (some) old ones.

The use of the Julian texts to contribute to our salvation from a *Gestell* subjectivity is to propose that the new 'habit' created by the niche of performative, porous interaction with the text will be of porosity itself. It could be thought that the porosity of the subject is a means, and once the niche is settled, it becomes buffered. But remaining porous will be critical to our salvation from *Gestell* subjectivity and our ongoing response to the ecological challenge. Julian remains an example of this as she establishes a habit of porosity in her early life, is porous to the revelations as they take place, and continues to be porous to new and deeper understandings of the revelations in the decades that follow.

I have harnessed niche construction, a term coined in evolutionary theory, in service of the third hermeneutical pillar, which recognises the significance of psychological and physical 'place' when we read. The niche in which the performative and porous encounter between Julian and her revelations, or reader and text, takes place influences the encounter, and is transformed by it, so that new niches emerge from the encounter. Niches contain affordances: those things within the niche which are dynamically interacted with, such as the crucifix held before Julian's eyes. They include other people, such as those who populated Julian's sickroom. Niches that are constructed from the performative and porous encounter can be said to embody them, as Julian's text embodies her revelations. And niches become habituated as the new place in which further performative and porous encounters can take place. 'Niche construction' thus describes how the same world can be so utterly different depending on our subjectivity.

Conclusion: a three-pillared, post-Ricoeurian hermeneutical approach

This chapter has built a three-pillared hermeneutical framework which is now ready to be used as we come to read the Julian texts. To recap: its initial foundation is Ricoeurian, based on his assertion of the autonomy of the text, the interpreter *in medias res*, the transformative effect of poetic texts on their reader and the asymmetrical summoning of the reader who is not, therefore, able to be a controlling or *Gestell* self in relation to the text. On that stable foundation, drawing additionally on the insights of enactivism and niche construction as well as theology and philosophy, I built three interdependent pillars of, first, 'performative interaction' where the meaning of the text emerges in real time as the reader encounters it and engages performatively with it; second, of 'porous interaction' of the reader with the text which brings about the realisation of our *a priori* porosity and also gives rise to newly creative porosity; third, of a 'niche' where the reading takes place, which participates in and is transformed by the performative and porous interaction of the encounter.

The ground has been prepared to read the Julian texts. We will read the texts as they stand and we will enter into Julian's experience as it is described there. We will not look for her outside that experience recounted in the text. We do not know for certain if she was a 14th–15th-century anchoress writing in the cell next to the church of St Julian in Norwich, so we won't try to put her there. Nor will we place ourselves among her medieval (we surmise) audience. But everything that is in the text about Julian and her audiences, and everything the Julian of the text says, will be valid for our purposes. With these, both the Long Text and the Short Text, we will bring ourselves actively into encounter. They will be our world for the next three chapters. In that world, with our three-pillared hermeneutical framework to guide us, we will uncover rich, creative wisdom to help change our *Gestell* subjectivity that is so harmful to the planet.

3 Julian's Wounds

Introduction

Julian interacts performatively and porously with her revelations, and the interaction in turn affects her subjectivity and her world, creating or re-alising a new niche embodied in the text. In what Oliver Davies refers to as the 'intimate communication' of her writing (2017 pp 15, 22), she in turn effects a performative, porous interaction between her readers and the text, which has the power to change our subjectivity and make possible the imagination and perception of new worlds or niches that do not harm the planet.

To unpack this a little further: the revelations themselves were a performance in which Julian participated interactively and porously: she took an active part in them, interrogating them visually and verbally and musing over them; her subjectivity was wholly involved in the performance and open to be changed by it, hence porous; and the niche in which the revelations took place, which influenced them, was also changed by them. Julian's performative, porous, niche-constructing encounter continued throughout the revelations themselves and, as the text indicates, for many years thereafter (LT p 520.86), in what Davies has characterised as a *lectio divina* on what she saw (p 44).

Wounds as porosity

Julian's porosity can be identified as a 'wound'. In her text, 'wound' carries the force and effect of the porousness of self that leads in turn to porous encounter. It resonates with Michael Scott's anthropological interpretation of the Arosi people (2014), whose 'wonder' at the land 'wounds' them so as to make the strength of the land available to them, and Mary-Jane Rubenstein's etymological suggestion (2008 p 9), connecting 'wound' with 'wonder'. 'Wound' is of critical importance to Julian's method interpreted by the post-Ricoeurian triad. The asymmetry of woundedness generates encounter; woundedness is the porous nature of the subject and what it interacts with; and woundedness is realised performatively in interaction.

DOI: 10.4324/9781032623948-4

Julian's wounds

Julian asks for wounds at the beginning of her text, as she describes, according to the Short Text, hearing the story of St Cecilia's three wounds which were her martyrdom, a story that awoke in Julian the desire to be wounded. This is when the participative porousness that will lead to her revelations and her text is set in motion:

> I harde a man telle of halye kyrke of the storye of saynte Cecylle, in the whilke schewynge I vndyrstode that sche hadde thre wonndys with a swerde in the nekke, with the whilke sche pynede to the dede. By the styrrynge of this I conseyvede a myghty desyre, prayande oure lorde god that he wolde grawnte me thre wonndys in my lyfe tyme, that es to saye the wonnde of contricyoun, the wonnde of compassyoun and the wonnde of wylfulle langgynge to god.
> (ST pp 204.46ff)

This was the third of three gifts she had asked of God, the first being to have deeper knowledge of the Passion and the second to have an illness that brought her to the brink of death. Both these gifts could be characterised as woundings too, for both have the quality of interactive participation (of Julian with Christ) and will be addressed as such when we study her eighth revelation. The third gift of three wounds, conceived as a 'mightie desyre', was asked for 'mightly with out anie condicion' (LT p 288.44f), unlike the first two, which were asked for on condition that they were God's will. The first two 'passid from my mynd', but the third 'dwellid contynually' (LT p 288.45f). Julian wishes to remain constantly and consistently porous to God. The third gift of three wounds are the means by which she may be so. They can thus be thought of as a continuous presence running under the text, making an appearance from time to time: for example towards the end of the eighth revelation when Christ is said to suffer his Passion 'with a contriccion and compassion' (LT p 378.35); and later as gifts of God, visited by his grace to prepare us for 'blysse', 'made evyn with seyntes' (LT p 451.24f):

> whom oure lord wylle he vysyteth of his specialle grace with so grett contricion, and also with compassion and tru longyng to god.
> (LT p 451.21ff)

Identified with 'wonder' and 'marvelyng', the wounds are even more obviously present as a continuous dynamic force within the text, rendering the encounter between Julian and her revelations asymmetric, as she never ceases to wonder and marvel at what she is shown: from her 'full greatly was I a stonned for wonder and marvayle' (LT p 296.17f) at her first revelation to her 'I wondryde and mervenlyed with alle the dylygence of my soule' (LT p 510.6) at the 14th. 'Marvelyng' is the porous means by which Julian's subjectivity is transformed as she looks at that which she does not yet understand. She uses it of herself throughout her text.[1]

The wounds are gifts: Julian does not assume she has them, but she asks for them continually, and the asking creates the asymmetry which in our terms is needed to energise the encounter's performative and porous power. Thus Julian opens herself to interactive porosity from her early life and remains 'wounded' thereafter, creating the conditions under which, first, the revelations then come to pass when she is 30 years old and a half (LT p 289.2); second, the revelations are made meaningful by her interaction with them at the time; and, third, Julian continues 'wounded' to their meaning 'oftyn tymes': 'fro the tyme that it was shewde [...] xv yere after and mor' (LT p 732.13f); and in respect of the 14th revelation, 'twenty yere after the tyme of the shewyng saue thre monthys' (LT p 520.86).

Christ's wounds

Christ is wounded. The porosity is on both sides of the encounter in the revelations, most of all in the 14th, where the subjectivity of Christ and the subjectivity of Adam are so porous to each other as to be indistinguishable, a remarkable insight to which we will return. The wounds of the Passion which Julian porously and performatively experiences are described in detail in the eighth revelation, to which we will also return. Other references to Christ's woundedness are found in the 10th revelation:

> Oure good lorde lokyd in to hys syde and behelde with joy, and with hys swete lokyng he led forth the vnderstandyng of hys creature by the same wound in to hys syd with in;
>
> [...] he brought to mynde hys dere worthy blode and hys precious water whych he lett poure out for loue;
>
> [...] he shewyd hys blessyd hart clovyn on two.
> (LT pp 394.3ff)

The meaning of these wounds is endless love: 'he shewyd to my vnderstandyng [...] to mene the endlesse loue that was without begynnyng and is and shal be evyr' (LT p 395.10ff). Christ is wounded in all eternity which means that his wounds participate in the 'blyssydfulle godhede' (LT p 395.11). Thus the revelation shows that not only is Christ wounded, but that God himself is porously interactive, the 'endlesse loue' an endless flow of participation within himself as Trinity and with his creatures.

In her later discourse on Christ as mother, Julian refers back to the wound shown in the 10th revelation, drawing an analogy between the mother giving her child suck and Christ feeding us from his wounded side: 'Oure tender mother Jhesu, he may homely lede vs in to his blessyd brest by his swet open syde' (LT p 598.38f). The link is explicitly made with the eucharist as Christ feeds us with himself as a mother feeds her child:

> The moder may geue her chylde sucke hyr mylke, but oure precyous moder Jhesu, he may fede vs wyth hym selfe, and doth full curtesly and full tendyrly with the blessyd sacrament, that is precyous fode of very lyfe.
> (LT pp 596.29ff)

The wounded side is the location of the performative interaction between Christ and his beloved, the place where his motherhood is expressed. The effect is powerful as the subjectivity of Christ's love is identified as that porous, unfailingly tender and vulnerable love of a mother, as delicate and capable of hurt as an open wound. Motherhood and woundedness continue to be identified with Christ's porous subjectivity as he is that by which childbirth takes place, in the bloody, scatological event of 'bodely forthbryngyng' (LT p 599.49), a reference that brings to mind Julian's earlier observation that Christ is in the earthy bowel movement of the 'purse fulle feyer' that is 'openyde and sparyde ayen fulle honestly [...] it is *he* that doyth this' (LT p 306.36f, my italics). And it is the 'deerworthy blode and precious water' (LT p 608.64f) that flow from his wounded side to make us clean, when we run to him having made ourselves 'foule' (LT p 606.50), as a child to its mother: 'The blessed woundes of oure sauiour be opyn and enjoye to hele vs' (LT p 608.65f).

The references display all the features of our three-pillared hermeneutical framework, as the subjectivity of Christ and that of Julian interact performatively and porously. This is demonstrated in Julian's experience in the 10th revelation of entering Christ's body through his wounded side. It was Christ's 'swete lokyng' that was the means by which he 'led forth the vnderstandyng of hys creature' into the wound in his side (LT pp 394.4ff). Christ's looking and Julian's looking interact porously (the first pillar). Their mingled looking also interacts performatively (the second pillar) as by means of it Julian enters his side. And, true to Julian's method, the reader is in turn drawn in to the new niche that has been created (the third pillar): 'ther he shewyd a feyer and delectable place, and large jnow for alle mankynde that shalle be savyd' (LT pp 394.5ff). As Bernadette Lorenzo observes, Julian is reborn (1982 p 170), but so is her reader. In this exquisite performative intermingling of porous subjectivities the revelations may be seen as a 'joint project' (Raczaszek-Leonardi, Debska, and Sochanowicz 2015).

The text's wounds

The text itself displays wounds. That is to say, Julian's theological 'musings', as Kevin Magill describes them, are integrated into the visions themselves. She interweaves bodily sight, ghostly sight, words spoken to her in dialogic and monologic form and her own theological responses (Magill 2006 p 78). Writing of the composition of the Julian texts, Nicholas Watson observes how the revelations, Julian's understanding of them and the writing have become inextricably intertwined with one another in the texts (1993). For example, there is a chronological porosity in Julian's declaration, as she is describing the eighth revelation, that: 'this hath *evyr be* a comfort to me, that I chose Jhesu to be my hevyn' (LT p 371.17f, my italics), as Watson discusses (p 658); and again the chronological but also theological porosity of the text of the 14th revelation, so much so that it is not described as an 'example' in the list at the beginning of LT (LT p 284.43ff): it had become

> irrecoverably mingled with two other layers of apprehension [...] first, the insights produced by Julian's prolonged attempt to grasp the exemplum; second, her growing understanding of the meaning of her revelation as a whole.
> (Watson 1993 p 677)

Barry Windeatt notices that Julian gives no primacy to the original of what she saw over what she was then shown, in extended time, about their meaning (2015 p xxv), as the narrative sometimes seems pushed to the outside and the 'musings' become central. Julian's narrative of two days 'ends up almost splitting at the seams under the exploration of its own implications' (Windeatt 2016 p xxiv). Evoking an apt and striking image, Nicholas Watson writes: 'It is as though the Biblical text in the centre of its manuscript page were literally to "overflow" and to merge with the surrounding apparatus' (1993 p 93). The revelations are in this way themselves porously involved in a joint project with Julian's interpretation of them in the performative encounter that becomes the 'niche' that is the text. The ongoing 15 or 20 years of 'wounded' interaction with the revelations she describes in the text could thus be extended even further into the time she spent creating the text. The niches of revelation; *lectio divina* on revelation; and the bringing of revelation into linguistic embodiment are all porous to each other, and in turn, in unbroken continuity, the text we receive, in the same modality, is porous to our reading, as it yields still more meaning into today: a 'never-satiated process' (Watson 1992 p 100).

We have established Julian's own woundedness as critical to her response to the revelations, for which she specifically importunes God, and which she sustains as an attitude prior to her revelations, throughout her encounter with them and thereafter as she reflects and writes about them. Christ too is wounded, and so, intriguingly, is the text itself. The next three sections will follow Julian's way of reading and look ever more closely at her woundedness and its intimate identity with porosity.

The wound of 'verie contricion'

The wound of 'contricion' (contrition), the first of the three wounds for which Julian asked, can be understood as that which engenders humility through deep penitence. Interpreted through our three-pillared framework, contrition brings Julian porously and asymmetrically to the encounters of her revelations. The self that is wounded by contrition is a willingly summoned self, not 'master' of her revelations but 'disciple of the text' (Ricoeur 1975 p 95). She has no prior sense of absolute certainty about the world and herself. With her wound of contrition, she declares herself a penitent, ready to learn. Under the theme of contrition we will consider first, Julian's hard-to-define subjectivity; second, the significance of 'holy chyrch' for her subjectivity; and third, the significance of 'reuerente drede', which is urged throughout the text.

Julian's subjectivity of contrition

The person of Julian as she emerges in the text is true to the porous subjectivity of contrition in the sense that she refuses any special status or identity separate from her readers. The title of anchoress is reserved for the rubrics and not claimed by the Julian of the text. She does not refer to herself as a nun. She explicitly denies being educated: 'This reuelation was made to a symple creature vnlettyrde' (LT p 285.1). She also explicitly denies being a teacher: 'god for bede that ye schulde saye or take it so that I am a techere, for I mene nouyt soo, no I mente never so' (ST p 222.40f). As Ritamary Bradley notices, although the texts are in the pedagogical tradition or category, Julian's device is to become invisible so Christ becomes the teacher. 'By using the concept of Christ as teacher, Julian creates a rhetorical strategy which sets her work apart from other writings of its kind' (1982 p 127). Bradley regards Julian's mysticism (if that is what it is) to be summed up in Poiret's cataloguing of her as 'taught of God, profound and ecstatic' (p 138).[2] Unlike the Wisdom writers who portray themselves as instructors of their readers, Julian passes back all pedagogy to Christ, so that her readers see not her but Christ. She might be thought of as standing alongside her readers, as one taught of God, but among us: hard to see.

It can even be misleading to regard Julian as a mystic, as Denys Turner (2011) and Kevin Magill (2006) have both argued, writing of her as a theologian and a visionary respectively. Julian's nature might have been captured in Jean-Luc Marion's 'new phenomenology' whose challenge is 'to go to the limit of what gives itself without limits' (Caputo and Scanlon 1999 p 7). But for Marion, 'mystical theology' is needed, because of the 'excess of intuition' experienced by, for example, the disciples at the Transfiguration or on the road to Emmaus. There is no concept to match the experience, there are no words to describe what they saw (p 69). For Julian, by contrast, there are usually plenty of words to say, words which emerge like St Paul's *phusis* (Breton 2011 p 124) out of her wish to describe what she saw accurately, including what she saw theologically, and she thereby does go some way to giving material form, the 'thickness' Julia Kristeva (1984) accords poetry, to the 'excess of intuition' she experienced in her showings. The friendly way in which Julian strives to communicate to her 'evyn cristen' all that she saw is quite unmysterious, so that, by participating performatively in seeing what she sees, we can know as she knows, including those mysterious things over which she puzzles, such as the 14th revelation. The mystery is reserved for the privity of God, not the person of Julian. Windeatt calls her a 'contemplative' (2016 p vii), whose meditations on her revelations become as narratively important as the revelations themselves (p xxiv). Julian does not say that God wanted her to write down her revelations, but she does understand that God wants them to be made known (p xx). For Nicholas Watson Julian is a theologian for whom the Trinity is the exegetical key in the 'polyphonic complexity' of her revelation (1992 p 86), seen in the 'process of abstraction from the visual to the theological' (p 88). In the same way as the persons of the Trinity are impossible to separate, so her showings, her understandings of her showings, and her reader's reception of both cannot be disentangled; and the Trinity is present in all stages of seeing, receiving and understanding (pp 98f). Vincent Gillespie calls Julian a 'vernacular theologian' whose text 'subverts normal critical (and perhaps theological) reading. Originality is not the issue: truth to her showing is' (2011 p 404).

While Vincent Gillespie calls Julian a 'master of multiple discourses, capable of alluding to and pastiching various contemporary styles of religious and philosophical writing' (2011 p 403), Colledge and Walsh (1978) see her rather as a scholar of theology, noting throughout the text numerous resonances and echoes of the writing of her (14th century assumed) day. The Julian of the text, meanwhile, describes herself as 'a symple creature vnlettyrde' (LT p 285.1). We might favour the description the Julian of the text uses of herself, partly because we are taking seriously what is in the text and only that, but also because it evinces her porosity through humility. However we simply cannot match the adjective 'unlettered' to her mastery of language. She is an exquisite, accomplished writer in the poetic nature of the text as a whole, in her vocabulary and syntax, her use of rhetoric, puns, poetic forms, narrative voices, allegory, simile, metaphor and imagery, which Gillespie honours as 'skilful' (2011 p 403). We can only make sense of 'unlettered' by assuming it refers to Julian not having knowledge of Latin, and the internal evidence of the text bears witness to this. Julian's only use of Latin appears to be liturgical: she 'seyde oftynn tymes: Benedicite Dominus' (ST p 217.4); she 'never stynte of these words: Benedicite Dominus' (LT p 317.2); and she refers to the 'Pater noster, Aue and Crede' (ST p 258.9). These indicate that the Latin Julian knew was what she heard and recited at Mass. She gives one direct quotation from the Bible, Philippians 2.5 which is, intriguingly, an exact translation from the Vulgate Latin Bible: the syntax is identical. Julian's rendering is: 'ylke saule aftere the saying of saynte Pawle schulde feele in hym that in Criste Jhesu'; the Vulgate Latin is: '*Hoc enim sentite in vobis quod et in Christo Jesu*' (Colledge and Walsh 1978 p 234.25f and fn). There are many resonances with Biblical texts, but no other quotations, and this one is only in ST.[3] Julian clearly knows her Bible, referring to a number of characters: David, the Magdalene, Peter and Paul, Pilate and Thomas whom she refers to as 'Thomas of of Inde' (ST p 255.19f; LT p 446.14f), 'of Inde' a tradition, not described in the New Testament, in which the disciple Thomas was said to have sailed to India to establish a church there. Julian also produces some non-scriptural characters: Saint John of Beverley to whom she refers as if he were a local and well known saint (LT p 446.16ff), and Saint Cecilia (ST p 204.47ff). In her eighth revelation she refers to 'Pylate' and 'Dyonisi of France' (LT p 368.27) legends about whom are to be found in the *Gospel of Nicodemus* and *The Golden Legend* (Watson and Jenkins 2006 p 186). *Pace* Colledge and Walsh, these are not theological scholars whose works Julian draws upon, but lively characters populating her text, participating in its drama and manifesting its effect. The resonances with other writers and their theology are never direct quotations and could be accounted for in what the historical Julian would have heard in homilies. Nicholas Watson writes:

> the flexibility of her exposition, the variety of its strategies, and the rapidity with which it shuttles between particular moral points and far-reaching theological ones all suggest the influence of biblical exegesis – mediated, perhaps, mainly through preaching – on her writing and thought.
>
> (Watson 1992 p 92)

Julian expressed ideas that were the theological currency of the day. As Benedicta Ward puts it, she could have worked them out for herself: an original thinker like Anselm of Canterbury, neither had footnotes to their texts (Ward 1995 p 26). Julian is highly intelligent, but that does not mean, Ward wryly observes, that she must therefore have been taught by men (p 26). In a rare specific self-reference Julian does claim her womanhood, but only to confirm the fragility (porousness) of her subjectivity: 'I am a womann, leued, febille and freylle' (ST p 222.41f).

The contrite Julian claims no fixed prior subjectivity, then, of anchoress, nun, teacher or scholar. She is 'liminal' (Davies 1992 p 39); 'poised' (Turner 2011 p 15). This lack of fixity places her, for us, in porous, interactive movement. Andy Clark (2011) would make sense of her subjectivity's emergence as a dynamic expression of numerous encounters, not a thing with edges. She is (always) ready to be transformed, receiving her visions which she sees performatively, porously and interactively. From her transformed subjectivity she in turn offers dynamic porous interaction with her 'evyn cristen' by means of her text, itself 'pressed' from encounter (Clark 2011 p 60). The contrite, hard-to-see Julian gives birth to her text, which is not itself divinely inspired, so noted by Davies (1992 p 40), but is the *phusis* born of her porous encounter, which *was* divinely inspired, and it carries the transformative power of the original vision, inviting its readers into interactive porous encounter in turn.

Contrition and 'holy chyrch'

One fixed base which Julian, however porous she herself might be in receiving her revelations, does not surrender is the presence and teaching of 'holy chyrch' (holy church). But as we will see, Julian's refusal to deny holy church, despite its teaching's absence in her revelations, not only, counterintuitively, increases the porosity of her own subjectivity, but because she is so identified with it, brings holy church itself into the niche of her revelations, making its subjectivity porous too.

Julian had a habit of holiness, as Clare Carlisle (2014) would express it, a habit established from her youth (LT p 351.3f). Julian's repeated assertion that she was grounded and knowledgeable in the teaching of holy church means that holy church had been, for all her life before the revelations, the place of her performative expression of that holiness through contrition. For example, she writes of the importance of turning to one grounded in holy church as contrition quickens in a penitent soul:

> contriscion takyth hym by touchyng of the holy gost [...] Than vndertakyth he penannce for every synne enjoyned by his domys man that is groundyd in holy chyrch.
>
> (LT pp 449.6ff)

With a typical humility, Julian writes of seeking solace in holy church while she waits to be shown the 'great privity' which is in God. Having seen that 'moch pryvete is hyd whych may nevyr be knowen in to the tyme that god of hys goodnes hath made vs worthy to se it', she falls yieldingly back into the arms of holy church, to sustain her habit of holiness, keeping her contrite until such time as God is ready to reveal his great secret. 'And now I yelde me to my modyr holy chyrch, as a sympyll chylde owyth' (LT p 494.49f).

Holy church is thus present, non-adversarially, in the niche of Julian's encounters. She asserts its right to be there through her firm belief in what holy church teaches. She had believed it before her revelations and still believes as she is writing her text:

> But in all thing I beleue as holy chyrch prechyth and techyth. For the feyth of holy chyrch, which I had before hand vnderstondyng, and as I hope by the grace of god wylle fully kepe it in vse and in custome, stode contynually in my syghte, wyllying and meanyng never to receyve ony thyng that myght be contrary ther to.
>
> (LT p 323.21ff)

She sees, continuously, the fixed poles of 'endless love' *and* 'the teaching of holy church':

> And ytt in alle this tyme fro the begynnyng to the ende I had ij manner of beholdinges. That one was endlesse conntynuant loue with suernes

of kepyng and blysful saluacion, for of this was all the shewyng. That othyr was the comyn techyng of holy chyrch, of whych I was befor enformyd and groundyd and wylfully hauyng in vse and in vnderstondyng.
(LT pp 491.15ff)

Holy church has not been dismissed by the revelations. It keeps its porous place within Julian's niche, participating and interacting with what we might call, with McGann (2015) and Laroche (2015), her other 'affordances'. It is present, for example, in Julian's armoury as protection against the fiend that threatens her in the 16th revelation:

My bodely eye I sett in the same crosse there I had seen in comforte afore that tyme, my tong with spech of Cristes passion and rehersyng the feyth of holy church, and my harte to fasten on god with alle the truste and the myghte, that I thought to my selfe, menyng: thou hast now great besenes to kepe the in the feyth, for that thou shuldest nott be taken of thyne enemys.
(LT pp 650.2ff)

The habit of holiness remains, after all the revelations are over, with holy church a continuing affordance in the niche alongside reason and the holy ghost:

By thre thynges man stondyth in this lyfe, by whych iij god is wurschyppyd and we be sped, kepte and savyd. The furst is vse of mannes kyndly reson. The seconde is the comyn techyng of holy chyrch. The iij is the inwarde gracious werkyng of the holy gost; and theyse be alle of one god. God is grounde of oure kyndly reson; and god is the techyng of holy chyrch, and god is the holy gost, and alle be sondry gyftes, to whych he wylle we haue grete regarde, and accordyng vs therto.
(LT p 707.2ff)

Holy church is thus established as an affordance not only in Julian's niche within which the revelations take place, but also in the transformed niche generated by her encounter with the revelations. But its presence causes two difficulties. First, the contrition that it generates falls short of the contrition that recognises God, even blinding the soul to God because of a false meekness. Second, it teaches that the soul will be judged, whereas the revelations contain no judgement, only endless love. Characteristically, Julian refuses to assert an excluding theology that will explain away the contradictions, but rather keeps both in her sight. This generates asymmetry, a transformed subjectivity of herself and, by association, of holy church itself. It keeps its place in the niche, as it were, by participating in the transformation of subjectivity the paradoxical revelations bring about.

So, first, Julian has shown that holy church has established in her a habit of holiness from her youth, but it is not, of itself, enough. Through the understanding that the revelations give her, she sees that her own contrition born of her habituated holy church faith falls short. Holy church helps us to repent of our 'synne that we know', but the wretchedness we feel because of this holy church version of contrition blinds us to the most important thing that God wishes above all: 'our beholdyng and oure enjoyeng in loue' (LT p 668.27f):

> that [god] is alle loue and will do alle, there we fayle [to beleue] [...] for whan we begynne to hate synne and amend vs by ordynannce of holy chyrch, yett ther dwellyth a drede [...] And thys drede we take some tyme for a mekenes, but it is a foule blyndnes and a wekenesse; and we can nott dyspyse it as we do another synne that we know.
>
> (LT pp 668.30ff)

Not only is the ordinance of holy church not enough, it can have a blinding effect, making us think that the wretchedness we feel at our sin is a right feeling of meekness, when in fact it, too, is a kind of sin, because it blinds us to God's love. The wound of contrition, for which Julian asked, she understands *not* to be the false meekness that buffers the self and makes it blind to God.

Second, if judgement is of such importance to the teaching of holy church, where is it in the intense encounter she is experiencing through the revelations? She writes that she wishes to have 'som syght of hel and of purgatory' (LT pp 427.2ff). She does not do so, she adds, in order to undermine what holy church has taught: for 'I beleued sothfastly that hel and purgatory is for the same ende that holy chyrch techyth it for' (LT p 427.3f). But for all her asking, she is not shown more than that the devil is damned: 'the devylle is reprovyd of god and endlessly dampned' (LT p 427.10). She is not shown, at any time, any person who is damned (not even 'the Jewes thatt dyd hym to deth' (LT p 428.21f)[4]). Julian cannot be 'fulle esyd' (LT p 487.17); the 'dome' or judgement is 'medelyd', mixed. One is 'hyghe endlesse loue, and that is that feyer swete dome that was shewed in alle the feyer revelation in whych I saw hym assigne to vs *no maner of blame*' (LT p 487.13ff, my italics). The other is 'hard and grevous', requiring the Passion of Christ which 'reformyth it', as holy church had taught. So why was only the 'hygher dome' showed to her, when she knew only too well the 'lower dome' of holy church?

> The hygher dome god shewed hym selfe in the same tyme, and therfore me behovyd nedys to take it. And the lower dome was lernyd me before tyme in holy chyrche, and therfore I myght nott by no weye leue the lower dome.
>
> (LT p 488.23ff)

Julian presses the point: how true in God's sight is the 'dome' of holy church? The longing in her to see and understand is born of the asymmetry of God's 'dome' and the 'dome' of holy church.

She expresses the way in which her own subjectivity is changed by this unanswered paradox but it is risky: she hopes God's mercy and grace will protect her uncertainty. I will, she declares, 'kepe me in the feyth in evyry poynt, and in all as I had before vnderstonde, hopyng that I was ther in with mercy and the grace of god' (LT p 429.24ff). In this she is like the saints. There are some things that we cannot yet understand, some things that are hidden in God; she would try to be like 'the seyntes in hevyn' (LT p 429.31f) and wait with the paradox: 'than shalle we only enjoye in god and be welle apayde both with hydyng and shewyng' (LT p 429.32ff). Julian's niche contains an attentive waiting with paradox, but it is an active attention: she cannot leave the question alone. Dispensing with saintly patience, she returns with increasing urgency to the paradox over the ensuing chapters of her text, her importunity finally giving birth to the 'example' of the lord and the servant, her 14th revelation. This is the culmination of the revelations, the most mysterious and the most theologically insightful, original and challenging, even today. This showing, which we will come to, emerges from and for a transformed Julian, whose porous subjectivity is able to see what would have been invisible to her if such urgent, asymmetric questioning had not been generated. Even when she did see it, she barely understood what she was seeing, and spent 20 years (LT p 520.86) re-inspecting it in order to draw out its meaning. Julian's subjectivity, then, was brought into porous interactivity by her insistence on keeping holy church non-adversarially and troublingly in her niche.

The presence of holy church in this niche of transformational seeing brings it, too, into porous encounter, by means of its influential and unmovable presence in Julian's selfhood. I am suggesting that Julian's subjectivity is so identified with holy church that when her subjectivity is transformed, so is that of holy church. Brought into performative encounter with the revelations, Julian realises the porosity of her contrition and its porous subjective intermingling, ultimately, with God's love. But the implication of this performative encounter of Julian's subjectivity, which has been so defined by holy church, is that holy church itself is participating in the porous encounter. Its subjectivity, too, is realised as porous and interactive. Nicholas Watson notices that for Julian, 'even the truth God revealed to the Church is provisional' (1992 p 93), because the 'nott yett performyd' (LT p 731.2f) meaning of the revelations is the 'never-satiated process of love' (p 100). Furthermore, Julian identifies those, including holy church, who are God's lovers, who will be 'scornyd and mokyd and cast out' so as to 'breke' them from their 'veyne affeccions' (LT p 409.14ff). Holy church specifically 'shall be shakyd in sorow and anguyssch and trybulacion in this worlde as men shakyth a cloth in the wynde' (LT pp 408.6ff). Like Julian's habit of contrition, like her 'evyn cristen', and like our *Gestell* subjectivity, holy church's stability is undermined, 'shaken' into porous performative interactivity.

The intersubjective interactivity of holy church is not to destroy it or reform it; that is not Julian's concern. Rather it is to be restored to its 'belonging-to' in Christ, and thus our three-pillared framework helps reveal Julian's insight. As a mother gives suck to her child, she sees, Christ gives us suck through the sacrament, and what he means by that is what holy church means. All it preaches, teaches, all the health and life its sacraments proffer, and all the goodness it ordains: 'I it am':

> The moder may geue her chylde sucke hyr mylke, but oure precyous moder Jhesu, he may fede vs with hym selfe, and doth full curtesly and full tendyrly with the blessyd sacrament, that is precyous fode of very lyfe; and with all the sacramentes he systeynyth vs full mercyfully and graciously, and so ment he in theyse blessyd wordys, where he seyde: I it am that holy chyrch prechyth the and techyth the.
> (LT pp 596.29ff)

The porous, loving subjectivity of holy church is restored through Christ's own porous selfhood, in performative interaction as he feeds us with the sacrament, as intimately and tenderly as a mother offers her breast and gives suck to her child. Julian's seeing creates a niche in which holy church becomes an affordance, drawn into the interactive performance of sacramental sustenance by means of which Christ himself feeds his 'evyn cristen', such that holy church's subjectivity cannot now be separated from his.

Contrition and 'reuerente drede'

'Reuerente drede' (reverent dread) runs like a golden thread through Julian's text. As with the teaching of holy church, she returns to it many times, suggesting that it, too, is her lifetime's habit. I connect it with the wound of contrition because, in Julian's careful definition of the phrase, it evokes an attitude of attentive, open, humble asymmetry, hence porosity and a consequent performative response. What is being attended to is so important and so holy that our watching must be for the slightest move, our listening for the subtlest sound. Reverent dread is the attitude Julian brings to her revelations and is at the performative heart of her method from the start:

> And alle thys our lorde shewde in the furst syght, and yave me space and tyme to behold it. And the bodely syght styntyd, and the goostely sygte dwellth in my vnderstondyng. And I aboode with reuerent dreed, ioyeng in that I saw, and desyeryng as I durst to see more, if it were hys wylle, or lengar tyme the same syght.
> (LT pp 318.17ff)

Reverent dread is part of Julian's subjectivity, readily available and active in her, making her porous to the revelations and willing to see more or to look for longer at what she is shown, as God wills. It can be thought of as an essential psychological affordance in the niche of the interactive project of the revelations. She knows how it is evoked:

> For of alle thyng the beholdyng and the lovyng of the maker makyth the soule to seme lest in his awne syght, and most fyllyth hit with reuerent drede.
> (LT p 309.64ff)

Steadily beholding and loving God, Julian's established habit, evokes reverent dread in the realisation of the 'littleness' of the soul. This introduces asymmetry into the interaction in Julian's niche and ensures the porous openness of the soul to God:

> The reverence that I meane is a holy curtious drede of our lorde to which meekenes is knyt; and that is that a creatur see the lord meruelous great and her selfe mervelous litle.
> (LT p 628.9f)

Reverent dread is not to be wasted upon, for example, sin, except insofar as it makes us hastily return to God: 'be we nott a dred of thys [synne] but in as moch as dred may spede' (LT p 615.19). We should 'nothyng dred but hym' (LT p 629.23). Indeed, dread of sin brings about the mistaken meekness that blinds us to God's love, as we saw, and keeps us from the reverent dread that is our contemplation of God. Nor should other kinds of dread be mistaken for reverent dread, though they have their relative value. 'Dreed of afray' which comes suddenly to us in our frailty, has a value because it purges us as do other kinds of pain or illness that are not sin, if we bear it patiently (LT p 671.2ff). 'Drede of payne' generates a response which has an initial value, and here Julian makes a distinction that clearly illustrates the porosity of the triadic encounter we have been using. She writes of the 'drede of payne' as 'harde' whereas the comfort of the holy ghost, associated with reverent dread, is 'softe'. 'Drede of payne' works for the one who is 'harde of slepe of synne', whose heart, we might say, is hardened. Our nonporous self has to be woken up and made porous again. The dread of pain does this; importantly it awakens contrition, and then we are receptive or porous enough to receive the 'soft comforte of the holy goste'. The dread of pain penetrates: it is an 'entre' (LT pp 671.6ff). The other dread that is distinguished from reverent dread is 'doughtfull drede', which draws us into despair. This bitter despair God turns into sweet love by grace: 'the bytternesse of doughte be turned in to swetnes of kynde loue by grace' (LT p 673.13ff).

These other kinds of dread highlight by contrast the fact that although reverent dread reveals asymmetry and evokes a response, it does not do so by being fearful. It is associated for Julian with enjoyment and sweetness, such as the experience of the time when prayer comes to an end in the simple, joyful contemplation of God, when with 'speciall grace' God 'shewyth hym selfe to our soule'. As our sight is 'onyd' with that which caused us to pray, so then are we 'mervelously enjoyeng with reuerente drede and so grett swettnesse and delyght in hym' (LT p 477.24). Prayers come to an end because there is nothing more to do or want except to behold him. Reverent dread is thus a form of deep and joyful contemplation whose asymmetrical humility energises the interactive encounter. It is inseparable from love. Love and reverent dread are, says Julian, 'bredryn and they are rotyd in vs by the goodnesse of oure maker' (LT pp 673.20f). Love and reverent dread are interactive performers in the heart of our subjectivity and at the heart of Julian's niche of revelation, giving birth to more of themselves: the more we see God, the more we love, the more reverent dread. The contemplation that is reverent dread is performative, energising the post-Ricoeurian triad, giving birth like Breton's *phusis* to a new subjectivity in Julian, to the text and, by our encounter with the text, in us. Reverent dread is *realised* by the revelations. The more it is practiced, the more it is understood, the softer it becomes, the more our subjectivity is transformed into or by it so that we no longer feel it as a separate affordance: 'there is no drede that fully plesyth god in vs but reverent drede, and that is softe, for the more it is had, the less it is felte, for swetnesse of loue' (LT p 673.17ff). A reverent dread that is present but not felt resonates with Schilbach's 'dark matter' (Schilbach et al. 2013): the response stirs and is active in the face to face encounter with God, without any consciousness of it. It is there already in our subjectivity.

The niche in which the performative contemplation of reverent dread takes place is not limited to a few people. Heaven and earth and all creatures are included: as the great cause and purpose of God become manifest, so 'for wonder an merveyle all creatures shulde haue to god so grett reuerent drede' (LT p 681.27f); the reverent dread is so activating that 'the pyllours of hevyn shulle tremylle and quake' (LT p 681.29). And later, Julian writes again of the cosmic niche quaking because of the 'over passyng' love and reverent dread all heaven and earth has towards God:

> For this reverent dred is the feyerrer curtesy that is in hevyn before goddys face; and as moch as he shall be knowyn and lovyd, ovyr passyng that he is now, in so much he shall be drad, ovyr passyng that he is now. Wherfore it behovyth nedys to be that alle hevyn, alle erth shall tremylle and quake whan the pillers [of heaven] shall tremylle and quake.
> (LT pp 682.42ff)

For Julian, reverent dread is an indispensable attitude in her experience and sense-making of her revelations. It is evoked through contemplation of God, which creates the asymmetry of longing as the soul sees its littleness in contrast to God and is made reverent thereby. Julian characterises reverent dread as 'softe' contemplation (LT p 673.19), which in its softness makes the self realise its porous subjectivity and openness to transformation. It is not fearful. With patient practice of prayer it emerges as a joyful oneness with

God. Not only the single soul but all heaven and earth are included in the niche of reverent dread as God makes his meaning manifest.

We have explored Julian's porous subjectivity through the lens of her asked-for wound of contrition. She defies categories of scholar, teacher, mystic and theologian, though her writing displays all of these qualities. Rather she retains, in her unwillingness to be the object of the text, a porous subjectivity. This she brings to her revelations. She also brings a fierce loyalty to holy church, but the paradoxes that this evokes serve to increase the dynamic interactivity of the revelation-niche and deepen her questioning. The attitude of reverent dread ensures a sustained openness to transformation. Next, we shall read of the wound of compassion and see how it makes Julian porous to others, including us, her readers.

The wound of compassion

We can understand Julian's wound of 'compassion', as 'suffering with', and it becomes a way into exploring her porosity to the subjectivity of others. The revelations are no individualised message to a special mystic visionary whom we look up to with awe and envy:

> leue the beholdyng of a wrech that it was schewde to.
> (LT pp 320.36f)

nor have they turned Julian into a teacher:

> god for bede that ye schulde saye or take it so that I am a techere, for I mene nouyt soo, no I mente never so.
> (ST p 222.40f)

They are, insists Julian, for all Christians:

> Alle that I say of me I mene in person of alle my evyn cristen.
> (LT p 319.33f)

and she looks beyond even this limitation of participation in the niche of her revelations. Julian is thus a kind of everyman and the niche formed by her subjectivity is porous to all.

Those whom Julian was with

We begin our exploration of Julian's 'compassion' with those physically closest to her: the people who populate her sick room when she experiences her revelations. A 'niche' is formed by the room in which Julian lay in her bed, ill to the point of death, with various characters who make their appearance in the narrative, participating interactively with the 'joint project' of Julian's revelations. One is her curate, called to her bedside. He holds before her face a crucifix, so that she can steadfastly behold her redeemer. She is half sitting up, and had kept her eyes fastened upwards, towards heaven, but understands that as her body fails, she will be able to rest her eyes on the crucifix her curate holds for longer. She consents to do so, and the crucifix, held all the time by the curate, becomes the affordance on which the revelations take place. All about the crucifix becomes dark, but the crucifix itself is held in 'a comon light, and I wiste not how' (LT pp 290.20ff). The curate holding the crucifix is thus present throughout the revelations and the text, in the shadows. We know nothing of him, nor of how he responds to what is happening to Julian. After his invitation to Julian to 'looke ther vpon and comfort thee ther with' (LT p 291.23f), he does not speak again, but only laughs (see below). He is a crucial affordance in the niche, however. He is the armature for the Cross of the Christ whom Julian encounters so powerfully. When in the eighth revelation Julian is offered the choice of looking upwards and away from the bloody, dying Christ, towards heaven, she refuses, despite having had her gaze so fixed before the curate arrived, and her niche is dramatically re-imagined as she understands that this bloody, agonised, foul-faced Christ *is* her heaven. The curate is the steady, attentive presence, like the supportive audiences of Koubova's experiment (2015), who turn space into 'place', the niche in which transformational interaction can safely happen.

Julian's mother is a second character, who at a critical point in the eighth revelation thinks Julian has died and seeks to close her eyes:

My modere that stode emangys othere and behelde me lyftyd vppe hir hande before my face to lokke mynn eyenn for sche wenyd I had bene dede or els I hadde dyede.

(ST p 234.29ff)

The Long Text omits this passage, which falls at a climactic moment of the eighth revelation of Christ's Passion, a moment when it would have been of supreme importance to Julian to be able to see. As we will discover when we explore this revelation in detail, the action of Julian's mother has its interactive effect in the niche of the revelation, making the encounter of Julian with Christ ever more porous, their subjectivity intermingling as the mother's action emphasises the merging of Julian's experience with Christ's Passion, both in Julian's nearness to death and in the witness of her mother as Christ's mother witnessed his dying. Apart from this dramatic intervention which influences the encounter of the revelations, Julian's mother remains another Koubovian attentive presence, like the curate, present throughout in the shadows.

A third character is in the form of a religious person who is not present throughout, but comes to Julian at the conclusion of the 15th of her 16 revelations. He is thus a critical first audience for Julian's expression of her revelations. And to her first audience, Julian is, astonishingly, utterly dismissive of them:

> Then cam a relygyous person to me and askyd how I faryd, and I said I had ravyd to day. And he loght lowde and interly. And I seyde: The crosse that stode before my face, me thought it bled fast.
> (LT pp 632.16ff)

This is the first chance Julian has to say what has happened to her and she summarises her revelations as hallucinations: all they amounted to was a crucifix that seemed to her to bleed as she raved. But her visitor takes a different view:

> and with this worde the person that I spake to waxsed all sad, and merveylyd.
> (LT p 633.19f)

The seriousness with which the religious person responds completely changes Julian's attitude to what has happened. His first witness is the performative interaction that 'explodes' (Ricoeur 1995 p 61) Julian's world in which she has as yet made nothing of the revelations. His response means that Julian will ultimately write the text we now have, because she would never have reflected so long and hard on what had happened, and written down her experience, if she had thought the revelations were those of a raving woman.

> And anone I was sore ashamyd and astonyd for my rechelesnesse, and I thought: this man takyth sadly the lest worde that I myght sey, that sawe no more thereof.
> (LT p 633.20ff)

The man did not see her revelations, and yet he believes; the oblique reference to the biblical story of Thomas (whom Julian has mentioned among those saints who had erred (LT p 446.14)) sets the man in an honourable place in the niche as one whom Christ specifically blesses, having believed and not seen (John 20:29). This 'affordance' in Julian's niche establishes the veracity of her revelations and of her own subjectivity: he is an independent non-witness responding to her words only, confirming in Julian that she should take herself very seriously indeed. The encounter is of critical importance. The interaction of Julian and her religious visitor is performative intersubjectivity for both of them and, in the world of the text that then emerged, for all of us as we encounter it:

> I beleft hym [the visitor] truly for the tyme that I saw hym, and so was than my wylle and my menyng ever for to do without end.
> (LT p 634.26ff)

Julian, her subjectivity changed by this encounter, will now 'without end [...] loue [the revelations] evyr joyeng' (LT p 652.24). She will look at them again and again within her soul. She had called the revelation 'ravyng', but Christ 'wolde nott lett it peryssch, but shewde hyt all ageene within my soule' (LT p 653.31f). Her porosity to the revelations will become a habit as she relives them in real time: 'wytt it *now* [...] *now* thou seest it (LT p 653.36, my italics). Her attitude will be, like the religious person's, one of 'marvelling' (LT p 296.18), which, as we saw, critically maintains Julian's porosity throughout the text and the revelations of which she writes: the retrospective 'marvelling' is rekindled in her looking again, and is repeated throughout the text, emphasising the immediacy of communication as the text, the revelations, and the readers all retain their porosity to each other.

Julian's porosity as one among her 'evyn cristen' is established by this encounter: she is not some special mystic, since she nearly missed the whole point of her revelations and so should not be rated as anything special, as she observes self-deprecatingly of the episode with the religious person: 'Here may yow se what I am of my selfe' (LT p 634.30ff). We are to understand from Julian that this meeting is described in order to show us that it is the revelations, and not she, to which we should be attending. And yet it is she whom the religious person took seriously, and so her subjectivity remains a critical participant in the niche, not least because her subjectivity is identified with everyman, as we shall see.

There are two references to Julian's interaction more generally with those who are in the room with her. At the point, just after her first revelation, when she believes she is about to die, she thinks that what she has seen is for the living, so they are to share it with her:

> In alle this I was much steryde in cheryte to myne evyn christen, that they myght alle see and know the same that I sawe, for I wolde that it were comfort to the, for alle this syght was shewde in generalle. Than sayde I to them that were with me: It is this daye domys day with me [...] This I sayde for I wolde they schulde loue god the better [...] For in alle thys tyme I wenyd to haue dyed, and that was marveyle to me and wonder in perty, for my thought this avysion was schewde for them that shuld lyve.
>
> (LT p 319.22ff)

Her 'avysion' or revelation was for the living, her 'evyn cristen', represented by those who were in the room with her and, by that token, to 'thee', that is, we her readers. She herself was going to die, so she had to pass on what she had seen to those about her, for clearly her revelations were for them, not just for her. Her niche, formed by the revelations, is porous, folding into its seeing the subjectivity of others, so that Julian's subjectivity becomes universal. The niche of the sickroom populated with its characters becomes the microcosm of the niche that includes all 'evyn cristen'. Later, when Julian laughs at the overcoming of the fiend, she makes those around her laugh also, and this puts her in mind of her 'evyn cristen':

> I thought that I wolde that alle my evyn crysten had seen as I saw. Then shoulde all they a lawchyd with me.
> (LT p 348.24ff)

Julian's sickroom companions can thus be understood as critical affordances in the niche of her revelations. They ensure she shares the revelations, right at the start understanding they are for all and not just for her, and at the end being assured that they are not the ravings of a dying person but to be taken seriously. The small group that is around her becomes the porous gateway to all her readers, identified by her as her 'evyn cristen'.

Julian's wound of compassion is consonant with her recurring insistence that she is identified with her 'evyn cristen'. She is not a special individual teacher of mystical truth but engaged in a 'joint project' with her readers. The revelations she experiences, the energy or passion of that encounter, are for all. We see together with her. Her method is to make herself invisible, in so doing enabling the creative encounter that she has experienced to be experienced directly, in turn, by her 'evyn cristen' that is her reader. This has consequences, which we will consider both for Julian's subjectivity and also for that of her readers; as 'evyn cristen' reveals itself to be everyman.

Julian's 'evyn cristen'

Julian's subjectivity is 'evyn cristen'

Julian's subjectivity is interwoven with her reader who is her 'evyn cristen'. She insists that all that happens to her, all that she sees, is for her 'evyn cristen'. Thus, in the text, 'I' *means* 'evyn cristen'. Julian's subjectivity is already interactive, already in porous relationship: 'Alle that I say of me I mene in person of alle my evyn cristen' (LT p 319.33). If she looks just at herself she is nothing; but she is one with her 'evyn cristen':

> For yf I looke syngulery to my selfe I am ryght nought; but in generall I am, I hope, in onehede of cheryte with alle my evyn cristen.
> (LT p 322.9f)

In order for her 'evyn cristen' to receive as Julian has received, she must become invisible among them. Maurice Merleau-Ponty articulates this soft and porous subjectivity, that melts to allow the other to be as they are, when he writes of perceiving only when there is total negation of the I. Then 'what there is' is also 'such as it is' (1968 p 53). Further: 'I do everything that depends on me in order that the world lived by me be open to participation by others' (p 53). Julian's self-negation makes her everyman, and her task is, it seems to me, accurately described by Alain Badiou (2003) with reference to St Paul:

> Whoever is the subject of a truth (of love, of art, or science, or politics) knows that, in effect, he bears a treasure, that he is traversed by an infinite power. Whether or not this truth, so precarious, continues to deploy itself depends solely on his subjective weakness. Thus, one may justifiably say that he bears it only in an earthen vessel, day after day enduring the imperative – delicacy and subtle thought – to ensure that nothing shatters it. For with the vessel, and with the dissipation into smoke of the treasure it contains, it is he, the subject, the anonymous bearer, the herald, who is equally shattered.
> (Badiou 2003 p 54)

Julian, like Paul, will destroy the thing she has seen and carries if she herself becomes too 'hard' a vessel. Julian's soft porosity has her among us, an 'evyn cristen' herself, thus placing her, too, among the Koubovian audience, allowing others to perform. She is 'softe' (LT p 673.19) but present, and her presence in the niche makes possible the transformed subjectivity and new niche of her reader.

The 'evyn cristen' reader's subjectivity is made porous in turn

For the readers, the effect of Julian's identity with us is to engender participative response. We do not sit back and admire Julian as she and only she receives her 'marvellous' (LT p 296.18) revelations. We too receive them, by our performative, 'marvelling' porous participation. 'For the slow, deliberative and prayerful reader, the written *Revelation of Love* must be, or be meant to become, the showing' (Watson 1992 p 96). Badiou writes that the truth Paul declared was 'militant', creating a new kind of subject, a new kind of 'me', for all, equally: '[t]he production of equality is the material sign of the universal' (2003 p 108). Julian's revelations are for all: 'for alle this syght was shewde in generalle' (LT p 319.24). The meaning of the revelations for the reader is experienced enactively, not passively, and there is no step, or distance, between what Julian encounters and what the reader encounters. It is the power of Julian's text that is working on us and in us. Oliver Davies accounts for our participative response thus: 'the transformation which began as an interior movement in the soul of the mystic is itself incarnated in literary form and becomes communicable to those of us who come after' (1992 p 52). Marion Glasscoe suggests that Julian is thinking aloud rather than presenting polished ideas, and 'the reader is [thus] involved in a primary mental process, and this in itself is an essentially creative element in the response evoked by Julian's account of her revelation' (1993 p xviii).

Julian's intention, established in her description of her first revelation, is that the reverent dread she brings to her showings should be the same as that which her 'evyn cristen' will bring:

> In alle this I was much steryde in cheryte to myne evyn christen, that they myght alle see and know the same that I sawe.
> (LT p 319.22ff)

The meaning of the revelations will remain hidden if this participation is not entered into by the reader. Julian sees inwardly, 'by goostely syght', that which she cannot show as openly as she wishes, but the readers will see for themselves, better than Julian can describe, because our encounter will be direct:

> but I trust in our lord god that he shall of his godnes and for iour loue make yow to take it more ghostely and more sweetly then I can or may tell it.
> (LT p 323.32ff)

The Julian of the text wishes us not to look at her but directly at what the revelations reveal: 'leue the beholdyng of a wrech that it was schewde to, and myghtely, wysely and mekely behold in god' (LT pp 319.33ff). Of course we, her readers, *do* look at Julian, because we learn from the way she encounters her revelations how we in turn should encounter them in their literary form in the text. Julian through her text demands the same porous, performative, interactive subjectivity of us as the revelations have done of her. Meaning, for us, then emerges in the performative encounter, as our three-pillared hermeneutical framework has shown. It is the asymmetry of our own contemplative reverent dread – not Julian's, even though we learn from her – that will activate the porous encounter between us and God in the revelations, to transform our subjectivity and consequently our niche.

'Evyn cristen' is everyman

Julian's subjectivity is porous to all creatures, not just to some (Christians). First, we can establish that Julian's invitation to contemplative reverent dread was to all, unlike, for example, the author of *The Book of Privy Counselling* (Hodgson 1982a) and *The Cloud of Unknowing* (1982b). The anonymous author of *The Cloud* was clear that his or her work was only for those especially called to perfection. The Short Text includes one passage that could indicate that Julian agreed there were special men and women 'that desire [...] to lyeve contemplatifelye' whom she contrasts favourably with 'thaye that er occupied wilfullye in erthelye besines, and evermare sekes worldly wele' (ST p 215.41ff), but this passage is alone in the distinction it makes. The parallel passage in the Long Text has no such division. Rather it enjoins all 'evyn cristen' to prefer God to worldly things, because there is rest in God, whereas there is none in things that are made. We:

> nedeth vs to haue knowledge, that vs lyketh nought all thing that is made, for to loue and haue god that is vnmade [...] we seeke heer rest in this thing that is so little, wher no reste is in, and we know not our god, that is almightie [...] for all that is beneth him suffyseth not to vs.
>
> (LT p 301.24ff)

And elsewhere in the Short Text the division is not maintained, eg:

> And in alle this I was mekylle styrrede in charyte to myne evynn cristene, that thaye myght *alle* see and knawe the same that I sawe.
>
> (ST p 224.8f, my italics)

The contemplative prayer that 'onyth the soule to god' (LT p 475.2), we can conclude, is to be experienced by all Julian's 'evyn cristen', if their enactive reverent dread is kindled. But who are Julian's 'evyn cristen'? She worries regularly at the question. 'I speke of them that shalle be savyd', she writes, 'for in this tyme god shewde me no nother' (LT p 323.20f) but she keeps looking beyond the group, to try to see those whom holy church has said are damned. She never sees them; for all her asking, she is not shown more than that 'the devylle is reprovyd of god and endlessly dampned', and can only infer, because holy church taught her thus, that 'alle the creatures that be of the devylles condiscion' (LT pp 427.10ff) are included among those who are damned. Her inference is not convincing.

Julian *is* convincing when she writes of what she sees rather than what she infers, and in her looking, 'evyn cristen' becomes 'evry man' (LT p 403.16). For example, she writes of a 'serteyn creature that I louyd yf it shulde contynue in good levying' (LT p 432.3), but she is given no answer in respect of her friend. She is told '[t]ake it generally' (LT p 432.7). It is more worship to God to 'beholde hym in alle than in any specyalle thyng' (LT p 432.9f). When God shows her that she will sin, he shows that he means all will sin: 'I was lernyd to take it to all my evyn cristen, alle in generalle and nothyng in specialle. Though oure lorde shewyd me that I shuld synne, by me aloone is vnderstonde alle' (LT p 442.6ff). When in the 10th revelation Julian is shown the wound in Christ's side, it is a 'feyer and delectable place', a 'niche' that is 'large enow for alle mankynde that shalle be savyd' (LT pp 394.6f).

But 'mankynd that shalle be savyd' is not just 'evyn cristen', it is not even just all mankind. It is all that is made and unmade:

> And he that generally lovyth all his evyn cristen for god, he lovyth alle that is. For in mankynd that shall be savyd is comprehendyd alle, that

is to sey alle that is made and the maker of alle; for in man is god, and in god is alle. And he that lovyth thus, he lovyth alle.

(LT p 322.9ff)

We saw that the 'ovyr passynge' reverent dread will shake *all* creatures, the earth and heaven itself (LT pp 682.40ff). She repeats this learning at the end of her revelations: 'I saw that his menyng was for the generalle man, that is to sey alle man [...] of whych man I am a membre' (LT p 702.5ff).

As we will see, in the eighth revelation Christ identifies with the whole creation at his Passion, and in the 14th both with Adam who is everyman and with all the Earth. The niche of participative encounter into which Julian draws us is for all. Her wound of compassion, then, identifies her as everyman and her revelations are for everyman:

evry man, aftyr the grace that god gevyth hym in vnder standyng and lovyng, receyve them in our lordes menyng.

(LT p 403.16f)

The 'evyn cristen' do not need to be thought of as 14th-century people with 14th-century ears, utterly different from our own, because the Julian of the text is addressing all 'evyn cristen', whoever and whenever they are: the niche that her texts give birth to stretches out in time and even when Julian is done, the book itself is 'nott yett performyd' (LT p 731.2f). The performative encounter continues in her readers, whoever and whenever they are. For our purposes, this means the category of 'evyn cristen' is at the very least porous to all, and quite possibly, in the end, inclusive of all, as Julian's promise of a mighty 'prevyte' that God will in time 'clerly show' (LT p 430.2f) suggests. Reading Julian today places me, the reader of the text, among the 'evyn cristen', because the text is addressing me, whoever I am (I could be a Jew, for example). This point is not a theological claim that Julian was offering universal salvation 'which Julian never declares' (Windeatt 2016 p xxxvi) but that the niche of God's love excludes nothing that is made. The invitation to performative porous interaction is, through Julian's identification as everyman, to all. Julian, identified with her 'evyn cristen', is thus also identified as everyman.

The wound of compassion has provided a broad category for us to explore Julian's porous subjectivity expressed in her participative interaction with others in her niche. We saw how her interactions with those in the room with her affected both her and her encounters with her revelations, and they became porous to the intermingled subjectivity of Julian and her readers, identified as her 'evyn cristen', from whom she becomes impossible to distinguish. We saw that her porous melting into the audience of her readers has the effect of engendering an active participative encounter between her reader-'evyn cristen' and the revelations. Julian's text has the lasting power to do this. And we saw that by 'evyn cristen' Julian means 'alle'; thus identifying herself and her reader as everyman.

The wound of longing to God

I understand Julian's third wound of longing to God as that which sets the direction in which she faces, bringing her into encounter with Christ in her revelations and determining what she is looking for. 'Seeing' is, unsurprisingly, the most-used verb in her writing of her participative interaction with her revelations. In this section, I explore how Julian's looking is performative and porous as it penetrates through the detail of what is seen to God; and I also explore her meditations on prayer, which for Julian is seeking and ultimately beholding God.

Looking

Looking is Julian's way of understanding. It is the test of veracity, as we saw in her struggles with the teaching of holy church on the one hand and the revelations on the other. If she sees something, even if it contradicts what she knows, she will not deny it, and if she does not see something, even if all that she has been taught makes her expect to see it, without denying what she has been taught, she nevertheless admits to the truth that her not-seeing reveals. The asymmetry of the paradox which she retains in her niche then gives birth to new imaginative insights, as we saw in the subjective transformation of holy church, restored to its 'belonging-to' in Christ.

As Guy Bourquin notes, mystics (for him Julian is a mystic) see visions in great detail. Like the medieval mystery plays, the detail of what is shown and seen is not merely a decorative addition but 'precious evidence of something mysteriously at work within the very process of writing' (1982 p 194). In each revelation Julian looks carefully at what she is shown, and finds its meaning in her seeing, not by developing proofs through argument. Hers is a poetic text, as Ricoeur would define it. She describes this method as being one that she was taught to use for the allegorical or 'example' 14th revelation of the lord and the servant, which is the most mysterious to her, and the looking she is advised to undertake is entirely practical:

> I had techyng inwardly as I shall sey: It longyth to the to take hede to alle the propertes and the condescions that were shewed in the example [...] I assented [...] seeing inwardly with avysement all the poyntes and the propertes that were shewed in the same tyme [...] at the manner of syttyng of the lorde and the place he satt on, and the coloure of his clothyng and the manner of shape, and his chere withoute and his nobley and his goodnes within; and the manner of stondyng of the seruannt, and the place where and how, and his manner of clothyng, the coloure and the shape, at his outwarde behavyng and at his inwarde goodnes and his vnlothfulnesse.
> (LT pp 520.87ff)

Julian brings this exegetical practice to all her revelations. It is by looking closely at exactly what is shown that the sense is revealed, the performative porous encounter is enacted and the new niche is created. Julian is 'watching with the greatest possible attention', says Bernadette Lorenzo (1982 p 171). 'The intensity of the scrutiny magnifies the minutest details', points out Bourquin, and the detail is the 'pregnant substitute for the ungraspable signatum' (1982 p 194). Julian looks with a 'pathological' eye on the detail in order to meditate on it (Windeatt 2015 p xviii). The sense that is made is participative, not theoretical, and for the reader, the same detailed, participatory attention to the words of the text as Julian gives to her revelations yields a transformative power. Seeing is performative, both for Julian and for her attentive readers. From an enactivist point of view, 'seeing' is 'action', since perception is always already a 'coordination' with the agent's environment (McGann 2015 p 21): on this account Julian 'seeing' her revelations, and the reader 'seeing' her text, create the niche in which performative interaction takes place. Other scholars comment on the participative effect of Julian's way of seeing. Kevin Magill calls it 'integrative perceptual' (2006 p 78). As Marion Glasscoe has observed, Julian translates what she has seen into words rather than, as in *The Cloud of Unknowing*, for example, offering a manual for how to have a mystical experience. In so doing, Julian 'closes the gap' (1993 p xv) between what Glasscoe calls knowing, but I would call seeing, and the language that expresses what is seen. Her words are not only 'painterly' (Baker 2005 p xii) but also 'performyd' (LT p 731.1f). They have 'transformative materiality', as Bourquin puts it (1982 p 194). Marion Glasscoe further elaborates: 'the very process by which the words are understood may act as a metaphor for the experience to which they relate' (1993 p xix), referencing TS Eliot's poetic demonstration that, like music, it is the form or pattern of words that reach the stillness, rather than the words by themselves. This is Davies' insight. The text re-enacts what Julian enacted, making possible the reader's performative re-enactment of the porous encounter, all taking place through Julian's and her reader's 'seeing'.

Seeing, for Julian, is an expression of her wound of longing to God: her 'pathological' looking at the detail of her revelations has a penetrative effect. As Merleau-Ponty recognised, it is the opaqueness of the material that signifies the presence beyond it: the exterior renders the '*ipse* nothing-that-I-am' partially visible because it gives the 'nothing-that-I-am' an outline for others to see (1968 p 63). Koubova's experiment, predicated upon this insight, released the creative 'inner excess' with the simple participative perception of the audience and the person in the performance space. In her first exploration of 'seeing', in the second revelation, Julian writes in detail of what she sees:

dyspyte, spyttyng, solwyng and buffetyng, and manie languryng paynes, mo than I can tell, and offten chaungyng of colour. And one tyme I saw how halfe the face, begynnyng at the ere, over yede with drye bloud, tyll it closyd in to the myd face, and after that the other halfe beclosyd on the same wyse.

(LT pp 324.5ff)

Despite such minute detail being available to her – even the 'ere' – she desired more light because the vision was so dim. 'I saw him and sought him' (LT p 325.14), she writes: she knows there is more to see. She is answered in her reason: 'If god will shew thee more, he shal be thy light; thou nedyth none butt him' (LT p 325.11ff). She is reminded of a vision she had had in her earlier life of being underwater, and had understood then that 'if a man or woman wer there vnther the brode water, and he myght haue syght of god [...] he shoulde be safe in sowle and body, and take no harme' (LT p 326.21ff). 'Syght of god' brings protection. Although the seeing is of the material detail, the seeking is of God. She looks at the detail but by means of it she looks to God: an asymmetry that keeps the porous encounter active. Contemplative seeing, reverent dread, is always to God. The encounter in her revelations takes Julian beyond the merely visible because she is looking, not over and above, but through, the detail of what she is shown, even the foul, tortured beauty of the dying Christ, towards God, as she discovers this same bloody Christ is her heaven in the eighth revelation.

Not seeing God is the cause of sorrow 'that servyth to synne' (LT p 496.21). Sin, as the 14th revelation shows Julian, is due to blindness. But she reflects that however much this may be so, and however much man may be blinded and prone to sin, the feeling of this is 'but lowe and small in regard of the grett desyer that the soule hath to se god' (LT p 497.24f). In her extended discourse on prayer, which we will consider next, it becomes clear that 'seeking' is as important, and the same in God's eyes, as 'seeing', which is to say, seeking without seeing has the same force (possibly another oblique reference to the biblical Thomas narrative). We already see the dynamic interactive tension of seeing and seeking in the second revelation, the asymmetry of 'I saw him and sought him'. She understands, from this revelation, that we do not seek God 'till what tyme that he of his goodnes shewyth hym to vs' (LT p 325.15f), and it is this seeing 'ought of hym' that stirs us to 'seke with great desyer to see hym more blessedfully' (LT pp 325.16ff). Thus, she writes, 'I saw him and sought him, and I had hym and wantyd hym; and this is and should be our comyn workyng in this life, as to my sight' (LT p 326.18ff). Julian sees that she must seek, and this sustains her (and her reader) in an asymmetric and porous performative interaction with God.

In the same revelation, in understanding that 'sekyng is as good as beholdyng' (LT pp 332.74f), Julian also sees that the one quickens into the other: the habit of seeking penetrates through into beholding. '[I]t is gods will that we seke into the beholding of hym' (LT p 333.76). Paul Janz's enactive response to the command of grace resonates here. Our seeking into encounter with God is attentive, not cognitive (2009 p 9), and it pulls us into the unseen. Janz compares it to the desire for a drink: it is not the drink (which we can see) that we truly desire but the cessation of thirst (which we cannot see) (p 84). The desire calls us into performative response to the command of grace, and our subjectivity emerges from that (pp 174ff). Philip Sheldrake offers another resonant insight: that desire is 'the *condition* of our openness to […] the infinite' (2016 p 103, my italics).

Looking, then, for Julian, is porous, performative interaction as she steadfastly watches with the greatest possible attention all that she is shown, and through all that she is shown to God. She looks through the made to the unmade, because that is what she is looking for. This penetrative looking transforms her subjectivity as it quickens the revelations into life and ultimately into the creation of the new world of her text. The readers' performative seeing of the text quickens it into creative life and transforms our subjectivity, which then sees differently: our *Gestell* subjectivity is undermined so that our looking, in Janz's terms, ceases to be cognitive and consequently exploitative, and becomes appetitive and consequently, as Janz brilliantly recognises, calls us into service: 'it demands sacrificial action in embodied life' (2009 p 175).

Praying

In her seeing of prayer at the beginning of the 14th revelation, Julian understands further the dynamic performative dance between seeing and seeking. I include it in the category of the wound of 'longing to God' because it is both an expression of longing to God and also creates the 'wound' that brings about a longing to God. Prayer makes the soul, in Julian's language, 'suppull and buxom' (LT p 478.31). Prayer is habitual repetition, and works, whatever we may feel. Prayer is evoked through the asymmetry of the soul's need and through God's call and response and thus brings God's subjectivity into interactive performance as well as that of the soul. Prayer brings heaven *and* sensuality into Julian's niche. Prayer ones the soul to God and sometimes brings about an end to all seeking, leaving the supplicant simply and blissfully beholding.

The asymmetry that evokes the porous encounter of prayer is the soul feeling that it is 'temptyd, troblyde and lefte to her selfe by her vnrest' (LT p 478.30f); she is cut off from porous encounter and prayer makes her porous to encounter (LT pp 478.31ff). Prayer is evoked by the soul whose desire for God deepens and strengthens 'the more the soule seeth of god' (LT p 478.27); and also when she does not see God, she then feels 'nede and cause to pray' (LT p 478.28f). Rehearse the 'blessyd passion and his grett goodnes' (LT p 467.63f), enjoins Julian, and so the words will turn 'in to the soule and quyckynnyth the hart and entryth by hys grace in to tru werkyng' (LT p 467.64ff). The words of the Passion 'turnyth in to the soule' (LT p 467.64f), becoming affordances in the niche of prayer. The interactive porosity of the soul is expressed most beautifully as its becoming 'suppull and buxom' (LT p 478.31) to God. The effort comes to fruition as we 'enjoy in his louyng and delyghte in his goodnesse' (LT p 480.43f). The niche of prayer is deeply interior to the soul, whether the soul knows and feels it or not:

> Pray interly, thoughe the thyngke it savour the nott [...] though thou fele it nowght. Pray interly, though thou fele nought, though thou se nought [...] for in dryenesse and barnesse, in sicknesse and in febelnes, than is thy prayer fulle plesannt to me, though thou thynk it saver the nott butt little.
> (LT pp 464.42ff)

By this means all of one's life becomes prayer to God: 'And so is all thy lyvyng prayer in my syght' (LT p 465.47).

In the interactivity or 'werkynges' of longing and trust, God 'beholdyth vs contynually' (LT p 473.60). It is the interaction of our duty and his goodness that brings about the performative, enactive, porous encounter. The subject may feel nothing, but the bliss and goodness is there in God who beholds us continually, and our subjectivity is porous to that, as our 'wekenesse' and any 'doutfull dredys' (LT p 477.68f) are overcome by our steadfast practice and God's steadfast gaze. '[W]e do as we may [...] and alle that vs felyth we shalle it fynde in hym' (LT p 474.63ff).

Prayer is also thankfulness, which Julian calls 'a true inward knowyng' (LT p 466.56f); it is a continuous porosity maintained by seeing the utter dependence of creation upon God, as the 'little thing, the quantitie of an haselnott' has shown (LT pp 299.9ff). Thankfulness in turn keeps the soul in interactive porous subjectivity with God's subjectivity: 'turnyng oure selfe with alle oure myghtes in to the werkynge that oure lorde steryd vs to' (LT p 466.57f).

The niche of prayer includes all that is made, ourselves and the Earth. Julian writes of the importance of understanding the 'grounde' of our prayer, the ground where 'he wylle that we take oure stede and oure dwellynge' (LT p 470.31f). There are three aspects to this niche: first that we are excellently made, second that we are born again, and third that the whole creation is there to serve us:

> The furst is our noble and excelent makyng, the seconde oure precious and derwurthy agayne beyng, the thyrde althyng that he hath made beneth vs to serue vs and for oure loue kepyth it.
> (LT pp 470.34ff)

Julian would have us understand that God is responsible for everything, including our materiality. The asymmetry between God and us calls us to prayer: 'that we se that he doth it, and we pray therfore' (LT p 472.44f), and the inclusion of creation in the prayer-niche also dignifies materiality, as Barry Windeatt observes: our 'sensory being' (which is how he translates Julian's 'sensualite') is kept together with 'substance' by means of God, according to Julian, 'so that they shall never separate' (2015 pp xxviiff). Materiality is in porous interaction with soul in Julian's niche: 'For I saw full suerly that oure substannce is in god, and also I saw that in oure sensualyte god is, for in the same poynt that oure soule is made sensuall, in the same poynt is the sytte of god' (LT pp 566.22ff). The union of our substance and sensuality is located *in* God (Windeatt 2016 p xxxii).

The asymmetry that evokes prayer also comes from God's longing, for God is 'couetous to haue vs prayeng contynually' (LT p 465.49). Julian sees that God is the ground of our praying: 'it is my wylle that thou haue it, and sythen I make the to wylle it, and sythen I make the to beseke it' (LT p 461.11ff). It follows that any goodness and grace that comes from our 'beseking' is of God's 'propyr goodnesse'; it is not caused by our 'beseking', and yet our 'beseking' provokes the porous triadic encounter into performative interaction: through our 'beseking' God makes himself beholden for each good deed that we do, even though he causes the goodness in the first place. We beseech him to do as he wills; he wills that we beseech; thus is the subjectivity of God and the soul brought into porous performative interaction, and the soul aligned, 'acordyd', with God (LT p 476.17).

The niche of prayer includes heaven. Julian writes that our prayer is received by Christ, who in turn 'sendeth it vppe above, and setteth it in tresure wher it shall nevyr peryssch' (LT p 463.34f). Prayer remains in continuous interactive performance in heaven: 'It is ther before god with all hys holy seyntes, contynually receyvyd, evyr spedyng oure nedys' (LT p 463.35f). Prayer as the active performance in the niche transforms the soul into porous openness to the fullest bliss of heaven, giving it a 'ryghtwys vnderstandyng' through 'tru longyng' and 'very trust' (LT p 473.55f). The porousness of 'trust' comes from 'trew vnderstondyng and loue with swete menyng' (LT p 473.57f). The porousness of 'tru longyng' comes from 'saworyng or seyng oure blysse that we be ordeyned to' (LT p 473.56f), an experience that prayer sometimes evokes, when God reveals himself and all seeking is at an end. Then the the soul's longing overpasses all her imagining and all that she can work out or intend herself (LT p 480.40f); it is heightened until we 'dye in longing for loue' (LT p 481.49). Then Julian invites us into the niche of heaven to savour God:

and than shall we alle come in to oure lorde, oure selfe clerely knowyng and god fulsomly hauyng, and we endlesly be alle hyd in god, verely seyeng and fulsomly felyng, and hym gostely heryng, and hym delectably smellyng, and hym swetly swelwyng.

(LT p 481.49ff)

The niche of prayer could be said to be the ultimate restoration of Ricoeur's 'belonging-to' of the self. It 'onyth the soule to God', restored by grace, however much it is 'ofte vnlike in condescion' (LT p 475.3f). Prayer becomes a witness, sees Julian, that the soul is aligned with God, her will is God's will, and prayer softens the soul so that she becomes porous to the grace that restores the alignment. And so there comes a time when all 'beseking' ceases, because God of his goodness chooses to show himself to our soul:

> then we se nott for the tyme what we shulde more pray, but all oure entent with alle oure myghtys is sett hoole in to the beholdyng of hym.
> (LT p 477.19ff)

The triadic encounter is resolved because 'beholdyng' is no longer of subject soul to object God but all one seeing of that which is mysteriously not seeable: it is 'hygh vnperceyvable prayer', and we are 'onyd in to the syght and the beholdyng of him to whom we pray' (LT p 477.21ff). The niche of prayer is the soul finally fulfilled and satisfied as nothing less than God can ever satisfy: unlike the 'little thing, the quantitie of an haselnott' (LT p 299.9) which is made, his unmade 'fulsom goodnesse fulfyllyth all our myghtys' (LT p 479.37f). Encounter with that which is made is not generative of new niches, it will not last, because the soul which is one in kind with God will never be satisfied with it, and nor will it engender porous response. Encounter with that which is unmade is constantly creative of surprising new worlds. Our 'meke continuall' prayer engendered by his 'swete grace' means that we 'come in to hym' in this life by 'many prevy touchynges of swete gostly syghtes and felyngs' (LT p 480.45ff), like continuous gentle wounds that keep us in lively porous encounter.

Prayer, then, in Julian, is a demonstration of our three-pillar hermeneutical encounter of porous self in performative interaction with God, giving rise to new niches. The soul is already one in kind with God, but she does not feel it is so, and so God stirs in her the need to pray. She responds out of duty or a longing for sight of God, with tastes of which he has 'softened' her many times, awakening her 'ghostly' senses, and her prayer is partly savouring these tastes of God, partly just habitual rehearsal of the teaching of holy church in repeating the story of the Passion, but all the time making herself 'suppull and buxom', soft and obedient, hence porous, to God who covets her prayer. Her subjectivity is being transformed, whether the soul feels it or not. She has only to turn her eyes towards God, as it were, and even if her eyes are blinded and we 'se nott' (LT p 472.45) her intention and duty is towards God and she continually 'besekes' him. Sometimes the seeing clears and she ceases all 'beseking' simply to behold her God who is forever satisfying to her, with whose own steadfast beholding of her she is now aligned, so that there is no subject-object divide, and only one looking.

The third wound of longing to God has provided a context for our exploration of Julian's 'seeing' and 'praying'. Seeing for Julian is the performative means by which the self is wounded and opened to transformation by porous interaction with that which it gazes upon, in the greatest possible detail, looking always through what is made to God who is unmade. Praying is seeking and also beholding, and both performative interactions are the same in God's eyes. God himself participates porously: he covets our prayers as we covet him. Our sensual being is caught up in the interaction of prayer within the niche of God.

Concluding summary

God visits us of his special grace with the three wounds of contrition, compassion, and true longing to God, says Julian, so that we are delivered of all sin and pain, and are taken up into bliss and made even with the saints. Contrition makes us clean, compassion makes us ready, and true longing to God makes us worthy. The wounds are the means: they make the soul porous to heaven. Contrition, compassion and longing to God are wounds and they are also medicine, which cleans and heals the wounds, transforming them into worship (LT pp 451.21ff). This is Julian's language, and in this chapter I have sought to draw out themes in the text that resonate with her concept of wound, itself so resonant with the hermeneutical triad of porous or wounded interaction between reader and text or Julian and her revelations giving birth to new worlds. Thus Julian's contrition ensures her subjectivity is porous: she will not draw attention to herself and she remains impossible to categorise as teacher, theologian or even mystic. Her contrition is born of her learning from holy church, whose teaching she will not betray and whose subjectivity itself becomes porous because of her determined inclusion of it in the niche of her revelations. Her compassion is shown in her interaction and identification with the people immediately surrounding her in her sickroom and then extending to her 'evyn cristen', a category so inclusive that she can with integrity call herself everyman. Julian's wound of longing to God is enacted through her constant, steady learning through looking that is oriented towards God, and her prayer that is so directed.

Julian's wounds and our ecological consciousness

I have argued that the cause of the ecological crisis facing the 21st century is the enslavement to *Gestell* that has bound humanity's subjectivity and given rise to the objectivising exploitation of nature that has done such harm. The ecological challenge is not, in the first instance, to find more technological solutions to climate change, destruction of habitat and biodiversity loss, but to release our subjectivity from its buffered enslavement to *Gestell* and restore its ancient, as Taylor would put it, and originary, as Schilbach would put it, porosity. Technological responses can then be employed by the porous self in order to serve, not control, the environment.

Julian's embodiment and enactment of woundedness offer an example of porosity and they also invite her readers, through the intimate power of her language, to be summoned and transformed into wounded porosity ourselves. The move is a theological one but not in the sense that Julian has constructed theological arguments for a porous subjectivity to save the planet by which we may or may not be persuaded. Julian's writing manifests truth by poetry, in Ricoeur's terms: it does not demonstrate it by argument. Just as she interacts with her revelations, allowing them to summon and change her self whom her asked-for wounds have already made porous, so her readers are invited to interact with her text, allowing it to summon us and change us. Our willingness to be summoned is our awakening to porosity, the first stirrings of the slaves who seek to escape captivity from a *Gestell* subjectivity. If the foregoing exploration of Julian's wounds have demonstrated that this is so – and for consistency the demonstration should be experienced in real-time reading, not as a theory – then it has gone some way to showing how Julian can help our 21st-century ecological crisis.

The following are some specific observations from each of the sections of study of the Julian texts on her three wounds. These are not conclusive but rather indicative of how our subjectivity, if we have chosen Julian as our means of escape from *Gestell* and our restoration to porosity, might then embody a new ecological consciousness and inhabit a new ecological niche.

We learned from the general passages on woundedness that porosity is the state in which transformation of heart and behaviour becomes possible. The technological, *Gestell* self is able to be transformed if it is open and receptive. The implication from Julian, however, is that porosity has to be asked for and received as a gift; that is to say, it requires recognition of a giver. In Julian's case this is God. For a deep ecologist like Arne Naess or an environmental writer like Michael McCarthy it might be nature itself. It is an openness to a greater other at which we can wonder. Wound and wonder are very close, so our wonderment can reveal our woundedness. Wonder will also help to ensure that the woundedness is received as a gift, with the readiness to learn that it implies. It is not difficult to wonder at the Earth, and the universe in which it floats suspended, if we take the time to look at it and understand it. Julian also indicates that our woundedness has to be sustained. Our porous subjectivity is not an initial impulse into enquiry that then departs, but a way of being in and with the world. Like the Arosi people whom Michael Scott studied, we have to wonder at the Earth and *stay* wondering. Philip Sheldrake points to the wounded Christ as an 'important icon of the risen life' (2016 p 112), a 'perfectly liminal state' (p 103).

From the passages that defined, or rather failed to define, Julian's subjectivity, we have a pedagogic example of a non-*Gestell* self, one that is summoned to her revelations and ready to learn and be changed by them. Julian's self-negation points to an ethic which allows the other: like Simone Weil's definition of prayer as attention in which the question 'what are you going through?' is asked by one who has emptied her soul in order to see the other, 'in all his truth' (1951/2001 p 65). So the 21st-century self empties itself in order to see the Earth and its needs. In such a way we might present ourselves to the Earth, as it were, in order to learn from it rather than to make use of it. Wise husbandry does this, attending to the rhythms and patterns of soil, weather and water, supplicating the Earth for our food and shelter rather than dominating it.

From the 'holy chyrch' passages we learn the generative power of paradox held non-adversarially and interactively in a niche. This delicate art of not damaging important but incoherent principles, policies or practices as they jostle for their place in our 21st-century world, and seeing what hitherto unthought-of possibilities emerge from their interactive proximity, may be important as we wrestle with competing moral imperatives in facing the ecological crisis, such as the imperative to feed our families today and the imperative to ensure the Earth remains healthy enough to feed the families of tomorrow.

From the 'reuerente drede' passages we can understand the power of contemplation with which it is associated. Contemplation as, for example, Evelyn Underhill has described it, involves the reverent observation of anything at all 'from Alp to insect' (1915/2000 p 48). The effect of such loving contemplation is to dissolve boundaries between oneself and that which is being contemplated, so that St Francis was being 'accurate as well as charming' when he referred to Brother Wind and Sister Water (p 48). Julian's attitude of reverent dread has the same quality: it makes love active in connecting the one contemplating and the object of contemplation which ceases to be 'object' under her loving gaze. Such an activation would change perception and hence behaviour towards the planet.

From the reflection on Julian's sickroom companions we can draw an indication of the nature of response to the challenge. When the problem seems huge, and everyone needs to be involved in addressing it, one starts with one's immediate neighbours; but one does not stop with them.

Julian's subjectivity as everyman, drawing all that is made into the niche of her revelations, reiterates her insight that there is nothing made that God does not love: indeed without God's love there would be nothing, because that love is what gives and sustains existence. If all of creation is loved by God, 'there is nowhere called away where we can throw things', a wonderful saying whose source I have not been able to find. I heard Sally Bingham quote it at a sustainability conference in Kathmandu in 2001 and have used it ever since.

The passages that indicate that the reader is part of everyman establish the foundational social interconnectedness and interdependence recognised by Taylor's account of history, modern enactivist science and in our triadic hermeneutical encounter. For our ecological ethic, it points to a recognition of the universalisability of personal responsibility and also of unselfishness, the recognition both that my actions have their ongoing effect like ripples in the lake of the cosmos which, once created, never cease, and also that actions undertaken selfishly are in no one's interests, including my own. It means that I am drawn in to Julian's 'unperformyd' work; involved in the primary process of giving birth to new worlds, of imagining hitherto unimaginable selves. Out of this primary possibility comes the recognition that there may be a way of making our habitat or niche in Earth without harming it, even though we have not seen that way, yet.

From Julian's steadfast looking that sees every detail and through the detail to God because, as we saw, it arises from and is oriented by her wound of longing to God, we can learn the power of watching with the greatest possible attention. Wisdom emerges in looking porously at and thus learning from the thing seen: not away from the thing seen. Julian's way of looking is, to use Janz's categories, appetitive rather than cognitive. For our 21st-century ecological consciousness, cognitive looking is to be rejected because it will lead to exploitation, whereas appetitive or attentive looking, which we should choose, will lead to interactive encounter: the looking is beyond and therefore performatively through porous encounter. If our looking stops where a thing materially stops, the triadic encounter dies and new worlds are stillborn. Our looking as Julian looks will 're-enchant' nature, in the Taylorian sense (2007 eg pp 35, 74, 85, 98, 553). Our appetitive encounter leads to service, not exploitation: 'sacrificial action in embodied life' (Janz 2009 p 175).

The challenging proposition from the prayer-revelations is that the porous triadic encounter that is productive of new selves and worlds is only productive when God energises the encounter. Simply attending to 'what is made' without attending also to 'what is unmade' will produce stillborn worlds and leave the self buffered and unchanged. It is Evelyn Underhill's contention, which the Koubova experiment also implies, that attentive contemplation of anything that is made will bring about this encounter with what is unmade, because it lies just behind it. The implication is that such looking will bring God into emergent play in the encounter, given the chance. Julian's God is 'covetous' of our prayers. Prayer makes intentional our seeking of what is beyond, and by means of it what is material is known also to be 'ghostly': the Earth is, in Taylor's terms, re-enchanted.

The recognition in the prayer revelations of God as the ground of all being, as the creator of all that is made, engenders thankfulness and humility, both of which responses are essential to an ecological consciousness that does not exploit but rather receives and understands before acting. This way of seeing is challenging even to religious 21st-century ears because it feels like a renunciation of responsibility: but that is what is needed if the *Gestell* self is to be transformed.

The ecological consciousness that emerges from a porosity learned from Julian's wounds can be summarised as one which empties itself of its own concerns and priorities, simply contemplating the Earth or an aspect of the Earth, allowing boundaries to dissolve, allowing the underlying interdependence and relationality to rise to the surface and be seen and acknowledged, allowing the attentive looking to penetrate through (not over) what is made to what is unmade. From that steady, contemplative, prayerful looking emerges wonder at what is; thankfulness for it as gift; recognition that every part of it is loved by God; humility in the recognition of the beauty and wisdom it manifests; and sense of responsibility towards it and each other, experienced as service, not control.

Notes

1 Eg (all LT) pp 300.13; 308.54; 315.55; 336.6; 338.23; 358.23; 363.30; 383.8; 384.23; 407.39; 424.37; 436.3; 437.11; 495.6; 505.2; 505.7; 510.6; 516.28, 32; 519.65; 524.130; 527.161; 528.171; 529.185; 530.189; 531.203; 532.210; 539.268; 546.9, etc.
2 Quoted in the Colledge and Walsh introduction: 'The Protestant Pierre Poiret, who knew of Julian from the [1670] Cressy published text, has, in his "Catalogue Auctorum Mysticorum", an entry "*Julianae, Matris Anachoretae, Revelationes de amore Dei. Theodidactae, profundae, estaticae. Anglice*"'(Colledge and Walsh 1978 p 14).
3 If we date the ST in the 14th century, this is an early translation of the Bible into the vernacular, perhaps the first by a woman. The suggestion was made by Julienne McClean in the 'Roots of Mysticism' course, London, 2003. It is historically plausible to suggest that the direct translation was dropped from the (therefore later) LT from fear of Lollardy, since part of that heresy was to produce translations of the Bible in the vernacular.
4 As Denys Turner points out, this anti-semitic stab, however historically explicable, shows a side of Julian many readers would rather not see (2011 p 18).

4 The Eighth Revelation

Introduction

The eighth revelation is longer and more complex than those that have gone before. In it, Julian encounters and is changed by the dying Christ upon the crucifix her curate holds before her eyes. She experiences Christ's transforming, dying body through death into new life porously and performatively as she undergoes the pains of the Passion herself. Through her experience, Christ's transformation comes into porous encounter with all. The eighth revelation reveals a Christ that is identified with the whole cosmos, and the world Julian expresses through language is as all encompassing as a photograph of planet Earth could (or should) make our world. In identifying with his pain and not looking away from it, asserting that this Christ who is dying on the Cross is her heaven, Julian creates a niche that is as much within her as it is within Christ. But she has to travel, as it were, into the revelation; she has to follow Ricoeur in taking no 'short cuts'. She nearly stops short, because of regretting her wish to experience Christ's pains, but chooses to stay with the Christ-on-the-Cross, and so journeys with him from death into life, a mysterious and hidden transformation that she nevertheless fully participates in because, having so chosen, she remains in intense and porous encounter with him. Time is an important affordance in the niche of this revelation, seeming to stretch into 'sennyght' (LT p 358.25), and so is place, from the focussed point of the crucifix itself to the cosmos that it ends up encompassing. Thus the eighth revelation has the subjectivity-changing, niche-creating features of our three-pillared hermeneutical framework. We will read the revelation in narrative order as it is recounted in the text.

Twenty disconcerting alternations

In the revelation described immediately prior to the eighth revelation, Julian experiences strong alternate emotions, changing from one to the other 'I suppose about twenty tymes' (LT p 355.17f). First she knows a sureness

DOI: 10.4324/9781032623948-5

without pain: a 'sovereyne gostely lykynge in my soule [...] everlasting suernesse, myghtely fastnyd withougt any paynefulle drede' (LT p 354.3ff) and then she feels utterly weary and bereft: 'left to my selfe in hevynes and werynes of my life and irkenes of my selfe' (LT p 354.8f). She makes the transition from one state to the other so quickly that she cannot infer any goodness in herself to cause the 'gostly lykynge' nor any sin that she may have committed to cause the 'irkenes'. There simply was not time. Julian's subjectivity is disconcerted in the face of its inexplicable experience, finding itself changing in ways of which it cannot make sense, neither Julian nor, in turn, her readers, who, drawn by the power of the text, empathetically experience her changing by means of the clarity and forthrightness of her description. Even if we manage to withhold disbelief, we still cannot make sense of what is happening to Julian, or why. Julian's state changes not through her own merit or fault. Her willingness to accept that familiar explanations of culpability are not valid allows a porous openness to other possibilities.

The niche of this revelation is Julian herself, the states she experiences are states of her own body and soul. There is porosity in the internal interactive encounter, in that the 'sovereyne gostely lykynge' Julian attributes to God, the 'hevynes and werynes' to God leaving her alone. Julian is in porous encounter with God himself, who is a dynamic and disconcerting presence and withdrawal within her. Julian's state of mind changes with the movement, not through her own volition but by the encounter. We can see our triadic framework in Julian's own self, its encounter with the God who grants her soul's ease, and in the form of the strange, changing states for which she cannot claim responsibility, located within her body and soul. The text that emerges from the dynamic niche constructed in Julian herself describes her as open to new encounters and worlds. What she understands and articulates is that God's gift of 'gostely lykynge' is freely given, and that it lasts, whereas the 'hevynes and werynes' passes. The revelation prepares Julian for the wrenching experience of what is to follow, where she will be called to enter into and experience the Passion of Christ so powerfully that she will regret ever having asked for it, and where God's 'sovereyne gostely lykynge' seems to withdraw from the whole cosmos. Julian's summoned self is made wounded and porous but also stronger by this preparation for the more deeply transformative and interactive experience of the Passion. Here she identifies with Paul and Peter:

> And in the tyme of joy I myght haue seyde with seynt Paule: Nothyng shalle departe me fro the charyte of Crist; and in the payne I myght haue sayd with seynt Peter: Lorde, saue me, I peryssch;
>
> (LT p 355.18ff)

soon she will identify with Christ himself.

98 *The Eighth Revelation*

The dying, drying Christ

The eighth revelation then begins with Julian observing closely Christ's Passion:

> After thys Crist shewde a parte of hys passyon nere his dyeng.
> (LT p 357.3)

From earlier in the text, we know that Julian has her eyes fixed on the crucifix being held before them, having stopped trying to look upwards towards heaven, which was more difficult and painful in her feverish state:

> [My curatte] set the crosse before my face, and sayd: I haue brought the image of thy sauiour; looke ther vpon and comfort thee ther with. My thought I was well, for my eyen was sett vpright into heauen, where I trusted to come by the mercie of god; but nevertheles I ascentyd to sett my eyen in the face of the crucyfixe, if I might, and so I dide, for my thought I might longar dure to looke even forth then right vp.
> (LT p 291.22ff)

This attitude will become critical to the meaning and effect of the revelation. We can picture Julian propped up in bed, herself dying, as she and all about her believe, watching the revelation of Christ's death. Her physical state mirrors that of the Christ she is shown on the Cross and their interactivity is thus already powerfully in process, the location now widened outwards from within Julian herself (in the seventh revelation) to her sick room and the figure raised in the bed facing the crucifix held before her eyes. The curate holding the crucifix so steadily in place is, as we saw, both a silent Koubovian witness and an armature for the crucifix and hence an essential affordance in the niche, as described by Laroche et al. (2015) and McGann (2015), albeit in the darkness that surrounds the Cross which is self-effulgent:

> it waxid as darke aboute me in the chamber as if it had ben nyght, saue in the image of the crosse, wher in held a comon light; and I wiste not how.
> (LT p 291.28ff)

As the revelation proceeds the location of the porous encounter closes in on the Cross itself. The curate's crucifix is the locus of the revelation, suffused with Julian's imagination, and so the niche of the performative encounter includes Julian herself and the dying Christ she is shown, as though Julian's subjectivity has moved into the place where the crucifix is: where, for her, Christ is.

The experience of the Passion is brought alive for Julian's readers by its focus upon the drying of Christ's flesh; this particularity greatly increases our porous response as Julian's *ipse* self is summoned to attend to the dying, drying Christ, and we in turn are too. The dreadful changes and intense pain of Christ's body are described with a detail that manages to be both tender and 'painterly' (Baker 2005 p xii). Julian's text avoids being morbidly fixated upon the foul details while at the same time giving them her full attention. The lack of morbidity comes, perhaps, from the intense interest Julian shows, and her readers share, in what is happening. Julian's attention is on the activity of the dying, drying flesh. (Watson and Jenkins note that typical medieval accounts of the Passion reflect on it as a static image (2006 p 178)). This interactive engagement in Julian's description shows her entering into the movement of the Passion, rather than the image of it: she writes of the changes in Christ's body. Julian's involved description brings her and us into performative encounter, the changing colours creating a porosity in the vision:

> I saw the swete face as it were drye and blodeles with pale dyeng and deede pale, langhuryng and than turned more deede in to blew, and after in browne blew, as the flessch turned more depe dede.
> (LT p 357.3ff)

Windeatt cites this relative colouring and contrast of the changing shades of blue as an example of Julian's visions being 'both fervently compassionate and yet also dispassionately analytical' (2016 p xxviii), which is why perhaps there is no descent into sentimentality, while at the same time we are drawn so closely and tenderly into the revelation ourselves. The focus of the Passion, for Julian, closes in on Christ's face and then even more closely on his lips:

> For his passion shewde to me most propyrly in his blessyd face, and namely in hys lyppes. Ther in saw I these iiij colours: tho that were be fore fressch and rody, lyuely and lykyng to my syght.
> (LT p 357.6ff)

Julian mourns the change in the lips. Her choice is striking, but again, her interest and focus are not on the lips themselves but the changes they go through. We readers follow her, as Popova (2015) would express it, hearing and interacting in turn with a narrative voice that brings the reality of the dying body home by focusing on detailed changes so that we feel as involved as Julian is. The involvement is painful: the pain crosses from Christ to the one seeing, as the pain of the Passion and the pain of seeing circle around the 'changing' figure on the Cross. The seer changes as the scene changes, creating porous subjectivity; but the energy of the encounter is pain. Thus Julian and her readers porously interact with the pain of the Passion:

> This was a peinfulle chaungyng, to se this depe dying, and also hys nose clongyn to geder and dryed to my syght; and the swete body waxid

browne and blacke, alle chaungyd and turned oughte of the feyer fressch and lyuely coloure of hym selfe in to drye dyeng.

(LT p 357.9ff)

Julian's eye lingers on the lips and nose and then extends its gaze to include the body, all changing colour, drying and dying. The niche incorporates more context as Julian's perspective widens further, connecting the dryness within with the cold and dryness without as she sees, with an imaginative eye, the elements of wind and cold that buffeted the figure on the Cross. The niche in time and space is now Christ's body in which her imagination is performing, a body worked upon and tortured within and without:

For that same tyme that oure blessyd sauyour dyed vppon the rode, it was a dry sharp wynd, wonder colde as to my syght; and what tyme that the precyous blode was bled out of the swete body that myght passe ther fro, yet ther was a moyster in the swete flessch of Crist as it was shewde. Blodlessehed and payne dryed with in, and bloowyng of the wynde and colde comyng from with out, mett to geder in the swete body of Christ; and thesse iiij dryed the flessch of Crist by prosses of tyme.

(LT p 358.13ff)

Colledge and Walsh suggest that the 'wynd' was inspired by John 18:18 ('Now the slaves and the police had made a charcoal fire because it was cold'), and that it was a common feature of medieval literature of the Passion (1978 p 358.14 fn), but Watson and Jenkins disagree, citing only the *Privity* which notes that 'the wedire was colde', and imagine, rather, the historical Julian feeling the easterly winds blowing off the North Sea across East Anglia on Good Fridays (2006 p 178). Windeatt cites a carol of c 1500 which refers to the cold wind (2016 p 210):

There blows a colde wynd todaye, todaye,
The wynd blows cold todaye
Cryst sufferyd his passyon for manys salvacyon
To kype the cold wynd awaye

Our concern is not historical but with the niche constructed by Julian as she identifies four affordances of cold and wind from without, and drying blood and pain from within, Christ's body. The niche constructed is internal and external: it is Christ's Passion, located in his body and in Julian, utterly material, particular, porous to the world without and interacting with it from within.

In the next passage, while the 'spirits' in Christ's flesh are dried up by pain, nevertheless the 'spirit' in Christ's flesh extend the dying, playing its part in the 'joint behaviour' (McGann 2015 p 24) that constructs the niche and introduces a temporal affordance: time extended to feel like a week:

> And thowe this peyne was bitter and sharp, yet it was fulle longe lastyng, as to my syght. And the payne dryede vppe alle the lyuely spyrites of Cristes flessh. Thus I saw the swete flessch dry in my syght, parte after perte dryeng with mervelous payne. And as long as any spryte hadd lyffe in Cristes flessch, so longe sufferde he. This long peyne semyde to me as if he had be sennyght deede, dyeng at the poynt of out passyng, alwey sufferyng the gret peyne.
>
> (LT p 358.20ff)

Julian is careful to ensure her account does not stray from the Gospel account, in clarifying that the 'sennyght' was a seeming, not a reality (Windeatt 2016 p 210):

> And ther I say it semyd as he had bene sennyght deed, it specyfyeth that the swet body was so dyscolouryd, so drye, so clongyn, so dedly and so pytuous as he had bene sennyght deed, contynually dyeng. And me thought the dryeng of Cristes flessch was the most peyne and the last of his Passion.
>
> (LT p 359.26ff)

but in so doing she emphasises all the more the niche of the revelation of the Passion her words are creating. She will later return to this seemingly endless suffering, understanding that Christ's spirit could withstand the pain and experience its own flesh dying longer than any other soul could, because it is the Godhead. The drawn-out process is described as an artist might: Julian lingers upon, but does not morbidly wallow in, what she sees. The niche that is created by Christ enduring the experience of his body's deterioration into decay is one in which Julian and her readers are held with Christ in agony, suspended, a moment of dying stretched beyond imaginable suffering, an awakeness to the moment of dying, which of course Julian is actually experiencing materially herself because her own body is ill to the point of death. It is drawn out further and the internal aspects of the niche are emphasised as Julian reflects next on the scriptural account in John 19:28 of Christ's thirst:

> And in this dryeng was brought to my mynde this worde that Crist seyd: I thurst. For I sawe in Crist a dowbylle thurst, oon bodely and a nother gostly. This worde was shewyd for the bodyly thurste and for the gostely thurst was shewyd as I shalle sey after; and I vnderstode by the bodyly thurste that the body had feylyng of moyster, for the blessyde flessch and bonys was lefte alle aloone without blode and moyster.
>
> (LT p 360.1ff)

102 *The Eighth Revelation*

Thirst, then, is both internal and external, joining forces in the construction of the niche of the Passion whose principal feature is dryness. The blood which flowed so plenteously is now dried, discoloured and obscuring. Julian has earlier almost rejoiced in the flow of blood from the crucifix in her fourth revelation, which should have soaked her bed: 'it shulde haue made the bedde all on bloude, and haue passyde over all about' (LT p 343.11f), and she compares it favourably to water, of which she says:

> Then cam to my mynde god hath made waters plentuous in erth to our servys, and to our bodely eese, for tendyr loue that he hath to vs. But yet lykyth hym better that we take full holsomly hys blessyd blode to wassch vs of synne; for ther is no lycour that is made that lykyth hym so wele to yeue vs.
>
> (LT p 343.13ff)

The flowing blood is life-giving as flowing water is, a porous interpenetration of 'ghostly' and material. Now, however, the life-giving blood is dried and caked on Christ's dying, drying body. The life-giving blood that, in the fourth revelation, had washed away sin and had so plenteously flowed, is in the eighth revelation dried up, as though it, like the rest of creation described later in the same revelation, freezes into immobility and stops its life-giving function for the timeless moment of the Passion. It could be said to have become non-porous. In niches of revelations that take place before and after this one, (for example the fourth and the 10th revelations) the flowing blood is the energy that brings about porosity between Christ and Julian and her readers; for the time of this revelation, the time of Christ's Passion, the only thing that flows is pain. Pain, not blood, energises the interaction in the niche.

Julian goes on describing in careful detail the loosening of the flesh as the thorns detach it from the bone.[1] Her detailed account draws the reader ever more closely into the experience of the Passion as her way of seeing means she and the reader enter into and journey with the Passion, so that the joint behaviour and interaction becomes more intense and performatively part of the niche that is being created: the Cross, the Christ figure, his internal and external suffering, the words Julian uses to describe the flesh, her readers following the words with breathless intensity, culminating in Julian's cry 'I wolde nott for my life haue seen it fall' (LT p 362.27f). I cite the description in full because it conveys the momentum of the dynamic performance in the niche, woven out of movement, whose energy is pain, and the only way for us to make sense of and be transformed by Julian's porosity is to follow her language with the same close attention with which Julian 'reads' the body of Christ:

> The blessyd body dryed alle a loon long tyme, with wryngyng of the nayles and weyght of the body; for I vnderstode that for tendyrnes of the swete handes and the swete feet by the grete hardnes and grevous of

the naylys, the woundys waxid wyde, and the body satylde for weyght, by long tyme hangyng and persyng and rasyng of the heed and byndyng of the crowne alle bakyn with drye blode, with the swet here clyngyng the drye flessch to the thornys, and the thornys to the flessch dryeng. And in the begynnyng, whyle the flessch was fressch and bledyng, the contynualle syttyng of the thornes made the woundes wyde. And ferthermore I saw that the swete skynne and the tendyr flessch with the here and with the blode was alle rasyd and losyde aboue with the thornes and brokyn in many pecis, and were hangyng as they wolde hastely haue fallen downe whyle it had kynde moyster. How it was goone I saw nott, but I vnderstode that it was with the sharpe thornes and the boystours grevous syttyng on of the garlonde, not sparyng and without pytte, that all tho brake the swet skynne with the flessch, and the here losyd it from the boone. Wher thorow it was broken on pecys as a cloth, and saggyng downwarde, semyng as it wolde hastely haue fallen for heuynes and for lowsenes. And that was grete sorow and drede to me, for me thought that I wolde nott for my life haue seen it fall.

(LT pp 360.8ff)

There is a dreadful irony, as Watson and Jenkins observe (2006 p 180), in the flesh 'saggyng' like a cloth for Julian, who uses the metaphor of clothing many times as an evocation of the porous subjectivity of Christ to her 'evyn cristen'. Like the blood which was life giving and is now dried, the flesh of Christ is now useless and helpless. It had clothed us: 'for loue wrappeth vs and wyndeth vs, halseth vs and all becloseth vs, hangeth about vs for tender loue, that he may never leeue us' (LT p 299.5ff). The niche of the Passion is affecting a revolution in the affordances that had been and meant one thing and now become something else, their meaning shifting in performative interaction with the energy of pain and the spreading dryness.

The process of drying and dying continues with Julian's description of the crown of thorns creating a terrible poetic beauty of concentric circles of thorns, blood and flesh; of the colour brown spreading as the dryness spreads, 'lyke a drye bord when it is agyd, and the face more browne than the body' (LT p 363.36f). The drying has four features: bloodlessness, pain, hanging like a cloth in the wind, and unslaked thirst. The intensity of the description, which grows as Julian herself moves closer and closer to the heart of it, descends into inarticulacy, not the Marian mystical silence of the unsayable (Caputo and Scanlon 1999) but a kind of despair that there are not enough words for what she saw:

A, hard and grevous was that payne; but much more harder and grevous it was when the moystur fayled, and all began to drye, thus clyngyng. Theyse were ij paynes that shewde in the blyssed hed. The furst wrought to the dryeng whyle it was moyst, and that other slow

> with clyngyng and dryeng, with blowyng of wynde fro without, that dryed hym more and payned with colde than my hart can thingke, and all other peynes, for which paynes I saw that alle is to lytylle that I can sey, for it may nott be tolde.
>
> (LT p 364.41ff)

The skin and flesh are moving: they are in danger of falling from the body altogether. The thorns seem to be tearing at the flesh as Julian watches, as though they had a life or intention of their own. Above all the pain that drives the movement of the interaction is fuelled by dryness. Christ's body is in destructive interaction with the affordances of the Passion and Julian's 'watching with the greatest possible attention' (Lorenzo 1982 p 171) draws her and us into the performance.

The Philippians quotation

A passage of scripture, a direct translation with the same syntax as that of the Vulgate, is in the Short Text but not in the Long. Whereas in the Long Text Julian lapses into the silence of 'it maye nott be tolde', in the Short Text she goes on to tell it through St Paul, that each soul should *feel in him* that in Christ Jesus.

> Swilke paynes I sawe that alle es to litelle that y can telle or saye, for itt maye nought be tolde [the Long Text passage ends here; the Short continues:] botte ylke saule aftere the sayinge of saynte Pawle schulde feele in hym that in Christe Jhesu. This schewynge of Criste paynes fillyd me fulle of paynes, for I wate weele he suffrede nought botte aney, botte as he walde schewe yt me and fylle me with mynde as I hadde desyrede before.
>
> (ST p 234.23ff)

Julian's translation is the exact syntax of the Vulgate's *hoc enim sentite in vobis quod et in Christo Jesu*. Whatever the reason for the quotation's absence in the Long Text it is entirely apt for our interpretation of the niche that has been constructed, in which Julian and Christ are in participative interaction. Julian's subjectivity is changing by means of this; she feels as Christ feels; like Paul, hers is an 'impassioned attachment that unhinges the coordinates of pre-established identity', as Ward Blanton puts it (quoted in Breton 2011 p 21). Theologian Paul Fiddes calls upon the Philippians quotation to help describe *phusis* as a mindset of ethical wisdom arising from a way of perceiving, learned (today) from phenomenological hermeneutics (2013 p 9). The feeling of identity with Christ is, according to Breton, the mark of Paul's conversion and that of the Christian: the experience changes the self. Ricoeur would say as much about the encounter with poetic text, and Julian's interactive porosity, and that of her readers, is resonant with this insight. The niche is intimate. The encounter is not, as Breton notes, bringing together 'what is far apart' (p 106), but already participative. Julian, like Paul, is in her writing bringing forth like childbirth the spontaneity of her experience, for her the direct experience of the dying Christ, for Paul a conversion in which his mind became that of Christ. Julian's *phusis* gave birth to her writings which in turn draw her readers into participative encounter. Each of us must have a mind which is Christ's; but that means our subjectivity has to be transformed, and for Julian in the eighth revelation, that means intense, porous, performative participation in the pains of Christ.

Julian's own experience of the pains of Christ

The next development in the niche of the eighth revelation is Julian's own suffering. She had asked for three 'graces' (ST p 201.6) or 'giftes' (LT p 285.4) in her youth, that she should receive a sickness unto death, that she should experience the pain of the Passion, and that she should receive the 'wounds' of contrition, compassion and a longing for God. She said that the first two she forgot, and the third she remembered continually. The first, the illness that takes her so close to death that she will have the last rites administered to her 'that I might in that siknes haue vndertaken all my rightes of the holie church' (LT p 287.22f) is upon her (LT p 289.2ff), and now her mother thinks she has actually died, 'lokking' her eyes (ST p 234.30), a reference to which we will return below. The second 'gift', that she will have more knowledge of the bodily pains of Christ and the compassion of Mary his mother and those who loved him truly (LT p 286.12ff), is also now upon her: at this point in the narrative of the eighth revelation, both desires are fulfilled together in one niche. The porousness between Julian's and Christ's subjectivity is as participative as it can be. The pain she feels at not wanting 'for her life' to have seen Christ's flesh fall, and the intensity of her witness, seamlessly transform into the direct experience of the pain of Christ, which becomes the transformational affordance (McGann 2015):

> The shewyng of Cristes paynes fylled me fulle of peynes, for I wyste welle he suffryde but onys, but as he wolde shewe it me and fylle me with mynde, as I had before desyered. And in alle thys tyme of Cristes presens, I felte no peyne, but for Cristes paynes.
> (LT p 364.50ff)

The authenticity of the experience is confirmed in the next passage, as Julian regrets her wish rather than revelling in it:

> Than thought me I knew fulle lytylle what payne it was that I askyd, and as a wrech I repentyd me, thyngkyng if I had wyste what it had be, loth me had been to haue preyde it. For me thought my paynes passyd ony bodely deth.
> (LT p 364.53ff)

The pain she feels, that 'passyd ony bodely deth' carries her through a barrier to a new perception. Now she is fully participating in the niche of the Passion, not just an onlooker, but, as Breton would recognise in his account of the Church's performative participation in Christ, *with* Christ, *in* pain passing death (2011 p 126). 'I knew fulle lytylle what payne it was that I askyd' is resonant with Matthew 20:22 and parallels, in which Christ asks the mother of James and John whether she knows what she is asking: 'Are you able to drink the cup that I am about to drink?'. Julian's regret that she had ever asked to feel Christ's pains give a human fallibility and a touching veracity to her experience. It is worse than she could ever have imagined. The pain does not go away and she is indeed summoned to drink of the cup from which Christ drank.

The passage continues, now resonating with Lamentations 1:12:

> I thought: Is ony payne in helle lyk thys? And I was answeryd in my reson: Helle is a nother peyne, for ther is dyspyer.
> (LT pp 364.56ff)

Watson and Jenkins note that this question: was Christ's pain worse than hell? was a common one of the 14th century, for example Edmund of Abingdon asks it (2006 p 182), noted also by Windeatt (2016 p 212), but whereas Edmund accepts the question as rhetorical, Julian, with characteristic theological intelligence, stresses the difference between the two pains which she is shown: unlike the pain of the Passion, the (eternal) 'dyspyer' of hell has no hope.

The reflection thrusts the narrative forward into a time when the pain will cease, and Julian goes on immediately to understand the nature of her pain, which is itself now transforming. It threatens to overcome Julian in what Emmanuel Levinas has called a displacement of self: 'I am because I have displaced another; my existence has depended upon the suppression and exploitation of the other' (1984/1989 p 82), but she sees, and understands, that the pain she feels arises from her love for Christ. So 'pain' becomes 'love', and 'love' is now the energetic affordance that creates porosity of the subjects in the niche. Love is transforming Julian's subjectivity, but it cannot be decoupled from pain: that is its cost, and Julian has felt it to her own dying core:

> But of alle peyne that leed to saluacion, thys is the most, to se the louer to suffer. How myght ony peyne be more then to see hym that is alle my lyfe, alle my blysse and alle my joy suffer? Here felt I stedfastly that I louyd Crist so much aboue my selfe that ther was no peyne that myght be sufferyd lyke to that sorow that I had to see hym in payne.
> (LT p 365.58ff)

The pain is translated into love in the eighth revelation niche by Julian's steadfast, porous, performative interaction with Christ's Passion.

Julian's mother tries to close her eyes

Julian's mother, thinking Julian is dead, tries to close her daughter's eyes. The act, recorded in the Short but not in the Long Text, adds to the components of the niche. As the mother moves, our attention as readers expands to encompass those who are with Julian in the room: we are aware again, for example, of the curate holding the crucifix before Julian's eyes.

> My modere that stode emangys othere and behelde me lyftyd vppe hir hande before m(y) face to lokke mynn eyenn, for sche wenyd I had bene dede or els I hadde dyede; and this encresyd mekille my sorowe, for nought withstandynge alle my paynes, I wolde nought hafe beenn lettyd for loove that I hadde in hym.
>
> (ST p 234.29ff)

The enactivist significance of this passage is its theme of light and seeing. We know that (for Julian and her readers) the light in the room is dim but the crucifix is self-effulgent (LT p 291.28ff). Julian has asked for more light but was told inwardly that if there was more to see, God would show it, emphasising that the seeing is not just bodily (LT p 29√1.325.11ff). This attempted action of closing Julian's eyes, ironically, will prevent Julian from continuing the one thing she longs still to do, that is, to see. But with the mother's action, the boundary between Christ and Julian is crossed, because it places Julian where Christ is: close to death. Her mother's action not only attests to the fact that Julian is (nearly) dead, but the movement of the mother's arm 'into' the revelation means the niche being created now widens to include the mother and this material act. Julian's dying is so tied into the Passion narrative that we readers may find we see Mary in Julian's mother, and the other witnesses to the Crucifixion in the 'emangys othere' where her mother stood in the sickroom, thus identifying Julian directly with the dying Christ being so watched. This is the implication of the Philippians injunction, which for Julian is never going to be theoretical. As Badiou puts it, the 'truth is supported only by itself and relates to a new kind of subject, a new kind of "me". The production of equality is the material sign of the universal' (Badiou 2003 p 108).

The attempt to 'lokke' Julian's eyes is significant, since the revelations are to be seen, by their nature. Julian 'sees' more than she does anything else in her narrative. She mourns the action taken at this precise, climactic moment in the revelation, as Christ is dying and she is dying, for it separates her from the Christ whom she loves. The connecting porous energy is through the interior and exterior eyes, through Julian's seeing, of the Passion being enacted before her, and she cannot bear to be disconnected. Magill sees irony in her mother trying to 'lokke' her bodily eyes when it is through these that what he calls the 'integrated perceptual' vision takes place, and doubly so when we remember that Julian's looking and suffering place her directly within the tradition of Mary looking from the foot of the Cross on her son's suffering (as distinct from having her own 'Mary' to look at her). Magill suggests that the Passion is the means by which the lesson of divine love is taught: and Julian *sees* it (2006 p 80f).

Julian's pains become Mary's pains

The passage about the lokking of the eyes by the mother is omitted from the Long Text but motherhood itself is not. 'Here', says Julian, 'I saw in parte the compassion of our blessed lady sainct Mary' (LT p 366.2). Julian's pain-that-is-love is precisely where she sees Mary's love. In the same place, the same niche, she finds the love that makes Mary's subjectivity porous with her son's. Just as Julian's love causes the greatest pain, to see her beloved in pain, so is Mary's love turned into pain: the great pain that surpasses all other, as her love for her son surpasses all other. And Christ's pain is in turn increased to see her pain. This circle, or spiral, of love-pain is performative energetic niche creation, in which Julian's own experience of pain puts her in the same place as Mary. As Mary and her son are 'onyd in loue' (LT p 366.3), so is Julian, and so in turn are her readers. In making this connection, the participative energy always being love, all that has been said of Julian and her readers can be said of Mary and, as the passage goes on to declare, of all Christ's lovers. The niche is constructed of love.

> Here I saw in parte the compassion of our blessed lady sainct Mary; for Crist and she was so onyd in loue that the grettnes of her loue was cause of the grettnes of her peyne. For in this I saw a substance of kynde loue contynued by grace that his creatures haue to hym, which kynde loue was most fulsomly shewde in his swete mother, and ovyrpassyng, for so much as she louyed hym more then alle other, her peyne passyd alle other.
>
> (LT p 366.2ff)

The 'kinde love' that is the substance of their relationship, and then extended to Christ's 'creatures', is mother-close, as Julian writes in her long reflection on the 14th revelation (LT pp 594.1ff). A study within the enactivist movement, of a firewalking ritual, showed that the heartbeats of the families of the firewalkers increased at the same pace as the firewalkers' heartbeats as they watched the ritual, indicating a porous connection (Konvalinka et al. 2011). But Julian's later reflections on motherhood in the 14th revelation take the porous subjectivity of mother and son further, again removing boundaries, because she draws the conclusion that the nature of the love of motherhood is the nature of Christ's love: 'the motherhed of mercy and grace' (LT p 594.4) and 'the moderhed of kynd loue, whych kynde loue nevyr leevyth vs' (LT p 594.5f). This exquisite discourse on the motherhood of Christ thus concludes:

> Thys feyer louely worde: Moder, it is so swete and so kynde in it selfe that it may not verely be seyde of none ne to none but of hym and to hym that is very mother of lyfe and of alle.
> (LT p 598.45ff)

The niche is expanded by the size of the love of a mother, felt in all Christ's creatures, beginning with its being pierced by Julian's mother's own act of love, mistaken and ironic, and ending with a mother's love so great that it is appropriate to identify it as Christ's love.

The pain spreads to the whole cosmos

The love of Mary sets the bar, as it were, for Christ's other lovers. The size of the love determines the size of the pain, and so all who loved Christ: the disciples and Julian herself, as she knows through her own experience, suffer pain.

> For ever the hygher, the myghtyer, the swetter that the loue is, the more sorow it is to the lover to se that body in payne that he lovyd. And so alle hys dyscyples and alle his tru lovers sufferyd more payn than ther awne bodely dyeng, for I am suer by my awne felyng that the lest of them lovyd hym so farre abovyn them selfe that it passyth alle that I can sey.
> (LT pp 366.8ff)

The niche expands to include those selves whose love makes them porous and whose subjectivity is changed through the pain they suffer because of their love. But the expansion of the niche does not stop at those who love Christ. Julian understands from her first revelation that Mary, 'a symple creature of [God's] makyng' (LT p 298.34), is the highest thing in creation:

> In this syght I did vnderstand verily that she is more then all that god made beneth her in wordines and in fullhead, for aboue her is nothing that is made but the blessed manhood of Christ, as to my sight.
> (LT pp 298.34ff)

Mary is a creature, and suffers pain as the manhood of Christ does. In the eighth revelation Julian sees that at the Passion all creatures that could suffer pain do so, and in this is their 'onyng' with Christ. Thus the niche expands again, not through love-pain any more but just pain:

> Here saw I a grett onyng betwene Crist and vs, to my vnderstondyng; for when he was in payne we ware in payne, and alle creatures that myght suffer payne sufferyd with hym.
> (LT p 367.14ff)

Because all creatures are of the same 'kynd' or nature as Christ in his manhood, they experience through sorrow the same failing that Christ suffers in the Passion. This is a strong assertion of creation theology in which Christ is identified in his humanity with the whole cosmos, 'the fyrmamente and erth' (LT p 367.17). Christ's subjectivity as mortal is in deep performative interaction with all creatures, because in him 'alle ther vertuse stondyth' (LT p 367.19f). The failing of the cosmos at the Passion is not through its knowledge of Christ but through its shared nature, or 'kynd'.

The creatures that 'knew hym nott sufferde all maner comfort saue the myghty pryve kepyng of god' (LT p 367.23f). This seeing of Julian resonates with her 'little thing, the quantitie of an haselnott' (LT p 299.9f) which 'lasteth and ever shall, for god loueth it; and so hath all thing being by the loue of god' (LT p 300.15f). Thus the 'kynd' of the cosmos, that 'little thing', as well as being porous with Christ's humanity, is also in porous interaction with his divinity, because without his divine nature creation would fail altogether. God's 'pryve kepyng' is formed of love, and this is why God will never be wrathful at our sins, because if God were wrathful, his love would fail, and creation would fail. God would not be wrathful against himself:

> our lorde god as aneynst hym self may not forgeue, for he may not be wroth. It were vnpossible. For this was shewed, that oure lyfe is alle grounded and rotyd in loue, and without loue we may not lyve.
> (LT p 505.3ff)

The porosity of subjectivity between creation and God is made plain. For Julian, creation is continually sustained by God's love. The porous interaction of creatures at the Passion in the eighth revelation can be seen to arise from Julian's theology of creation, their very being granted by love (LT p 300.12ff) and made for integration (LT p 304.2ff), articulated by John Webster in his account of the meaning of *creatio ex nihilo* (2013 pp 160ff). He writes that the participative relation of creatures made out of nothing by God 'constitutes' creatures. 'Existing belongs to God by his essence, and [...] to other things by participation' (p 164). Furthermore, God's act of creation is one of 'purposive' love: 'Love *gives* life, and love gives *life*' (p 168, author's italics). The integrity of creatures comes from the 'benevolent love' which 'establishes and safeguards' that which it creates' (p 168). Such created integrity means that the actions of creatures are themselves directed towards completion. In our triadic hermeneutical terms, and in Julian's understanding of 'beseeching and beseking' (LT pp 460.3ff), the asymmetry of creatureliness provokes a performative and porous response to God.

The niche of all creation is energised and the porous interactions take place through God's love, even when there is no knowledge of each other. The pain is still love, even though creation does not know it. Julian calls upon witnesses, 'Pylate' and 'seynt Dyonisi of France' (LT p 368.27), to the 'onyng' of creatures with the manhood of Christ even when they do not know him. Dyonisi is Julian's explicit witness: he was a 'paynym' (pagan) (LT p 368.28) and had no basis of love of Christ to see that the disturbance of the whole cosmos, the planets and the elements are caused by the Passion; and yet that is what he sees. Thus is the cosmos drawn into the niche. For as Julian quotes Dyonisi: 'Eyther the worlde is now at an ende, or elles he that is maker of kyndes sufferyth' (LT p 368.29ff). Pilate and Dyonisi are powerful witnesses precisely because they were not believers. Julian concludes her argument: 'Wher for it was that they that knew hym nott were in sorow that tyme' (LT p 369.34f). The lens of the revelation has widened to include the whole cosmos and so Christ is now identified with the whole cosmos. The niche is cosmic. Humanity's home is Christ, and the creation of that niche is won through pain, pain caused by the cosmos knows not what, as Julian herself knew not what caused her alternation some 20 times between the light and darkness of her soul in the seventh revelation. Julian's creation theology has not just herself, nor just herself plus all 'evyn cristen', but all of these *and* the whole cosmos as summoned selves to the Cross, participating in the niche that has been constructed of the Passion that she has been shown.

The niche Julian's eighth revelation has constructed includes all creation, whose elements porously interact through love which is fundamentally an expression of God's love, binding all creation in what Joseph Murray has described as a 'cosmic covenant' (1992).[2] Hence the Passion of Christ, whose intense pain was experienced by his lovers because of their love for him, was also experienced by all of creation because creation is the same in kind as Christ's manhood, and all creatureliness is absolutely dependent upon the same God's love.

Julian does not look away from the Cross

The breadth of Julian's vision of God's love universally encompassing creation makes the next stage in her revelation all the more powerful, for immediately following her seeing all creation 'onyd' (LT p 367.1) with Christ, the revelation moves back to the tiny, microcosmic place of the crucifix in front of her. As all creation is 'onyd' with Christ, so it is 'onyd' with his Passion: Christ is all creation; creation is sustained and made of God's love; love is the Cross. The Cross thus becomes a distillation of creation. As Julian's vision swiftly refocuses on the singularity and narrow clarity of the crucifix held before her eyes, she understands that all that she needs, all that is, is *here*,

112 The Eighth Revelation

not away in some other, seemingly larger, space. Julian's niche is essential: the distilled, intense and undiluted heart of suffering, the greatest suffering that could ever have been or ever will be experienced.

Julian writes:

> In this tyme I wolde haue lokyde fro the crosse, and I durst nott, for I wyste wele whyle that I behelde the crosse I was suer and safe. Ther fore I wolde nott assent to put my soule in perelle, for besyde the crosse was no surenesse fro drede of fendes.
>
> (LT p 370.1f)

All the commentaries attest to the medieval belief that the Cross was surrounded by fiends. In the text Julian has already indicated her fear of them. When the curate has set the crucifix before her eyes and she has assented to rest them on it, and her sight begins to fail and there is darkness all about except in the image of the crucifix, Julian adds: 'All that was beseid the crosse was oglye and ferfull to me as it had ben much occupied with fiendes' (LT p 291.30ff). In her final vision, which happens in her sleep following the much-regretted denial ('I had ravyd to day' (LT p 633.17)) of all the previous revelations, a clearly seen fiend actually attacks her, perhaps because she *had* 'looked away':

> Ande in my slepe at the begynnyng me thought the fende sett hym in my throte, puttyng forth a vysage fulle nere my face lyke a yonge man, and it was longe and wonder leen.
>
> (LT p 635.2ff)

In this eighth revelation, Julian is encouraged to look away from the Cross and straight up into heaven, a posture she had assumed before the curate placed the crucifix before her eyes (LT p 291.21ff). She refuses, thus refocusing her readers onto the concentrated place of the Cross itself, now known to be one with the whole universe, and at the same time exonerating her own regret for having sought Christ's pain. Julian's choice not to look away from the Cross is tested by a friendly voice:

> Than had I a profyr in my reason, as it had ben frendely seyde to me: Loke uppe to hevyn to hys father.
>
> (LT p 370.6f)

But she understands that her niche of love and pain is right here in the dying Christ himself, and there is no space between the Cross and heaven for fiends to interpose and hurt her:

> And than sawe I wele with the feyth that I felt that ther was nothyng betwene the crosse and hevyn that myght haue dyssesyd me.
>
> (LT p 370.7ff)

She understands she has to make an explicit decision:

> Here me behovyd to loke vppe or elles to answere. I answeryd inwardly with alle the myght of my soule, and sayd: Nay, I may nott, for thou art my hevyn.
>
> (LT pp 370.9ff)

She unequivocally affirms that her place is in the pain of Christ, not elsewhere:

> Thys I seyde for I wolde nott; for I had levyr a bene in that payne tylle domys day than haue come to hevyn other wyse than by hym. For I wyst wele that he that bounde me so sore, he shuld vnbynd me whan he wolde.
>
> (LT p 371.11ff)

Julian is in enactive encounter with Christ, who has 'bounde' her sore. In medieval iconography this image has erotic overtones.[3] Margery Kempe declares that 'al hir lofe & al hir affeccyon was set in the manhode of Crist' (Meech and Allen 1940 p 86.21f). But whereas Kempe is 'sor aferd of the Godhede' and distinguishes it from the manhood (p 86.20ff) Julian resists the suggestion from the 'profyr in her reason' (LT p 370.6) that in order to see 'hys father' she needs to look away from the Son. Julian's Trinity is integrated, as Watson emphasises (1992), and she knows this, I suggest, because of her performative participation: her 'onyng' with Christ teaches her through experience that all the Trinity is present here on the bloody Cross.

At the beginning of her revelations, in an act that initiates them, Julian had made a practical decision to lower her eyes, which had been fixed uncomfortably upwards towards heaven, and rest them on the crucifix her curate held before her because she could manage that for longer (LT p 291.22ff). Now this practical decision becomes a theological and cosmological one; the act is performative and it becomes porous, with profound consequences. Like the witnessing relatives in the Konvalinka fire walking ritual (2011) Julian experiences directly the pain of the Passion. Like the students in the Koubova experiment, despite the pain, she nevertheless remains, not going away, attending on the other. Julian's participative encounters that create this niche happen because she *does not look away*. Seeing that Christ in the midst of his Passion is her 'hevyn', a Passion whose pain she now knows only too well, she will not look away from the Cross. The crucifix lit by its own luminescence: 'he shal be thy light; thou nedyth none but him' (LT p 325.13f) emphasises the niche's concentrated self-sufficiency that is all-encompassing. Paradoxically, as it focusses in this tiny material space, Julian's niche is growing: it now includes not only all creation but 'hevyn' too, distilled in the drying, dying Christ whose manhood is also an expression of the Godhead, and whose pain, Julian has declared, is her heaven. Windeatt observes Julian's 'pervasive spatial discourse of enclosing and of a mutual indwelling – simultaneously enfolding and being enfolded – that explodes the limits of material spatiality' (2016 p xxvii). The niche is cosmic but it is also minutely focused: there is nothing between the Cross and heaven that would 'dysses' Julian: there is no room for the fiends between the two because they are in one niche. The Cross and heaven are affordances in the porous interaction between Julian and Christ; the Cross is heaven too. The niche is truly universal, itself and all it contains in porous intermingled interaction. Julian's creation theology, in which all things are 'onyd' in Christ, extends now, I propose, *contra* Windeatt, who, as we saw, writes that Julian 'never declares' universal salvation, and stretching even our own observations on 'evyn cristen' in Chapter 3, to her salvation theology. All things, including material ones, will be 'onyd in blysse'. The niche is universal, the encounter transformative, Julian is everyman and her flesh, through her porous interaction with Christ, all creation. We her readers are invited into this niche, not theoretically but as active, porous, performative participants.

The encounter is energised by paradox: regret at experiencing the pain of Christ she had so earnestly sought; choosing wilfully Christ on the Cross as her heaven; pain and love. The paradoxes are energetic and the dynamic movement between them creates the niche. Julian declares herself much relieved that she has learned to choose Jesus for her heaven, even though all she sees is his pain. This is the pain she had regretted asking to feel; now her regret is exonerated as she deliberately remains in it, feeling it, looking at it: porously and performatively interacting with it.

Through this seeing, pain and heaven are conflated. This is profoundly contradictory, but Julian has been prepared for it by her previous, seventh, revelation of the undeserved alternating weal and woe. Julian makes the encounter of pain and heaven pedagogic as she characteristically learns and thereby teaches that it is a constant and ongoing choice:

> Thus was I lernyd to chese Jhesu for my hevyn, whom I saw only in payne at that tyme. Me lykyd no nother hevyn than Jhesu, whych shalle be my blysse when I come ther. And this hath evyr be a comfort to me, that I chose Jhesu to be my hevyn by his grace in alle this tyme of passion and sorow. And that hath ben a lernyng to me, that I shulde evyr more do so, to chese Jhesu only to my hevyn in wele and in woe.
>
> (LT p 371.15ff)

The wilful choice of Jesus in 'wele and in woe' fold these cosmic insights back into the causeless 'wele and woe' of the seventh revelation. Julian has seen that weal and woe visit her regardless of her own sin; now she knows for certain that Christ is in the woe as much as the weal, and her choice can and will remain steadfast whichever she is experiencing. The Cross asserts the nature of the niche: it is the vulnerable, summoned self of Christ, who is himself done unto. *This* is heaven, not some other place.

The choice she made stands in contrast to her regret and repentance for having asked to experience Christ's pains (LT p 364.53ff), and she reflects on how the choices were made. It was her body that regretted the experience of pain, and God does not blame the body:

> And though I as a wrech hath repentyd me, as I seyde before, yff I had wyst what payne it had be, I had be loth to haue prayde it, heer I saw werely that it was grugyng and dawnger frealte of the flessch without assent of the soule, in whych god assignyth no blame.
>
> (LT pp 371.21ff)

Wilful choice, the choice she made not to look away from the suffering, was inward: her internal niche. The pain of the flesh and its desire not to experience the pain ('repenting' of the experience as Julian had) is outward, and to be understood as without blame. Inwardly right choices can be made:

> Repentyng and wylfulle choyse be two contrarytes, whych I felt both at that tyme; and tho be two partes, that oon outward, that other inwarde. The outwarde party is our dedely flessh, whych is now in payne and now in woo, and shalle be in this lyfe, where of I felte moch in thys tyme; and that party was that I repentyd. The inward party is a hygh and a blessydfulle lyfe, whych is alle in peece and in loue, and this is more pryvely felte; and this party is in whych myghtly, wysely and wylfully, I chose Jhesu to my hevyn.
>
> (LT p 372.24ff)

Julian's reflection on what this might mean for free will and salvation follows, a typical 'musing' (Magill 2006) on the theological implications of what she has seen and experienced, including what she has not seen:

> And in this I saw truly that the inward party is master and sovereyne to the outward, nought chargyng nor takyng hede of the wylles of that, but alle the intent and the wylle is sett endlesly to be onyd to our lorde Jhesu. That the outward party sholde drawe the inward to assent was not shewde to me; but that the inwarde party drawyth the outward party by grace, and both shalle be onyd in blysse without ende by the vertu of Christ, this was shewde.
>
> (LT pp 372.33ff)

The inner and the outer are porous to each other. Julian is shown that the inner leads the outer and this exonerates her from repenting her wish to suffer Christ's pains, which she bitterly regretted. She sees how God sees us in our sin. For there is no condemnation of the inner (substance), and the outer (sensory being) has no will, so there is no condemnation, a Ricoeurian 'explosive' realisation to which her subjectivity has been made porous by the seventh, weal and woe, revelation. Windeatt notes (2015 p xlvii) that in showing that the outward 'sensory being' does not harm the inward but both shall be united in Christ, the passage dignifies sensory being and gives it worth (2015 p xxviiff), because it, as well as the 'higher being' of substance, are both in Christ. Julian declares, in a comment on her eighth revelation later in the text:

> theyse two pertyes were in Crist, the heyer and the lower, whych is but one soule ... and theyse two pertyes were seene and felte in the viij shewyng, in whych my body was fulfyllyd of felyng and mynd of Cristes Passion and hys dyeng.
>
> (LT p 569.49ff)

But there is more to the passage than a recognition that the inner substance leads the outer sensory being, that the two are united in Christ, and that the sensory being is dignified by the unity. Julian *chooses* the sensory being of Christ, the scarred and disfigured, despised and buffeted Christ, and finds heaven there. By not looking away from the sensory being of Christ, the subjectivity both of her own sensory being and that of Christ become porous to each other without disappearing into each other. Then through the sensory being, not away from it, not by dismissing it or rejecting it or transcending it, but porously through it, divinity is seen. In her later comment on the revelation, Julian writes that she had:

> a suttell felyng and a prevy inwarde syghte of the hye partys, wher I myghte nott for the mene profer loke vp in to hevyn. And that was for that ech myghty beholdyng of the inwarde lyfe, whych inward lyfe is that hye substannce, that precious soule whych is endlessly enjoyeng in the godhede.
>
> (LT p 569.54ff)

Julian learns to look at, not away, and keep steadfastly looking at the outer sensory being, and in this way penetrate through to the 'precious soule' which is endlessly with and in God. Julian and her attentive readers are in profound porous and performative interaction, as what is seen and felt in all its intensity becomes a doorway into divinity.

Christ's final, terrible suffering

The final death pains of Christ follow, suffered all the more greatly and extensively through time because of the strength his divinity gave him to endure. His high sovereignty means he can suffer longer, but Julian focusses on the joining of high sovereignty with pain. This clear seeing in a niche where the pain and the divinity become one is the 'hyest poynt', the most important seeing, not the suffering *per se*, nor those for whom he suffered:

> And thus saw I oure lorde Jhesu languryng long tyme, for the vnyng of the godhead gaue strength to the manhed for loue to suffer more than alle man myght. I meene not oonly more payne than alle man myght suffer, but also that he sufferd more payne than all man of saluacion that evyr was from the furst begynnyng in to the last day myght telle or fully thynke, havyng regard to the worthynes of the hyghest worshypful kyng and the shamfulle and dyspyteous peynfull deth. For he that is hyghest and worthyest was foulest co(n)dempnyd and vtterly dyspysed; for the hyest poynt that may be seen in his passion is to thynke and to know that he is god that sufferyd, seeyng after these other two poyntes whych be lower. That one is what he sufferyd; and that other for whom that he sufferyd.
>
> (LT pp 374.1ff)

Christ is able to suffer for much longer because of the divinity in his flesh, and the reader is reminded of the earlier passage in the same revelation where the spirits of Christ's flesh are put out one by agonising one (LT p 358.20f). Julian uses the language of contemplation and her words might be read as stages of contemplation: to see, to think, to know. The highest point of contemplation is that it is God that suffers, and two other points which are lower are what he suffered and for whom he suffered. Colledge and Walsh argue that 'see' is 'apprehend' rather than 'contemplate' here, since contemplation 'feels', citing as their authority Guigo II: 'Lesson sekyth, meditacion fyndith, orison askith, contemplacion felith' (Colledge and Walsh 1978 p 375.10 fn). But the niche of this revelation is steeped in feeling, and Julian's readers are brought to that sharp feeling by our contemplation of the text that explodes our world as we see the Godhead *itself* in despiteful pain. God and pain now perform interactively and porously in the niche of the Passion, and Julian and her readers can feel what that means, not from a distance, but as beings embedded and embodied within the niche.

The paradoxical porosity of sovereignty's subjectivity including 'lothfullnesse' is emphasised as the theme recurs in Julian's seeing of Godhead 'onyd' with manhood and of divinity 'onyd' with pain. The dimensions of the niche are made vast by the inclusion of these asymmetric extremes, and its detailed particularity is made evident in the inclusion of 'every mannys synne [...] and sorow':

> And in thys he brought to mynd in parte the hygh(t) and the nobylyte of the glorious godhede, and ther with the precioushede and the tendyrnesse of the blessydfulle body whych be to gether onyd, and also the lothfullnesse that in our kynde is to suffer peyne. For as moch as he

was most tendyr and clene, ryght so he was most strong and myghty to suffer. And for every mannys synne that shal be savyd he sufferyd; and every mannes sorow, desolacion and angwysshe he sawe and sorowd, for kyndnes and loue.

(LT pp 375.14ff)

The 'suffering for sorrow' is made particular and real by reference to Mary: 'For in as mech as our lady sorowde for his paynes, as mech sufferde he sorow for her sorowse' (LT p 375.22f). The mother and son are caught in a dynamic interaction of sorrow for sorrow, an endless dance of porous subjectivity. Julian sees that the suffering continues after the passing of Christ's body in the Passion: his suffering is his subjectivity and it does not come to an end: 'for as long as he was passyble he sufferde for vs and sorowde for vs. And now he is vppe resyn and no more passibylle; yett he sufferyth with vs as I shalle sey after' (LT pp 376.24ff). Colledge and Walsh note the earliest example of 'passibylle' is in Richard Rolle where it carries the meaning of 'capable of suffering'. If Julian understood the word in this way, she is foregrounding a great paradox, indeed an impossibility: Christ is no longer capable of suffering after he is 'vppe resyn' and yet he continues to, 'myldely ... with grett joy' and wilfully (LT p 377.27f). The power of the porous interaction of Christ's suffering for each soul is love: 'and I beholdyng alle this by hys grace saw that the loue in hym was so strong whych he hath to oure soule' and the soul that, with Julian, sees this, also sees that the subjectivity of pain becomes joy:

for the soule that beholdyth thus whan it is touchyd by grace, he shalle verely see that tho paynes of Cristes passion passe all paynes; that is to sey, whych paynes shal be turned in to everlastyng joy by the vertu of Cristes passion.

(LT p 377.28ff)

In a sentence which might be a summing up of the whole revelation of Christ's Passion, Julian writes:

It is gods wylle, as to my vnderstandyng, that we haue iij maner of beholdyng of his blessyd passion. The furst is the harde payne that he sufferyd with a contriccion and compassion; and that shewde oure lorde in this tyme, and gaue me myght and grace to see it.

(LT pp 377.33ff)

Of the three 'maner of beholdyng', the first is the 'harde payne that he sufferyd' and the second and third, according to Colledge and Walsh, are the contrition and compassion to which Julian refers in this sentence. It is not at all clear from the syntax that 'contriccion' and 'compassion' are the two other 'maner of beholdyng', despite the fact that Julian does not, at that point, go on to say what the other 'maner' are, but hastens into her description of Christ's transition from death to resurrected life. Since Julian uses numbered lists all the time and she almost never fails to deliver the full list,[4] it seemed highly unlikely that she would fail on this score. Windeatt notices (2016 p 218), but neither Colledge and Walsh nor Watson and Jenkins do, that Julian does indeed deliver her promised list later in the text, and these 'beholdings' fill out her understanding of the eighth revelation. At LT p 386, in the ninth revelation, Julian hears Christ ask her if she is 'well apayd'. Christ's meaning is, she says, that because of his love he would 'dye so oftyn, havyng no regard to [his] hard paynes'. She immediately follows this by noticing:

> And heer saw I for the *seconde beholding* in his blessyde passion. The loue that made hym to suffer it passith as far alle his paynes as hevyn is aboue erth; for the payne was a noble precious and wurschypfulle dede done in a tyme by the workyng of loue. And loue was without begynnyng, is and shall be without ende.
>
> (LT pp 386.45ff, my italics)

This second beholding re-emphasises the character of the niche created by the Passion revelation. The pain is born of love and its performance emerges from its porous subjectivity with love. In the analogy of love with heaven and pain with Earth, Julian's readers understand that pain will ultimately pass while love never will, but because of the porosity of pain and love, wherever the pain in the Earth is, there is love also, and the love is without end.

The third beholding is found at the beginning of Chapter 23 of the Long Text:

> And heer saw I for the *thyrde beholding* in hys blessydfulle Passion, that is to sey the joy and the blysse that makyth hym to lyke it.
>
> (LT p 389.6ff, my italics)

By this third beholding the joy that Julian had seen in Christ's wilful choosing of suffering for each sin and each sorrow is brought to the fore, given its place in the niche, performatively interacting with pain and love. In the great performance of the Passion, pain, love and joy are themselves in porous interaction, as are those performers (God, Christ, Julian, her readers) who experience them.

Looking back at the first beholding with the second and third beholdings in mind, we hear again Julian's articulation that Christ suffered the 'harde payne [...] with a contriccion and compassion' (LT p 378.34f). Julian's own wounds, sought from her early life, are now found here in Christ, suffused with love and joy. Christ's subjectivity and her own become porous to each other as she is given 'myght and grace to see' (LT p 378.36).

The transition from death into life on the Cross

The transformation from death into life takes place in such a way that Julian does not see Christ dead. In this finale to the eighth revelation (I do not agree with the Colledge and Walsh edit which begins the ninth revelation here) Julian does not see Christ die. She does not see it because it is not there, like God's wrath (LT p 506.13ff). Not-seeing is as important as seeing for Julian, as Watson observes: 'Julian finds revelatory material in what she *does not see*' (1992 p 90, author's italics). Not-seeing itself gives insights. Julian's not-seeing of Christ's death is not simply a detail to emphasise the swiftness of the change. Time is not linear in this niche. All creation and all time is *here*, concentrated on this figure on the Cross, *now* horribly suffering, drying and dying, *now* transformed into blissful cheer. The suffering of Christ for humanity offers continuity: his physical suffering ends but his suffering for us remains, for the time being, 'monying and mornyng tylle whan we come' (LT p 706.37). But love, which cannot be divided from suffering, remains constant.

> And I lokyd after the departyng with alle my myghtes, and wende to haue seen the body alle deed; but I saw him nott so. And right in the same tyme that me thought by semyng that the lyfe myght no lenger last, and the shewyng of the ende behovyd nydes to be nye, sodenly I beholdyng in the same crosse he channgyd in blessydfulle chere.
> (LT p 379.1ff)

Just as Julian's heaven had turned out to be no other than or away from the bloody Christ on the Cross, so Christ's Resurrection is no other than his bloody self on the Cross. The resurrected Christ remains wounded, as Sheldrake observes (2016 p 112). In Badiou's account of the Resurrection, for Paul there is an absolute disjunction between death and Resurrection. Resurrection 'is neither a sublation, nor an overcoming of death. They are two distinct functions' (2003 p 71). The sudden and unnecessary emergence of the event of the Resurrection remains of the order of grace. The crucifix does not cease to be an affordance in the niche, but the transformation of Christ's subjectivity transforms what is in the niche, beginning with Julian herself:

> The channgyng of hys blessyd chere changyd myne, and I was as glad and mery as it was possible. Then brought oure lorde meryly to my mynde: Wher is now any poynt of thy payne or of thy anguysse? And I was fulle mery.
> (LT p 379.1ff)

The Passion itself is revealed as an 'act of joy' (Watson and Jenkins 2006 p 192), confirmed in Julian's third beholding (LT p 389.6ff), cited above. The subjectivity of Julian has been transformed by the transformation of Christ, and because Julian is everyman and we are her attentive readers, so is our subjectivity:

> I vnderstode that we be now in our lordes menyng in his crosse with hym in our paynes and in our passion dyeng, and we wilfully abydyng in the same crosse with his helpe and his grace in to the last poynt.
> (LT pp 379.11ff)

The inclusion of heaven in the niche of Christ's bloody Passion, in which we are all porously interacting, is affirmed:

> Sodeynly he shalle channge hys chere to vs, and we shal be with hym in hevyn.
> (LT p 380.14f)

That there is no linear time between the pain and the joy is affirmed:

> Betwene that one and that other shalle alle be one tyme; and than shall alle be brought in to joy.
> (LT p 380.15)

The performative and porous interaction of all in the Passion is confirmed as the 'blyssedfulle chere' of Christ. Christ's cheer has transformed the niche but denied none of the pain that is in it, and his 'chere of passion' porously transforms all our pain. Our porosity to him means that the pain that goes with our creatureliness, 'as our kynd askyth', is his pain, and so our pain is 'chere of passion' too:

> And so ment he in thys shewyng: Wher is now any poynt of thy payne or of thy agreffe? And we shalle be fulle of blysse. And here saw I verely that if he shewde now to vs his blyssedfulle chere, there is no payne in erth ne in no nother place that shuld trobylle vs, but alle thyng shulde be to vs joy and blysse. But for he shewyth vs chere of passion as he bare in this lyfe hys crosse, therfore we be in dysees and traveyle with hym as our kynd askyth.
> (LT pp 380.16ff)

The ground of the 'chere of passion' is 'pooled' and it is a 'joint project' (Raczaszek-Leonardi, Debska, and Sochanowicz 2015) between the porous subjectivity of Christ and the porous subjectivity of the reader, who is now an heir:

> And the cause why that he sufferyth is for he wylle of hys goodnes make vs the eyers with hym in hys blysse. And for this lytylle payne that we suffer heer we shalle haue an hygh endlesse knowyng in god, which we myght nevyr haue without that. And the harder oure paynes haue ben

with hym in hys crosse, the more shalle our worschyppe be with hym in his kyngdom.

(LT pp 381.23ff)

The seventh revelation, in which Julian learns that pain is passing, even though it will happen, is recalled as Julian concludes:

For it is goddes wylle that we holde vs in comfort with alle oure myght; for blysse is lastyng withought ende, and payne is passyng, and shall be brought to nowght to them that shall be savyd. Therfore it is not goddes wylle that we folow the felyng of paynes in sorow and mowrnyng for them, but sodaynly passe ovyr and holde vs in the endlesse lykyng that is god.

(LT p 356.29ff)

But Julian does hold fast to the sorrow while she is identifying with Christ's sorrow, and only passes over when Christ himself does. Christ in ugly pain is heaven. Christ, humiliated and disfigured like the 'vernacle of Rome' (LT p 331.65) (a relic which was believed to be the handkerchief with which Veronica wiped the face of Christ as he struggled with his cross on the road to Calvary, and which bears the imprint of his suffering face), that *same* Christ is 'blessydfulle chere'. And his changing, which is as swift as Julian's shifting moods in the seventh revelation, changes Julian: 'and I was as glad and mery as it was possible' (LT p 379.8f). The change is not linear: 'betwene that one and that other shalle alle be one tyme' (LT p 380.15). In an instant the cosmos is also the transformed, resurrected Christ, still on the Cross, still bloody, transformed nevertheless into the highest heaven, and drawing all with him.

Concluding summary

The eighth revelation is the culmination of Julian's wish in her early life to suffer Christ's Passion 'nere his dyeng'. The text offers us a clear picture of the scene of the revelation, in which Julian lies close to her own death, in a room in which, among others, her mother is attending her, and her curate has placed the crucifix under her eyes. In McGann's terms (2015), Julian is 'achieving' an encounter as she engages with her surroundings. For Julian, the crucifix is an affordance, which is to say it is a part of her niche whose meaning and even name is conferred by her interaction with it. The crucifix would not be an affordance for another who had not so earnestly sought the experience Julian was about to undergo, because it would not hold the same meaning for that other: he or she would not see in it what Julian saw, her seeing influenced by pictures (ST p 202.16) and, we infer from the text, homilies, possibly books that she had read, adding to the dramatic meaning of the crucifix being held under her downcast eyes as she lay propped up in bed.

Her crucifix is an affordance because it is not, in this precise circumstance, merely an aspect or property of the environment, but a relation that holds between Julian and her environment (McGann 2015 p 23); it has come to life, as it were, under her imploring gaze. Julian 'makes sense' of her crucifix through participation in it. Importantly, as McGann notes, this participative sense-making needs no mediation or creation of a perceptual image. Julian has a hinterland of meanings which forms her niche, arising above all from her readiness not only to experience the pain of the Passion but also herself to nearly die. When that near-death experience comes about, she is able to make sense using what was in her niche as affordances. But it is the crucifix itself, and not some imagined symbol or image, that is the ground of her revelation. Thus for Julian we can propose that the crucifix itself moved and spoke. Nothing else is happening for Julian at this moment. Externalities impinge later (her mother attempting to 'lokke' her eyes because she thinks she is dead) which only serve to emphasise the potent focus of the niche of the revelation itself. The reality of the dying body of Christ is revealed to Julian in such a way that she experiences it as closely as if it were happening to her, while retaining a sense of herself as a lover of Christ who suffers because of the love, not because she becomes Christ. The two are deeply and porously engaged in a performative encounter, made possible by the affordance that the crucifix becomes under Julian's very particular eye.

The encounter of the two students occupying the stage in the fourth part of the Koubova experiment (2015) provides insight into the niche that is being created. Julian is prepared in her life-long wish to nearly die, to experience Christ's Passion, and to be wounded, as perhaps Koubova's students were prepared in their courageous and patient attention to being alone on stage, in their discerning of a hidden, powerful self that can be born and take its part as a potent contributor to meaning and engagement. Thus prepared, Julian and the student can encounter the other – Christ or another student – in steady receptive acceptance, in allowing of the other, waiting for the other, being endlessly curious about the other, and being able to respond with great subtlety and attentiveness to the slightest move of the other (Koubova 2015 p 69).

The eighth revelation brings to Julian's subjectivity the porosity of an understanding of Christ identified with the whole cosmos, that identity being graphically felt by her through the prism first of her own identification with his suffering, then Mary's, then all his lovers, and then all that did not know him, including all creatures and elements. The identification is intensely felt because of the pain that Julian experiences, and it is precisely this Christ, the one who is so slowly and painfully drying and dying, in time stretched out, that is identified with the cosmos. Julian does not look up to heaven, away from the Christ on the Cross. She declares that Christ is her heaven. And it is that same Christ, the one she is looking at, that changes into 'joy and blysse' under her very eyes, with no moment of dying that she can detect. Thus the niche being created has a body in heaven. Davies observes that this representation of such 'heavenly dimensions' supports a 'cosmic level of human niche construction': our niche is the Creator's niche (2016 pp 106f).

Julian brings her already-porous subjectivity to the revelation in her lifelong wounds of contrition, compassion and longing to God, and in her readiness to experience the Passion. Through the long, painful, Ricoeurian journey of the revelation Julian's already-porous subjectivity is transformed to include the cosmos, heaven, and the Trinity itself. And at every stage her readers are invited to participate. Our triadic framework that focusses our reading on the text's capacity to transform Julian's subjectivity also draws its attentive readers into the same transformative niche. Inasmuch as we, the readers, are prepared to engage performatively with the text, so we allow ourselves to be transformed as Julian is. Julian is the mirror-into-doorway to Christ: 'leve the behaldynge of the wrechid worme, synfulle creature, that it was schewyd vnto, and that ye myghtly, wyselye, lovandlye and mekelye be halde god' (ST p 219.4f); and she is everyman: 'alle that I sawe of my selfe, I meene in the persone of alle myne evynn cristene' (ST p 219.1).

The eighth revelation and our ecological consciousness

As with the study of Julian's wounds in Chapter 3, if the very act of reading Julian's account of the eighth revelation has had the effect of transforming the subjectivity of her readers to restore its porosity, then the Julian texts have already done their work. From this Julian-led porosity, we can now begin to see some specific expressions of a restored ecological consciousness, and emergent ecological niches can be proposed.

From the seventh revelation of 20 reversals of subjectivity we learn, through Julian's clear-sighted account, of an inexplicable experience of change to which no cause can be attributed and therefore no blame attached. The disconcerting changes in climate and in the other spheres of the Earth can be attributed to human action but not to the wickedness of some humans. Mostly they came about with the best of intentions and inasmuch as they are caused by greed, all of humanity shares in the responsibility for that greed. We are not living in an enemy narrative: if we were, since the enemy is all of us, the only adequate response would be to rid the Earth of humanity altogether. Quarrels about culpability simply detract from the action that is needed. Julian learns right attitude of summoned porous self from the experience and that is what we have to learn in our encounter with the harm that has been done to the Earth.

Julian's close observation to the point of subjective participation in the dying, drying Christ, whose formerly life-giving blood dries him from within and cold wind dries him from without, who is identified with the Earth, can be translated into a close observation of the suffering creation as the waters dry up and the air becomes polluted. This careful looking leads to empathetic understanding, heartbreak, and a loving response.

From the Philippians quotation we gain the insight that the feeling that is in Christ is, or can be, in us. Christ identified as the cosmos is dying again through the ecological crisis. Less dramatically he dies and is reborn through the death and rebirth that is continuously taking place in nature. Our own sharing in that death and rebirth opens us to feeling the interaction inside ourselves and this in turn retunes us to the natural flow of nature, rendering it and us non-adversarial.

From Julian's granted wish to experience Christ's pains we learn that empathetic recognition of the ecological crisis means experiencing its pain but that pain, if not turned away from, is translated into love, and the response is greater love, not defensive fear.

From the passage describing Julian's mother trying to lock her eyes, and Julian's distress at the disconnection that would entail, we can derive an injunction not to close our eyes to the pain of creation. Through our clear seeing, love is learned.

The passage on the pain of Christ's mother that transformed into love, so that love energises the niche Julian has created, can open up a reflection on the nature of our response to the ecological crisis, as that of a loving mother, or perhaps of a memory of nature itself being nurturing like a mother.

The passage which establishes Christ's oneness with all creation, as attested by witnesses who are 'paynims', turns ecological damage into damage of Christ himself, while at the same time affirming the unbreakable love of God which sustains all creation.

The passage in which Julian chooses not to look away from the 'vernacle'-ugly Christ on the Cross is critical to the porous ecological seeing she is helping us with. She has discovered, through that hard choice not to look away, the privy inward sight of divinity right there in the heart of the disfigured physical. So for us, the not turning away from the pain of creation, but looking at it deeply and contemplatively, generates a porous interaction which reveals its divine origin that will satisfy humanity in a way that consuming never will. We attend to materiality still, but not in order to consume it. The problem, as Heidegger saw, is not materialism (technology) but the way we approach materiality.

In the final passage on the Passion, pain, love and joy become the heart of the niche, the expression of Christ's subjectivity, and they are deeply seen by Julian. There is a simple read across to the pain and joy of death and renewal that is constantly expressed by the Earth, which, seen through Julian's eyes, is love in performative interaction as the cosmos is identified with Christ. The experience of childbirth carries the same porous qualities of pain and joy and love. An ecological consciousness from Julian might see the Earth not as an inert thing that is a backdrop for merely human dramas, but animated by the pain and joy and love of Christ, expressed in every movement of 'rotting and renewal' of the ecosystems of the Earth, as feminist eco-theologian Catherine Keller notices (2000 p 195).

The seeing of and meditation on the Resurrection of the bloody Christ still on the Cross, whose pain is transformed into joy, resonates with nature's enactment of death and resurrection through the seasons in all species; moreover, ecosystems are complex performative interactions between creatures that kill and eat each other; also dead organisms bring new life in humus or compost. The new life is in the death and does not happen without it. A porous human response to this is to recognise that humanity participates in this 'rotting and renewal': we too must die to be (in Christian theology) resurrected; we eat and are eaten; our death can bring new life materially in, for example, posthumous organ donation but also with the ideas and good deeds, and above all the health of the planet, we leave behind us. The participation in death and new life can be intentionally beneficent.

The ecological consciousness that emerges from the porous subjectivity Julian has brought about in the text of the eighth revelation can be summarised as transforming the enemy narrative in which we are living as *Gestell*, buffered selves into a greater narrative enacted by Christ's Passion and the natural rhythms of ecosystems. If there is an enemy in the ecological crisis it is all of humanity, so the logical response is to do away with humanity altogether. Julian's way is to learn porosity, that is to say, humility, from being presented with causeless weal and woe. The ecosystems of the Earth are full of weal and woe, as creatures eat and are eaten: nature is bloody. But the pattern of death and new life is embodied in the Crucifixion and Resurrection of Christ. By identifying, as closely as Julian did with Christ, with the 'rotting and renewal' of the Earth, we identify with a universal narrative and take our part in it. For us, now, that identification means suffering the ecological degradation of the Earth, as Julian suffered the degradation of the Passion. By not closing our eyes or looking away from the pain of the Earth, as Julian did not, the pain becomes suffused with love, love as great as that of a mother, which is the same as Christ's love. The pain and love are themselves suffused with joy in the new life of the Earth and the Resurrection.

Notes

1 There is some evidence, cited by Watson and Jenkins and also Windeatt, of a tradition within medieval accounts of the Passion of Christ having extremely tender flesh, found in Bridget of Sweden (Watson and Jenkins 2006 p 180) and Richard Rolle (Windeatt 2016 p 211). Julian's 'I vnderstode', rather than 'I saw' implies she is referring to a tradition in which the harm the nails and the thorns would have done would be greater on Christ's body than on any other.
2 An account of Old Testament theology that highlights those passages which speak of the interdependent relationship between all created things and the God who made them and eternally keeps them, eg Psalms 89 and 104.
3 Watson and Jenkins (2006) compare the reference to Chaucer's *Troilus and Criseyde* 3.1358: 'How koude ye withouten bond me binde', and the *Ancrene Wisse* in Part 7 makes it clear that Christ is bound to humanity as humanity is to him: 'love binds our Lord, so that he cannot do anything except with love's leave' (2006 p 186).
4 From the LT see pp 281.3; 285.4; 288.41; 300.17; 317.4; 323.29; 334.83; 334.87; 352.13; 357.8 (here Julian refers to iiij colours and one has to work quite hard to find them, but they are there: 'rody', 'blew', 'browne' and 'blacke'); 358.19;

360.3; 363.38; 368.26; 372.25; 375.11; 383.9 (the list is of three heavens; Julian only tells us of one of them, but her point is that all three are of the manhood of Christ); 389.2; 389.3; 401.38; 410.24; 414.2; 423.20 (the v words Julian refers to are actually vi: 'I may make alle thing welle'); 430.2; 440.54f; 452.27; 460.4; 461.15, 17 (Paris MS says vj, corrected by Colledge and Walsh to ii to make sense; a fair editorial decision since it is so rare for Julian not to give a full list); 468.3; 483.8f; 487.11; 491.16; 495.2; 497.26; 512.29; 514.4; 515.22; 519.70; 527.164; 552.72; 553.83; 569.49; 574.44f; 575.55; 583.20; 585.30; 593.43 (the list promises three; Julian adds a fourth, however the poetry of the context allows it); 631.35; 654.2 (the vj words promised can be surmised to be: take, believe, keep, comfort, trust, [thou shalt not be] overcome); 656.25; 659.4; 665.54; 666.2f; 666.9; 671.2; 678.2; 679.9; 687.23; 696.6; 707.2; 722.2; 727.10.

5 The Fourteenth Revelation

Introduction

The 14th revelation is pressed from Julian's intense questioning about the nature of sin and the inexplicable paradox between what she has understood about it from holy church and as it is being shown in her revelations. Out of the paradox of these two accounts of sin comes an allegorical showing, which Julian calls an 'example', in which encounter is brought into porous participation in one character, the servant who is both Adam or everyman, and also Christ: the paradox and the encounter are embodied in one subjectivity. It is mysterious and provokes more questions, keeping the subjectivity of Julian and her readers porous. The revelation is a demonstration of the energy of encounter released by the asymmetry of Julian's refusal to explain away difference. She stands apparently mutually exclusive points of view, in this case about sin, together. This releases energy to flow between them, unblocking a fixed *Gestell* notion of control of one by the other or some kind of negotiated transactional stand-off which damages both or rather does not do justice to both. Julian's persistence with keeping paradox in porous proximity brings to birth hitherto unimagined niches.

The 14th revelation is complex and layered, as its initial, very simple showing – of a lord sending out his beloved servant, who runs in his eager obedience to fulfil the lord's will and falls into a chasm – is returned to again and again by a 'marvelling' Julian, who repeatedly brings it to life by re-inspecting its detail and making more transformative sense of it each time. In the ensuing sections we will follow Julian in her deepening, ever more porous understanding, using our triadic framework as an aid. As with our previous reading, our engagement with Julian's enquiry through the interactive power of her text should bring about the transformed subjectivity the ecological challenge requires, and once more I will conclude by suggesting some characteristics of a Julian-inspired ecological consciousness from our reading.

Establishing the niche of the 14th revelation

We will begin by following the narrative of the text, exploring the way that the paradox of what Julian sees and what she knows evokes a powerful longing out of which the 14th revelation is pressed. We will then unpack her method as she describes it at this point, and consider together the first, puzzling layer of seeing of the revelation.

Julian longs for seeing and knowing to become one

Julian *knows* by the common teaching of holy church and by her own feeling that 'the blame of oure synnes contynually hangyth vppon vs' (LT p 511.10ff), from Adam's fall until doomsday. She *sees*, however, that God shows 'no more blame then if we were as clene and as holy as angelis be in hevyn' (LT p 511.14f). She recounts the paradox between what she sees and what she knows:

> I *see* the that thou arte very truth
>
> I *know* truly that we syn grevously all day and be moche blame wurthy
>
> I may neyther leue the *knowyng* of this sooth
>
> nor I *se* nott the shewyng to vs no manner of blame.
> (LT pp 510.7ff, my italics)

Julian attributes her sense of this unfathomable and unsolvable paradox to her own 'blyndnes' (LT p 511.16). This attribution is characteristic of her method, and what we can gain from her: she understands not that there is something she does not believe and should believe that will explain away the paradox, rather, she understands that she cannot (yet) see all that there is to see. Thus she is greatly concerned that her revelations will cease and God will pass from her sight before she understands fully, leaving her 'vnknowyng how he beholde vs in oure synne' (LT p 511.18). For Julian the paradox is resolved in God's sight: how God sees us in our sin will in turn teach her how to see what blame she may carry. So she remains in encounter, in her showings-niche, like the Koubova performance space, fixing her gaze inwardly on God: 'my longyng endured, hym contynuantly beholdyng' (LT p 511.22). She has made her niche dangerous: she *will* learn how to see sin by seeing how God sees sin, but if all she has seen so far is indicative, she will learn that which is counter to what she has learned from holy church. For if sin is as God seems to see it, which is to say, that he does not see it, then 'we be no synners nor no blame wurthy' (LT p 512.24). She must accept that, but she must be sure, because if she is wrong, she falls into error. Her imploring is heartfelt: 'I cryde inwardly with all my myght, sekyng in to god for helpe' and her question is urgent: 'how shall I be esyde, who shall tell me and tech me that me nedyth to wytt, if I may nott at this tyme se it in the?' (LT p 512.36ff).

The longing is a forceful, energetic, asymmetric importuning by Julian to God. The niche has been created through Julian's longing, her refusal to turn away from the face of God which holds such paradox. We recall Koubova's students at the beginning of the experiment, standing in the performance space with nothing to do, experiencing 'extreme reactions (fight, flight, freeze, exhaustion)' (2015 p 65). Like the students, whose readiness to continue despite the extreme discomfort Koubova attributes to our wish not to act other than in a 'coded way' (p 65), Julian stays in the performance space of her revelations, refusing to go back, as it were, to the 'coded way' that holy church has taught her. Julian's insistence on not denying what she sees is already drawing her into a changed subjectivity and niche; as McGann would have it, perception is action so her seeing, and the seeing into which she draws her readers, is already a porous and interactive response (2015 p 22).

Persevering with this tension means that, ultimately, knowing and seeing will become one, and God wills it:

> desyryng with all oure hart and alle oure strengh to haue knowyng of them [the properties of our soul] evyr more and more in to the tyme that we be fulfyllyd; for fully to *know* them and clerely to *se* them is not elles but endles joy and blysse that we shall haue in hevyn, whych god wyll we begynne here in knowyng of his loue.
>
> (LT pp 574.47ff, my italics)

The porosity between seeing and knowing 'oure owne soule' in order to have 'full knowynge of god' (LT p 573.32f) 'begynne here' even if it is only truly reconciled in 'hevyn'. We can understand this as an invitation to salvation from a *Gestell* subjectivity that is fixed in its knowing and not open to seeing new possibilities. The porosity into which Julian's and her readers' subjectivity is transformed is ongoing: the habit of porosity is a new niche; as Watson puts it, the 'never-satiated process' (1992 p 100) of the unfolding of meaning of love. Julian understands that after all her revelations are finished, the showings will 'passe', leaving no 'sygne ne tokyn' (LT p 652.18ff). But she will return to them again and again, as 'Jhesu [...] shewde hyt all ageene within my soule, with more fullehed with the blessyd lyght of his precyous loue' (LT p 653.30ff).

Sight to her understanding: Julian's method

The 14th revelation is the answer to Julian's longing:

> And then oure curteyse lorde answeryd in shewyng full mystely by a wonderfull example of a lorde that hath a servannt, and gave me syght to my vnderstandyng of both.
>
> (LT pp 513.2ff)

What Julian 'knows', having learnt it from holy church, will be changed by virtue of her allowing 'syght to my vnderstandyng'. She sees the example is 'wonderfull': her (thus) 'wounded' and hence porous self interacts with the showing, and by virtue of what it sees, which for Julian is being shown what God sees, her understanding changes. She sees both a 'bodely lycknesse' (LT p 514.8) and, as she is looking, God gives her 'gostly vnderstandyng' (LT p 514.9). She sees doubly, then, both the bodies of the actors in the revelation that is to be played out before her, and the seeing in her understanding of the meaning of what she is looking at. Julian is not, here, watching a scene that is played out *on* anything: we do not know if the crucifix is still being held before her eyes but if so, it is not an affordance in the niche of this 14th revelation. She is seeing the revelation internally, both the example itself and what is shown to her understanding of its meaning. But her understanding does not come straightaway. As she watches with the same attention to detail that we see in the eighth revelation, she is puzzled by many features. She is experiencing what Ricoeur would call a 'semantic clash', an 'interaction between contexts' that disorients the reader because the world of the parable does not make sense in the world of the reader (1995 p 161). The semantic clash will give rise to a 'progressive recognition' (p 161) of the nature of salvation. The porousness of her subjectivity is evident in her readiness to see and describe what does not make sense: in Fantasia and colleague's terms she in participating in 'enactive sense-making' (2015 p 113). As they would put it, her 'mind' emerges from the interaction as new domains are opened up in the interaction. This is how it is that Julian can come to see new worlds, and bring them to birth in her own writing so that her readers, too, can experience giving birth to meaning as we interact with the narrator (cp Popova 2015 p 320).

Thus for Julian the enactive sense-making and progressive recognition continue for many years. She 'culde nott take there in full vnderstandyng to my ees in that tyme' (LT p 519.66f). There were too many strange aspects to what she saw. But her 'techyng inwardly' which she is given, quite precisely, 'for twenty yere after the tyme of the shewyng saue thre monthys' (LT p 520.86) is not taking her away from what she saw originally. She is taught to look in ever more detail at it. '[S]yght to my vnderstandyng' came through steady and sustained looking, not through analysis or teaching to which the showing gives rise that would distract her from the showing itself. Julian has many levels of comprehension of the showing, and she returns again and again to what she sees to verify and deepen her understanding. The precise chronology of 'twenty yere [...] saue thre monthys' implies that Julian experiences some kind of breakthrough in her understanding at this specific time. She writes of being shown the meaning of the example 'in a touch' (LT p 527.158), like Darwin's precise memory of when and where he understood the importance of location in evolutionary theory (1887/1958 p 120f), and like Koubova's students, who stayed in the performative place of their experiment, allowing the time to discover the hidden subjectivity that turns out to be so creative. Her study over two decades bears fruit in herself and in her text, which attests to her obedience to the 'techyng inwardly' to look in ever greater detail at what she has been shown. She looks at everything: the way the lord sits, what he sits upon, what colour his clothes are and what they are like; his outer demeanour and what he is like inside; the way the servant stands, where he stands; the colour and shape of his clothing; his outward behaviour and his inward goodness.

As Julian has so closely observed, so in turn she gives her readers every possible detail of the vision; a practice which once again allows us to be as drawn performatively into the encounter as Julian herself is. We are to see for ourselves. Thus we, through her, are taught to 'take hede to the propertes and the condescions that were shewed in the example, though the thynke that it be mysty and indefferent to thy syght' (LT pp 520.87ff). What we then have is a layered account: the deceptively simple showing is recounted several times, each time taking us more deeply into its meaning. The effect on the reader is, with Julian, one of transformation through deepening participation, a gentle but inexorable, undeniable, effective rebirth into a new world born of seeing differently, seeing as God sees, over a long time, 'progressively', as Ricoeur would have it, but still 'explosively' (1995 pp 61, 161). What Julian learns through seeing over time is profoundly unsettling, turning upside down deeply held notions of blame and forgiveness. She thus embodies transformation and through language makes possible the readers' transformation in turn.

The first layer of seeing of the revelation

Julian first of all sees that the 'lorde syttyth solempnely in rest and in pees' while the servant 'stondyth before his lorde, reverently redy to do his lordes wylle' (LT p 514.9ff). Already, with the 'reverent readiness', there is a flow of energetic love from the servant to the lord. This is reciprocated: the lord 'lokyth vppon his seruannt full louely and swetly and mekely' (LT p 514.11f). The porous interconnection of this love and reverence is never broken; as we saw in Chapter 3, 'loue' and 'reuerente drede' are 'bredryn' (LT p 673.20). The love and reverent dread with which Julian sees her revelations, and which are revealed to her by her revelations, resonate as she sees the lord and the servant behold each other, their loving and interactive face to face encounter taking place in a niche pregnant with expectation.

For then the lord sends the servant 'in to a certeyne place to do his wyll'. The servant does so, and the manner of his going is significant. He does not just 'go', but 'sodenly he stertyth and rynnyth in grett hast for loue to do his lordes wylle' (LT p 514.14f). He leaps into action, spurred by his love and reverence and willingness to obey. There is no break in the love that holds the lord and servant in their niche, no disobedient pride. On the contrary, it is the same love that causes the servant to start and run. Love could command no other response. And yet it is precisely this loving, eager response that is the cause of his fall, literally, into a deep crevasse: 'anon he fallyth in a slade, and takyth ful grett sorow; and than he gronyth and monyth and wallowyth and wryeth' (LT p 515.15f). If he had not run as he did, he would not have fallen: 'oonly hys good wyll and his grett desyer was the cause of his fallyng' (LT p 516.35f). There is no 'defaughte' in the servant, nor does the lord 'assigne in hym ony maner of blame'. The servant is as 'vnlothefull and as good inwardly as he was when he stode before his lorde, redy to do his wylle' (LT p 516.34ff). This, then, most mysteriously, is what God sees when he sees us in our sin. Love and reverent dread are still 'bredryn', and the porous interconnectivity between the lord and the servant is not broken by the servant's fall. The niche holds steady, by means of energetic love.

But this is not what the servant sees. He has fallen into a 'slade', and the 'most myschefe' in this, as Julian sees, is that he has fallen in such a way that his face is turned away from the lord. The face to face encounter is broken and so, for the servant, the energetic flow of love *feels* broken: 'he culde nott turne his face to loke vppe on his lovyng lorde, whych was to hym full nere, in whom is full comfort' (LT p 515.17ff). The servant cannot see his lord, so he cannot see how 'thus contynuantly his loueyng lorde full tenderly beholdyth hym' (LT p 516.38f). Again, the Koubova experiment is illustrative, as the initial experience of the students, standing for the first time alone in the performance space and not looking at their audience, entirely exposed with nothing to do and no interaction to guide what they might do, are nevertheless supportively attended to by the audience all the while. Despite the loving audience, the students feel a horrible chaotic lostness, 'infinitely exposed', demonstrating that 'the isolation of the agent from the network provokes extreme reactions (fight, flight, freeze, exhaustion)' (2015 p 65). For the Koubova students, the experience of standing in the performance space, seen lovingly by their audience but not seeing that love and, in their fear and isolation, not knowing it either, exposes 'the rigid ego identified with the mask' (p 65) that is the persona worn in public. In the fall of the servant, although the love of the lord is unbroken, the servant's experience of isolation and loss is a necessary stage in his journey to salvation, an utter undoing of all his certainties of selfhood and relationality, in who he thinks he is in relation to the lord. This is the journey of the Koubova students, the Ricoeurian explosion of their familiar world with its 'rigid ego' unlocking new and profound creative possibilities in a new and porous niche. The transformation of the *Gestell* subjectivity of our 21st-century selves, by implication, will involve a similar journey to a restored porosity which we cannot yet see. The servant will also be restored in a way unimaginable to him as he lies in his painful isolation.

The servant has fallen and he is helpless: 'he may nott ryse nor helpe hym selfe by no manner of weye' (LT p 515.16f). The lord's loving gaze is not interactive without the returning gaze of the servant and the servant cannot be helped while he is thus disconnected. His troubles are manifold: he suffers 'soore brosyng'; 'hevynesse of his body' and 'fybylnesse'. The condition of fallenness is painful. But more than that, he is 'blyndyd in his reson and stonyd in his mynde so ferforth that allmost he had forgeten his owne loue' (LT pp 515.22ff). The damage is not just physical but mental and emotional. He cannot see the lord physically because of the way he has fallen, but he cannot see with his reason either, so that not only does he not know that the lord is still holding him in his loving gaze, he can barely remember the love in his own heart that generated his eager performance in response to the lord's request. He is bereft of the energetic love between himself and the lord. For Julian, the experience of not being able to see what is there is the cruellest punishment of all, entirely different from her experience of not-seeing because something is not there. It is more akin to her horror (we imagine) at the prospect of her eyes being 'lokked' by her mother who thought she had died in the eighth revelation (ST p 234.30), threatening her with being cut off from her performative, loving gaze on the dying Christ. She and her readers may shudder for the lonely, blinded servant's suffering, and thus we begin to experience in ourselves, rather than as objective teaching, the nature of sin.

The servant is also suffering, as Julian notices and marvels at, because he is by himself: he had 'payne most mervelous to me, and that was that he leye aloone. I lokyd alle about and behelde, and ferre ne nere ne hye ne lowe I saw to hym no helpe' (LT p 516.37ff). There is no other, not the loving lord and not any other other, to interact with. All the servant's relational references are internal: 'he entendyd to his felyng and enduryng in woo' (LT p 515.21f), and they are all painful (LT p 515.22). There may be an implicit reference here to the Great Commandment to love God and neighbour (Matthew 22:37ff and parallels): neither part of the Commandment can be kept by the lonely servant now. It might be suggested that the feeling the servant has is what the buffered *Gestell* self has, mostly without realising it, as his *a priori* porosity and relationality of selfhood, identified historically by Taylor (2007) and neurologically by Schilbach and colleagues (2013), is denied. The enactivists note, based upon their research, how very extreme is the torture of solitary confinement of a prisoner. There is a pathological loss of a sense of self and of 'realness' (eg Gallagher 2015 p 407). Fundamental relationality of the *ipse* self is cut, its journey to 'belonging-to' checked, or so it seems. The servant in Julian's example is in intense pain as his love finds no responding other in the place where he has fallen. The passage also resonates with John 12:24 where the grain of wheat 'remains just a single grain' unless it dies.

As Julian continues to watch, the niche of the 14th revelation expands from its focus on the fallen, lonely servant to include the 'slade' into which the servant has fallen as Julian is shown the features of the place where the servant fell. The 'slade' is 'alang, harde and grevous' (LT pp 515.20ff); 'long' meant in time as well as space, perhaps.

Julian continues to see the loving beholding of the lord, which has not faltered at any time, and which thus includes the fallen, lonely servant and the hellish place of his falling, holding the niche together. The loving beholding has two parts: the first, most obvious quality is its 'grett rewth and pytte' (LT p 516.40) that the servant should have taken such 'harme and dysses' in service of the lord, 'yea, and for his good wylle' (LT p 517.48f): reaffirming for Julian that the fall happened out of loving obedience, and that the lord knows this. The second way in which the lord looks is shown to Julian as an 'inward goostely shewyng of the lord's menyng' (LT p 518.54). She sees that the lord knows that the servant will come to a great reward, all the greater for the falling. The servant cannot know this, but he will be 'hyely and blessydfully rewardyd withoute end', rewarded 'aboue that he shulde haue be yf he had nott fallen'. The suffering itself would be transformed into 'hye ovyrpassyng wurschyppe and endlesse blesse' (LT p 518.57ff). The falling is necessary, or to use Julian's word, 'behovely' (LT p 405.13), for the transformation. Thus while the niche is held together by the affordance of the lord's unfailing love, the asymmetry that generates restoration comes from the feeling of separation and pain in the servant. The restoration will be interactive and mighty, all the greater for the suffering he is undergoing now. The journey to transformation seen here in the 14th revelation is illuminated by the experience of the Koubova students, the pain of whose solitary exposure, a 'cruel and unusual punishment' (Gallagher 2015 p 406), spurs them on to the next stages of the experiment, ultimately to knowing how to be face to face with the other in relaxed curiosity and playfulness, of which the supportive audience approves (2015 p 67). The subjectivity of the servant, as we will see, will be pressed from the fall into a glorious restored porous 'onyng' with Christ.

The 14th revelation is pressed from Julian's urgent longing to understand sin as God does, before God withdraws as her revelations cease. The response that gives 'sight to her understanding' establishes the method of the revelation's interpretation: it will transform Julian's subjectivity and that of her reader. The revelation, at first sight, unfolds as a simple parable narrative of a loving lord, a fallen servant, and a location which is long, hard and grievous. The niche of the revelation is held by love; its interactive energy is generated by the asymmetry of the servant who is cut off from the love of the lord by the manner of his falling: he cannot see it; moreover he is alone. In this showing, Julian and her readers have the advantage of the fallen servant because we can see that the lord's love is unbroken, and also that the pain is a necessary transformational step towards an almighty 'endlesse blesse'.

The meaning of the servant character

This was as far as Julian could see at the time of the revelation: 'at this poynt the shewyng of the example vanysschyd and oure good lorde ledde forth my vnderstandyng in syght and in shewyng of the revelacion to the ende' (LT p 518.62ff), meaning that the 14th revelation ended and the final two revelations followed at this time. But it remains with her: 'the marveylyng of the example went nevyr fro me [...] and yet culde I nott take there in full vnderstandyng to my ees in that tyme' (LT p 519.65ff). Much about what she has seen puzzles her. It is an answer to her longing to understand sin; and she still does not understand. If the servant is Adam, there is much about him that does not fit 'syngell Adam' (LT p 519.69). She waits in uncertainty and unknowing, and so do we her readers, because as Windeatt observes, in her text Julian has not interpreted the revelation with the benefit of her later hindsight, 'partial insights have not been revised away' (2016 p xl). The meaning emerges, as she says, over 'twenty yere after the tyme of the shewyng saue thre monthys' (LT p 520.86), a lengthy *lectio divina* of the revelation which brings greater understanding, perhaps in a 'touch' (LT p 527.158), and she 'document[s her] journey towards understanding' (Windeatt 2016 p xl). So we will continue to follow the narrative direction of the text, participating in Julian's unfolding understanding of the nature of the servant's subjectivity.

The servant is revealed as Adam and everyman

In her matured seeing of the example, Julian understands that the lord is God (LT p 521.99f) and the servant is indeed Adam, by which she understands that he is everyman: 'oone man was shewed that tyme and his fallyng to make there by to be vnderstonde how god beholdyth alle manne and his fallyng' (LT p 522.101ff). However, looking again at the fallen servant in the light of his being Adam, everyman, the paradoxical tension between what she sees and what she knows from holy church becomes even greater. She sees that in the falling, Adam was hurt and made feeble in body and reason, but not in his will, which continues to wish to obey God. Contrary to holy church, Adam in the example has not disobeyed God. Rather, his falling has happened because he obeyed God, and his wish to do that never changes. It is the feebleness from his falling that causes Adam to become blind to his own unchanged will: he is 'lettyd and blyndyd of the knowyng of this wyll' (LT p 520.108f). He has not stopped being the beloved servant of God. Only his perception is false. It is false not only in his blindness to his own unchanged will towards God, but also in his blindness to God beholding him in unbroken love. Julian calls this the 'begynnyng of techyng', referring, we might suggest, both to the servant whose perception will be transformed, and to herself and her readers, starting again in her understanding of what sin is in God's sight. In her, and our, intensely participative looking, the teaching of holy church is to be transformed. Merleau-Ponty says that the interplay of perceiving and being perceived is generative, in the light of which Julian's shifting perception is also changing her and our (and holy church's) subjectivity. She is beginning to see as God sees us in our sin, and in so doing sees already that 'oonly payne blamyth and ponyschyth' (LT p 523.117); God does not punish.

And so Julian's seeing deepens, taking us with her. We have observed the characteristics of the fallen Adam: bodily pain and heaviness; inability to move; stunned reason; solitude; long and bleak habitat; above all inability to see God's loving gaze. These punish. God does not blame or punish. Looking at the revelation in the visual detail her 'techyng inwardly' requires, she sees the lord's black eyes are full of 'louely pytte' (LT p 523.125). Inwardly he is 'an heye ward long and brode' (LT p 523.126), which carries the sense of a secure place of refuge, reinforcing the niche which has not been broken by the fall of Adam. His loving gaze is a steadfast longing, drawing us to him. Adam cannot see; but the subjectivity of Julian (and her readers) is beginning to be penetrated by God's 'louely lokyng' which sees the servant continually in his falling, as Julian comments: 'me thought it myght melt oure hartys for loue and brest them on twoo for joy' (LT p 524.127ff). If, in our ecological reading, the fallen servant is to be identified with the *Gestell*, buffered self that cannot change its harmful ways, this poetic language starts with 'prevy touchynges' (LT p 480.46) to prick its hardened selfhood, wounding it so that the buffered self lying alone becomes porous.

The servant is revealed as Christ

Julian's seeing-as-God-sees is a mixture ('medelur') of ruth and pity and also joy and bliss. 'The pytty was erthly and the blysse hevynly' (LT p 524.132f). The ruth and pity is for the falling of Adam, Julian understands, but the joy and bliss are 'of the fallyng of his deerwurthy son' (LT p 524.135f). This is the first mention of Christ in this revelation, and so it is at this point that Julian and her readers are introduced to the notion that, in the example, the servant is not only Adam but also Christ. This means that Christ's 'falling' into the Incarnation is identical to Adam's falling. And now some aspects of the example that had not made sense for 'syngell Adam' become clearer. The servant's standing ready to do the lord's will, his eager starting and running to obey his will out of great love for the lord, and the lord's great love for the servant, settle happily into Julian's (and our) understanding of the first two persons of the Trinity. For (of course) the Son willingly obeys the Father, taking on manhood and suffering even to death. That is what holy church teaches. The startling revelation is that Adam's falling is out of loving obedience too. And so Julian looks again at the example. Is Adam's falling identical to Christ's? Is the subjectivity of Adam or everyman to be identified with Christ in *this* way? Our perception stands ready to be transformed further, and it will be, but first Julian concentrates, at this stage in her understanding of the example, on the nature of the porous love of the lord, whose gaze is brought to Earth by its identification with Christ. She has already learned that the lord is God (LT p 521.99f)

The lord's 'erthly pytty' descends into the Earth through the falling of the Son 'whych is evyn with the fader' (LT p 524.136). Hence, through the Son, God's ruth and pity descend, conveyed through the 'mercyfull beholdyng of his louely chere'. Christ brings the loving gaze to Earth, and not only to Earth but through Earth and into hell, keeping Adam 'fro endlesse deth' (LT p 525.139). Christ draws the loving gaze to Earth because Adam cannot turn his head to heaven to see it. In this loving response to Adam's helpless blindness, Christ enters the Earth and his loving gaze is presented to Adam precisely where Adam is: on Earth. This 'mercyfull beholdyng [...] fulfyllyd all erth' (LT p 524.137). The niche expands: the 'slade' is all Earth, and now Christ is in it, identified with it.

Julian looks again at the lord who is God, and now other details become puzzling: the lord sits 'symply on the erth, bareyn and deserte, aloone in wyldernesse' (LT p 523.120f), though he remains inwardly a 'heye ward', which means he has not ceased to be the loving refuge of the niche. His 'full semely' countenance fixes its loving gaze, still, on the servant. Now that Julian can see his abode, she sees that it is no different from the lonely 'slade' in which the servant lies. She understands that his 'syttynge on the erth, bareyn and desert' means that he has taken his abode in 'mannes soule' (LT p 525.144ff), and in our post-Ricoeurian terms, is in porous interaction with humanity. God chooses to dwell in man's soul, to take on the embodiment of man, and God himself is thus identified with the Earth:

> [O]ure kynde fader wolde haue dyght hym noon other place but to sytt vppon the erth, abydyng man kynde, whych is medlyd with erth.
> (LT p 526.149ff)

Through Christ, enactive participation will take place. The transformation in man is to *see* this, but to see it in Julian's participative and penetrating manner, not as a theory. As Julian puts it, 'I saw that my vnderstandyng was led in to the lorde' (LT p 527.158f). Julian and her readers are in the performative, participative niche. Julian sees that the lord is enjoying himself, because he is restoring his servant. But she still marvels, which has the effect of keeping her subjectivity wounded and porous to deeper understanding. She too is in asymmetric enactive participation, and by her language, which expresses wonderment, not explanation, so are her readers. We are being shown things that continue not to make sense.

The servant takes his place in the Trinity

The triadic hermeneutical approach we have been using to understand the text now draws us with Julian into an interpretation of the nature of the Trinity itself, by means of the fall of Adam. The servant is both Adam, that is, everyman, and Christ: 'in the servant is comprehendyd the seconde person of the trynyte [...] whych is evyn with the fader' (LT pp 532.210ff), and 'in the seruannt is comprehendyd Adam, that is to sey all men' (LT p 532.212). The servant is both the Son, which is the Godhead, and Christ's manhood which is 'ryghtfull Adam' (LT p 533.215). The servant is near to the lord: that is because he is the Son of the lord; the servant stands to the left of the lord: that is because he is Adam. The 'evyn loue whych is in them both' is the 'holy gost' (LT p 533.217f). We understand that the lord, the servant, and the love that activates their porous subjectivity is the Trinity, and Adam, too, participates in the Trinity, because where the Son is, there is Adam.

'When Adam felle godes sonne fell' (LT p 533.218f); there is no temporal or spatial distance. With the falling of Adam comes the falling of the Son: this is their participative interactivity. As Andy Clark notices, interaction is non-linear (2011 p 73). Laroche and colleagues emphasise the spatial and temporal spontaneity of interaction: 'being together is neither mere co-presence in the physical space, nor a mere temporal correlation of activities in the physical time that can be observed from an external point of view. It is the co-regulated and skilful inhabitance of the complex, metastable, dynamical landscape that emerges spontaneously from the meeting of our embodied perspectives' (2015 p 51). Being together has to be enacted.

The oneness of Adam and Christ is made in heaven, before time, for all eternity:

[F]or the ryght onyng whych was made in hevyn, goddys sonne myght nott be separath from Adam, for by Adam I vnderstond alle man.
(LT p 533.219ff)

With the 'sterting and running' of the fall comes Adam's fall from life to death and into hell; and so comes God's Son's fall 'with Adam'. Christ also falls into the 'slade'; but his 'slade' is Mary's womb. He 'falls' into embodiment: into 'the feyerest doughter of Adam' (LT pp 533.221ff). Both Adam and Christ 'fall' as one man. It is the interactive participation, the energy between the Son and Adam, that determines the subjectivity of both. If this falling is characterised as sin, then sin, if that is the word for it, is in the Trinity.

The subjectivity of the servant has emerged, through Julian's and her readers' performative sense-making of the revelation, as Adam, everyman, and the Son, dynamically interacting in the Trinity. The performative participation of the (now much more interesting) Trinity includes Julian and her readers, because Adam is everyman, and 'oure good lorde shewed his owne son and Adam but one man' (LT p 534.228f). In as much as he is wise and good, he is Christ. In as much as he wears poor clothing and stands at the left hand side of God he is Adam, 'with alle the myschefe and febylnesse that folowyth' (LT p 534.227f). The 'vertu and the goodnesse' that we have is of Christ; the febilnesse and blyndnesse' is of Adam (LT p 534.229ff). The servant has both; Julian and her readers have both. Our subjectivity emerges from the participative interaction of the two 'partys'.

The servant is porous, participative and interactive

We penetrate with Julian deeper into the mystery of the 14th revelation, revealing first, that the subjectivity of the servant is porous and relational in that it emerges from the fall which is both the fall of Adam/everyman and the fall of Christ into Mary's womb and, second, that the work of the servant as Adam/everyman and as Christ is performative: it is gardening; and

The subjectivity of the servant emerges from the fall

Julian has understood that the lord and the servant and the love between them represent the Trinity. Because the servant is indivisibly both everyman as well as Christ, we too are included in the Trinity. Our participation is enacted by the starting, running and falling of the servant. Julian now separates them, seeing that the *starting* represents the Godhead of Christ, and the *running* is the manhood of Christ. Both then *fall* as one servant, whose subjectivity is both that of Adam and of Christ. The falling is the pain of the Incarnation and Passion, pain felt materially, as a human. 'The sore that he toke was oure flessch, in whych as sone he had felyng of dedely paynes' (LT p 540.280ff). Christ must fall into the womb of a daughter of Adam; his interpenetration of the Earth explodes humanity's blindness and feebleness, and the narrative changes, or rather is restored; because if Christ is to fall into the maiden's womb then Adam must fall into the 'slade' of blindness: this is the story. Adam and Christ are one, but the participative enactive encounter has to take place for the oneness to be realised: 'yett the redempcion and the agayne byeng of mannekynde is nedfull and spedfull in every thyng' (LT p 556.24f).

The falling is painful: the servant in the 'slade' suffers dreadfully. So does Christ suffer till we come to him, as a later passage indicates: like Adam the servant in the 'slade', Christ the servant 'abydyth vs, monyng and mornyng' (LT p 710.26). The text indicates the 'monyng and mornyng' is felt by us, but it is Christ in us who feels it. The suffering in the 'slade' goes on until we are restored: 'it passyth nevyr fro Crist tylle what tyme he hath brought vs oute of alle our woo' (LT p 711.30f). Dramatically, but unsurprisingly, the 'walowyng and wrythyng, gronyng and monyng' (LT p 541.294) that the servant in the example suffers in the 'slade' is unto death. He 'myght nevyr ryse all myghtly fro that tyme that he was fallyn in to the maydyns wombe tyll his body was sleyne and dede' (LT pp 541.295ff). This is the end of the suffering, and not before. Like the grain that is sown in the earth and dies in order to be reborn (John 12:24), the servant-Son must die. The participative porosity is culminatory: just as everything in the Earth, including humanity, dies, so does Christ.

The asymmetric desire that energises the performative interaction of the fall is expressed in 'longing and desiring': this creates the way. Heaven longs and desires (LT p 538.259f) and so does the Earth: '[a]nd all that be vnder hevyn, whych shall come theder, ther way is by longyng and desyeryng' (LT p 538.260f). The same longing is felt by the servant both as the Son and as Adam: 'whych desyeryng and longyng was shewed in the seruant stondyng before the lorde, or ellys thus in the son stondyng afore the fadyr in Adam kyrtyll' (LT p 538.261ff). The longing and desiring of humanity is held together in Christ's subjectivity: 'For Jhesu is in all that shall be safe, and all that shall be safe is in Jhesu, and all of the charyte of god, with obedience, mekenesse and paciens and vertuous that longyth to vs' (LT p 538.265ff). God himself wills it: '[T]he fader lefte his owne son wylfully in the manhed to suffer all mans payne without sparyng of hym' (LT p 541.287f). The longing that brings about the participative encounter, felt by Julian as she lies face to face with Christ on the Cross in her eighth revelation, is felt in all heaven and all the Earth, distilled in the second person of the Trinity who stands from all eternity waiting to do the will of the Father: 'Thus was he the servant before hys comyng in to erth, stondyng redy before the father in purpos tyll what tyme he wolde sende hym' (LT p 535.234ff), starting and running to enact that will, taking no thought for himself as he falls into the 'slade' and suffers the terrible pain of the Incarnation and Passion.

Julian's urgent wish to understand how God sees our sin is answered by the porous subjectivity of the servant. God *cannot* blame us: 'thus hath oure good lorde Jhesu taken vppon hym all oure blame; and therefore oure fader may nor wyll no more blame assigne to vs than to hys owne derwurthy son Jhesu Cryst' (LT p 535.232ff). Christ stands waiting to do the will of the Father, waiting for the time he will be sent: salvation is written into the narrative from the beginning. The cosmos was born to be saved. 'In his forseyng purpos, that he woulde be man to saue man in fulfyllyng the wyll of his fader' (LT p 535.239f). For this reason, 'so', he 'sterte and run' to fall into the maiden's womb, taking no thought for all the pain that would ensue, pain which Julian has herself undergone in the eighth revelation and knows full well. The fall is performative participation. Critically and paradoxically, although the falling is the blinding of Adam, it is also by virtue of the falling that our eyes are opened, so seeing can be identified with salvation:

> the lownesse and mekenesse that we shall get by the *syght* of oure fallyng [...] therby we shall hyely be reysyd in hevyn, to whych rysyng we myghte nevyr haue comyn without that meknesse. And therfor it nedyth vs to *see* it.
>
> (LT pp 603.28ff, my italics)

The subjectivity of the servant is called into being by the fall. The servant is both Christ and everyman; thus is our humanity drawn into the divine dynamic love of the Trinity. The fall is the narrative written into all eternity. It is 'behouely' (LT p 405.13); as Turner observes: '[S]in is behovely means that sin is needed as part of the plot – or, if you like, that the plot needs sin in the way that plots do – contingently indeed, but all the same just so' (2011 p 51). Sin has a necessary place in the story. It is painful and long lasting; it is suffered by the Trinity inasmuch as it is suffered by humanity. It is not the result of disobedience; on the contrary, the fall happens because of the eager obedience of Christ and everyman and the desiring and longing of all of heaven and Earth. It comes out of a 'single willing' (Turner 2011 p 118).

142 *The Fourteenth Revelation*

The servant's performative interaction is gardening

As Julian's gaze widens to see that the place that the lord sits is 'symply on the erth, bareyn and deserte, aloone in the wildernesse (LT p 523.120f), she notices that the lord sits 'as a man', with 'neyther meet nor drynke wher with to serue hym' (LT p 530.188ff), at which she marvels. She marvels secondly that he only has one servant, whom he sent out (LT p 530.190). In this next iteration of her seeing she also understands that there is 'a tresoure in the erth whych the lorde lovyd' (LT p 529.185), and this is what the servant is sent to bring to the lord. The treasure in the Earth is what pulls the servant into his hasty, disastrous, blinding, redemptive, sight-clearing errand. The treasure is not a thing that sits upon the Earth: it has to be dug for. It is the fruit of gardening, and so the labour that the servant is sent to do is gardening; and it is hard work, 'the hardest traveyle that is' (LT p 530.193). The servant:

> shuld be a gardener, deluyng and dykyng and swetyng and turnyng the erth vp and down, and seke the depnesse and water the plantes in tyme. And in this he shulde contynue his traveyle, and make swete flodys to rynne and nobylle plentuousnesse fruyte to spryng.
> (LT pp 530.193ff)

The detail of the work to be done connects the servant with the Earth, not just as someone who takes his place upon the Earth, but who enters fully into its substance, transforming it by his work. Our triad of performative interactivity is fully at play, as the niche of a tended, fruitful garden is created out of active engagement, generated by the love of the lord for 'a tresoure in the erth' and the willingness of the servant to bring it to him. The participative labour of gardening continues until the 'mett with the dryngke' are ready, and they can then be brought before the lord:

> And he shulde nevyr turne ageyne, tyll he had dyghte this mett alle redy, as he knew that it lykyd to the lorde; and than he shulde take thys mett with the dryngke, and bere it full wurschypply before the lorde.
> (LT p 531.198ff)

Julian sees that the lord 'hath within hym selfe endlesse lyfe and all manner of goodnes' (LT p 532.204f) but he does not have 'the tresure that was in the erth' (LT p 532.205). Although the foregoing passage depicts the lord *sitting* in a wilderness which the servant then tends, the following seems to imply that the wilderness to be dug is *in* the lord: The 'tresure' the lord seeks is 'groundyd *with in* the lord in mervelous depnesse of endlesse loue' (LT p 532.205f, my italics). Until that time, Julian sees, the lord '*was* ryght noght but wyldernysse' (LT p 532.205ff, my italics), not that he was *in* a wilderness. On this reading the garden to be tended and transformed is, mysteriously, the lord himself, who is thus clearly identified with the Earth. More mysteriously, Julian writes that the 'tresure' is to be brought 'in hym selfe present' (LT p 532.205ff).[1] On this reading, it could be understood that the lord identifies with the wilderness to be tended, and the fruit of the tending is the servant: the Son is born out of the Father by means of the fall. However the Earth is to be understood, its fruit is worship to the lord who treasures it, and it is the servant who is to dig for it. Performative interaction is needed to activate the triadic flow, and that comes in the responsive service of the lord, by the servant, through gardening the Earth.

As Windeatt notices, in this revelation tending the Earth is not a curse, as it is in postlapsarian Genesis. Nature is benign (2015 p xli). But the second creation story in Genesis has the *pre*lapsarian Adam 'tilling and keeping' the Garden (Genesis 2:15). We are out of time: the example simply shown leaves no space for the servant to do any gardening between starting, running and falling, so in Julian's sense-making, the servant's 'dyghting' is neither just Adam's prelapsarian 'tilling and keeping', nor is it just the (postlapsarian) hard labour he is condemned to, having fallen into the 'slade'. The example turns the niche of prelapsarian paradise inside out: the lord sits in the midst of, is identified with, hellish wilderness which the *servant* turns into a garden.

The gardening motif recurs as Julian describes the fall of the servant into Mary's womb and ultimately to death. In the eighth revelation the point of death is not seen: Julian looks with all her might and does not see it. In this parabolic 14th revelation the 'body ley in the graue tyll Easter morow' (LT p 542.302) but while the body lay thus, 'he beganne furst to show his myght' (LT p 542.299). This passage resonates again with John 12:24. In death (and only in death) is new life made possible. Christ in death delves deep into the Earth, as the gardener seeking to produce for the lord's pleasure and food the fruit of his gardening, and finds the root that is in hell: 'he reysyd vppe the grett root oute of the depe depnesse, whych ryghtfully was knyt to hym in hey hevyn' (LT p 542.300ff). Whereas in the eighth revelation Julian has been shown hell as that place only where the pain is worse than that of the Passion, because in hell 'ther is dyspyer' (LT p 365.58), now that despair is exploded by the interpenetration of Christ the gardener, even there where the 'grett root' is, deep within the Earth.

In this scene our triadic framework emphasises the performative interaction of subjects porous to each other in a joint project in a specific location. The scene is an enactment of McGann's 'behaviour settings' (2015 p 24) in which the environment is changed because of the enactive participation that takes place: the lord's desire and lack of fulfilment without the Earth being tended; the servant starting and running to tend it; and the tilled Earth that brings forth fruit which is Adam's release from hell, because of participative interaction. The Earth is not just a place where the lord sits but a dynamic affordance in a new niche. Laroche and colleagues would argue that embodiment, which with Julian we can call the Incarnation, arises from this 'agent-world' coupling (2015). For Laland and Sterelny, the dynamic embodiment that is the niche created by self in encounter, that is to say the tended Earth, 'is done when energy is made to flow' (2006 p 1759). Embodiment, Incarnation, is 'worked out' (Fantasia, De Jaegher and Fasulo 2015). The self is summoned to an interaction that is necessary to the completeness of God. In the eighth revelation Julian is in participative interaction with the Christ on the Cross before her dying eyes; in the 14th revelation the interactive porosity is between Julian (and us) and her mystifying example; between the lord and the servant in the example; and between Christ and the Earth all the way down to hell. Christ's 'digging' brings the Earth and hell transformatively into the Trinity.

The Earth that is the face of Christ gazing lovingly upon Adam ('the mercyfull beholdyng of his louely chere fulfyllyd all erth' (LT p 524.136f)) is made delightful to God when it is gardened. The Incarnation is enacted through gardening; the interactive participation of serving the lord is performed through gardening. Gardening ultimately brings about salvation as its digging is as deep as hell.

The servant's subjectivity as clothing and knitting

Clothing and knitting are important metaphors for Julian, acting as affordances in the niche of the 14th revelation and effectively expressing the participative interaction of the servant as Adam and Christ. The servant who is the Son wears Adam's 'olde kyrtyll' (LT p 543.305). The kirtle resembles the torn and broken flesh Julian sees so clearly in the eighth revelation (LT p 541.288ff). Adam is 'knyt' to Christ (LT p 542.301). The clothing of the lord expresses his steadfastness (LT p 526.153). When the servant-Son is restored in the Trinity, his clothes are 'rychar than was the clothyng whych I saw on the fader' (LT p 543.308).

Julian marvels because the servant stands before the lord with an inner and outer character that do not tally. Outwardly the servant is 'clad symply' and he stands on the inferior left side. He is as a labourer, 'dysposyd to traveyle' and his clothing is a white tunic that is short, old, and stained with his sweat. It is ready to be hitched up for work. It will be 'raggyd and rent' when he works (LT pp 527.165ff). Julian is experiencing another Ricoeurian 'semantic clash' where the events, what she sees, do not fit the semantic code of her own overarching narrative. Ricoeur is writing of Gospel interpretation, which he argues is not just a matter of reading a simple account of the life, ministry and death of Christ, but of a progressive recognition of him as Christ. It is 'the communicating of an act of confession – and the reader is in turn rendered *able to recognise*' (1995 p 161, my italics). The effect on Julian and her readers of the semantic clash of the clothing, which she is prepared to sit with for nearly two decades, is to look at and puzzle over as she is slowly 'rendered able to recognise' the meaning of the example. She 'marvelyd gretly, thynkyng: This is now an vnsemely clothyng for the seruant that is so heyly lovyd to stond in before so wurschypfull a lord' (LT p 528.171ff). We can surmise from her tone that, in Julian's inherited niche, great lords are served by well-dressed servants, so in the example the servant should, she believes, be far better dressed if he is to serve the lord, and is to enjoy such proximity to him. The semantic clash requires an interaction between contexts and is a driver for the dynamic asymmetric participative encounter that changes subjectivity. The servant's outward clothing makes it seem as though he has been 'a contynuant laborer and an hard traveler of long tyme' (LT p 529.181f); but his inward 'wysdom' (LT p 528.175) is that he is to respond for the first time to the will of the lord: a 'new begynnyng for to traveyle, whych servannt was nevyr sent out before' (LT p 529.188f). The semantic clash deepens. Not only does the servant not fit the clothes, neither do his actions. He is wearing an old and dirty kirtle, and yet inwardly he is as if he had never worked before. His labour is new.

As it becomes clear to Julian that the servant is not 'syngell Adam' (LT p 519.69) but also the Son, she understands that Christ takes on the filthy clothes of humanity and the Earth itself. The clothing starts to make some sense. The kirtle is white because it is flesh; it is single with no other clothing because there is 'noght betwen the godhede and the manhede'. It is 'strayght' because of 'povyrte'; old because it is worn out by Adam's wearing. The 'defautyng' is the sweat of Adam's labour, and it is short because the servant is a labourer: that is what Christ becomes. Christ takes on these characters: 'thus I saw the sonne stonde, seyng in his menyng: Lo, my dere fader, I stonde before the in Adams kyrtylle' (LT pp 535.244ff). Christ is as closely identified as it is possible to be with humanity in his performative interaction of vesting himself in Adam's kirtle. But his porous subjectivity extends beyond humanity. 'I wolde be in the erth', the servant declares, 'to thy worschyppe' (LT p 537.250). Julian has seen that the new labour, the 'worschyppe' to which he will be directed is gardening. The transformation is brought about by participative subjectivity: Christ takes on the materiality of the Earth as his clothing and as he gardens, he turns the earth, himself, to God.

Julian returns to the servant's clothing later in her 'musing' to understand more deeply its meaning and significance in the revelation. Now she sees that not only is the clothing indicative of humanity's labour transformed by Christ into worship of the lord, its torn and ragged nature also indicates the tender rent flesh of Christ at the Passion. The kirtle is also the torn flesh of Christ:

> By that his kertyll was at the poynt to be ragged and rent is vnderstond the roddys and the scorgys, the thornes and the naylys, the drawyng and the draggyng, his tendyr flessch rentyng, as I saw [in the eighth revelation] in some party.
>
> (LT p 541.288ff)

Her language vividly recalls the exquisite suffering of the Passion, which she herself had so interactively experienced:

> The flessch was rent fro the head panne, fallyng on pecys vnto the tyme the bledyng feylyd; and than it beganne to dry agayne, clevyng to the bone.
>
> (LT p 541.291ff)

The great cost of the servant's starting, running and falling in the example becomes evident as Julian understands the full implications for Christ's subjectivity of Adam's kirtle.

The clothing motif identified as the rent flesh of Christ becomes a means to draw Julian, together with her readers, into performative interaction, as she uses the metaphor to explain how it is that 'oure substance' is in God (LT p 562.17). As we saw in our reading of the eighth revelation, Julian describes the drying of Christ's body as he dies on the Cross as 'hangyng vppe in the eyer as men hang a cloth for to drye' (LT p 363.39f). This in turn recalls her reflections on the first revelation of the bleeding head of Christ, in which she is shown 'gostly' that God is 'oure clothing, that for loue wrappeth vs and wyndeth vs, halseth [embraces] vs and all becloseth vs, hangeth about vs for tender loue, that he may never leeue vs' (LT p 299.4ff). The 'beclosing' is how our participative subjectivity relates to God: he becloses and is beclosed by us:

> And I sawe no dyfference between god and oure substance, but as it were all god; and yett my vnderstandyng toke that oure substance is in god, that is to sey that god is god and oure substance is a creature in god [...] We be closyd in the fader, and we be closyd in the son, and we are closyd in the holy gost. And the fader is beclosyd in vs, the son is beclosyd in vs, and the holy gost is beclosyd in vs, all myght, alle wysdom and alle goodnesse, one god, one lorde.
>
> (LT pp 562.17ff)

The Trinity is both enclothing us and enclothed by us. The interactive participation is porous and denies any separation of materiality from divinity: where materiality is, there the Trinity is, in constant interactive participation. Here again is Julian's 'pervasive spatial discourse of enclosing and of a mutual indwelling – simultaneously enfolding and being enfolded' (Windeatt 2016 p xxvii). Julian's language, born of her own participative interaction, invites the same porosity with her readers; as Davies observes, she is able to communicate a world not as something to be referred to but to be 'shared' (2017 p 16). Because Christ has entered the Earth, the beclosing is with all materiality, and so the language effects a Taylorian re-enchantment of the Earth, experienced by the porous self.

Clothing is made from 'knitting' or weaving, and 'knyttyng' in Julian, a metaphor she uses extensively, makes the clothing itself porous. So not only do we have the porous subjectivity of Trinity, everyman, the Earth and hell explained by means of clothing, now the clothing itself is deconstructed, only to increase and bring together more closely the performative interactive porosity. Our subjectivity is enacted in the close interweaving of thread or wool out of which the cloth is made: 'this deerwurthy soule was preciously knytt to hym in the makyng, whych knott is so suttell and so myghty that it is onyd in to god' (LT p 560.59ff). Here Julian distinguishes between the 'soule [which] is 'made of nought' (LT p 558.41), that is to say, it is unmade, and our body, which is made from 'the slyme of the earth, whych is a mater medelyd and gaderyd of alle bodely thynges' (LT p 558.43f). But God is knit into both: 'oure kynde, whych is the hyer party, is knytte to god in the makyng, and god is knytt to oure kynde, whych is the lower party in oure flessch takyng (LT pp 577.17ff). The flesh interacts with 'all bodely thynges' of which the Earth is made; thus is God knit into all bodily things.

The renting of the cloth/flesh of the Passion tears apart the knitted knots as the gardener digs and turns the Earth and Adam falls into the 'slade'. This is necessary for our 'agayne beyng': 'nott withstonding this ryghtfull knyttyng and this endlesse onyng, yett the redempcion and the agayne byeng of mannekynde is nedfull and spedfull in every thyng' (LT p 556.23ff).

The knitting and the onyng are expressions of love: 'in the knyttyng and in the onyng he is oure very tru spouse and we his lovyd wyfe and his feyer meydyn, with whych wyfe he was nevyr displesyd; for he seyth: I loue the and thou louyst me, and oure loue shall nevyr parte in two (LT p 583.14ff). Thus, as Windeatt observes, is sensual being dignified and materiality taken seriously (2015 p xxviiff).

Just as in the eighth revelation the face of Christ changes into one of blyssefulle chere, there on the Cross as the culmination of (another piece of cloth) the 'vernacle'-ugly Passion, so in the culmination of the 14th revelation the same filthy kirtle, Adam's kirtle, is 'made feyer, new, whyt and bryght, and of endlesse clennesse, wyde and seyde', recalling the Transfiguration: the transformation of Christ is not away from or other than his Earthly ministry. Because of the profound interaction of Christ with Adam and all the Earth, as the kirtle is changed, so the subjectivity of Christ and Adam and all the Earth is changed.

In these deepening insights into the lord and servant revelation, Julian performatively and porously makes meaning out of the servant as one whose *a priori* relational subjectivity re-emerges from the starting, running and falling of Adam/everyman and Christ, such that her own subjectivity and that of her readers is transformed by this seeing. She explores and makes sense of the lord's wish for the fruit of gardening, with the lord participating in the work as it takes place in him, identifying him with the Earth which is tended by the servant; transforming his subjectivity of barren dryness into love which has to be dug for. The gardening is unto death, resonating with John 12:24. And Julian makes performative sense of Adam's kirtle as Christ's identification with everyman and the Earth, and in his flesh torn at the Passion in which she had participated, drawing her readers, too, into the porous interaction.

Restoration

Culmination and transformation

The culmination of the 14th revelation example is displayed in the visible transformation of all the parts. Adam's kirtle becomes as white as the transfigured Christ of the Gospels. The Earth is tilled and kept. God is worshipped. Now at the last the lord sits not on the barren Earth but is restored to 'his ryche and noblest seet' (LT p 543.313): the implication is that the Earth itself is transformed, participating in the restoration to become a seat worthy of the lord. God's subjectivity is seen to have changed. He makes his seat 'to his lyking' (LT pp 543.313f), as though the seat is not there before the servant's transformative fall into death brings the fruit of the deep root in hell before him. He can, or will, not move from the barren Earth until it has been tilled and kept by his Son, Adam, everyman, and then there is no need to move, because now the niche includes heaven, Earth and hell, but the three are in one, represented in Adam's transformed kirtle. The Son no longer stands as a servant, hardly clothed, 'in perty nakyd' but 'ryghte rychely clothyd in blyssefull largenesse' (LT p 544.316). There is a crown upon his head of 'precyous rychenes' (LT p 544.317). This, sees Julian, is us: 'it was shewede that we be his crowne' (LT p 544.317f). The crown of the Son is humanity: the 'faders joy', the 'sonnes wurshyppe' and the 'holy gostys lykyng' and to all that are in heaven 'endlesse mervelous blysse' (LT p 544.318f).

The final seeing of this revelation is a niche that resembles a montage. The Son stands no longer on the left as a labourer but sits on the father's right hand side, representative of being 'ryght in the hyest nobylyte of the faders joy' (LT p 545.326). The Son's spouse, Mary, 'feyer mayden of endlesse joy' (LT p 545.328) is there, in peace and not in pain. The montage niche extends into something our imaginations find hard to picture, affecting a Daviesian 'shared world' (2017 p 16) as we recognise that we, too, are included in the family portrait. 'Now syttyth the son, very god and very man, in his cytte in rest and in pees', which is assigned ('dyghte') to him by his father, 'of endlesse purpose' (LT p 545.328ff). The city in which the Son sits is our sensual being: 'that wurschypfull cytte that oure lorde Jhesu syttyth in, it is *oure sensualyte*, in whych he is enclosyd; and oure kyndly substance is beclosyd in Jhesu' (LT p 572.23ff, my italics) and later: 'oure good lorde opynnyd my gostely eye and shewde me my soule in the *myddys of my harte* [...] I vnderstode that it is a wurschypfulle cytte, in the myddes of that cytte sitts oure lorde Jhesu, very god and very man' (LT p 639.2ff, my italics). Time is not linear: the Son sits in man's soul for all time, gardening the barren Earth to find and save him, all in the purpose of God for all time. The Father is in the Son in the city; the Holy Ghost is in the Father and in the Son, all in the midst of the city that is our soul and our sensual being that is in heaven and in Earth, God and humanity together in the Son.

As the persons of the Trinity take their rightful places in Julian's restored niche, the sensual being of humanity and all the Earth take their places too, included in the porous subjectivity of the continuous dance of loving interaction of the culminatory montage.

The 14th revelation and our ecological consciousness

As with our previous readings, the primary gift from Julian to our 21st-century *Gestell* selves is the transforming effect on our subjectivity of, in this case, her penetrating understanding of the 14th revelation. If the ecological challenge is fundamentally caused by a buffered and *Gestell* subjectivity, Julian can spring the trap of our enslavement to that way of being and thus of seeing, by recalling us to our porosity. Everything follows from that.

We can also take from the foregoing passages some examples, led by Julian, of an emerging ecological consciousness for a new possible niche in which humanity lives with the Earth without harming it.

On to Julian's deep longing out of which the 14th revelation emerges we can map our paradox of today: what we *know* as *Gestell* selves is threatened by what we *see* happening to the Earth. What we know of the life we take for granted is not sustainable, but how do we address the dilemma? It cannot be solved transactionally. The Earth cannot be part of a trade-off within a policy based upon the benefit-cost ratio. Following Julian, we do not solve the dilemma. Instead we address it by not turning away from what we see but demanding to understand the paradox; she with Christ, we with the environment, allowing herself and ourselves to be taught, in order to change what we *know*. We keep looking without closing the subject.

From Julian's method of 'sight to her understanding' in this revelation we can derive a similar discipline of patient looking and looking again at the natural world. The more we observe the natural world, the more extraordinary it is. An exploitative attitude, seeking to use the natural world for the ends of humanity, will try to make immediate sense of it in order to use it. Julian's way is slow and receptive. Sense-making happens over a long period but it bears profound fruit, which could not be imagined by the self that initially comes to the encounter.

In the light of the first seeing of the example, the necessary stage of undoing of the self, when its fixed identity is undermined and lost, can be understood. The servant will be restored in ways unimaginable to him as he lies there alone and in pain. This is a necessary step, which the lord understands. Do we have to experience this terrible undermining of our *Gestell* self before it can be restored? Julian is struck by the loneliness of the servant as he lies, helplessly cut off from the lord's love; we can consider the Taylorian buffered and lonely self having to negotiate relations with the Other, rather than have the Other confirm *a priori* relationality. EO Wilson foresees the Eremezoic era, the 'era of loneliness' (2006 p 91) which humanity's denial of relationality with the natural world brings about. James Martin suggests that there will be a period of great stress, like a canyon through which humanity must pilot itself, when all the threatening ecological disasters will hit: global warming; rising oceans; emission of greenhouse gases; scarcity of water; growth of deserts; peak populations and mass migration (2007 pp 30ff). If Julian's example is true, then our experience of loneliness and struggle is only because we cannot turn our heads to face the love that is waiting and has held us all this time of trying to work out how to run the creation without God. We cannot turn our heads of our own volition: we have to realise our helplessness and pray. In this way, the world on the other side of Martin's canyon has the chance of being one of compassion, not of enmity, strife and ultimate destruction.

Julian gives her account of fallen man as he is shown to her at this stage of her understanding. He is bruised and heavy, in pain, unable to move, helpless, unable to think, almost (but not quite) forgetting the energetic flow of love between himself and God. He is alone. With his face turned away from the lord who loves him, and lying on his own, there is no interactive encounter. Fallen humanity is *Gestell*, buffered and separate, lonely, cut off. And his location, the 'slade' which is his habitat in his loneliness, is 'long': we can read this chronologically as well as geographically. But it is also the precursor of restoration. In the great narrative in which humanity is in performative interaction with the Earth, there is perhaps terrible failing, with the best of intentions, before there can be restoration. The servant's 'slade' could be James Martin's canyon. The fossil fuel age came about with the best of intentions but now we should bring it to a close, with suitable mourning and gratitude for all it gave us, as George Marshall suggests (2014 p 232). In order to learn, we had to fail, and the failure is what pricks our *Gestell* selves to make us look again at who and how we are.

When the servant is revealed to be not only Adam but also Christ, Julian sees that thereby the loving gaze of God is present, through Christ, in all the Earth. This showing, as it emerges in Julian's own seeing and as her text shows us, identifies Christ with the Earth that continually sacrifices for us, dying and being reborn through the seasons of the year, maintaining diverse life so we can live, making the air breathable by its continuous 'rotting and reviving' (Keller 2000 p 195), supporting us and providing means for shelter and for food. Julian sees the loving gaze of God shining through all the Earth, who through Christ takes his place in the Earth. Our realisation of this comes through participation.

The love between the lord and the servant is the Holy Ghost, thus establishing the Trinity in the niche. Adam's place is in the Trinity and his fall, which is also Christ's fall, is his interactive participation in the Trinity. The wounded everyman becomes less helpless. There is participation in the salvific act of Christ. There is a possibility that our feeble inability to perceive differently may shift, resulting in the discovery of a new niche of participative interactivity with the Earth that is not harmful.

The subjectivity of the servant emerges from the fall; the fall is both Adam's descent into hell and Christ's descent into Incarnation, and both are enacted out of eager obedience. The fall thus understood is longed for by all of heaven and all the Earth. The theological nature of the Julian texts is made plain to us: in her eyes our salvation from *Gestell* subjectivity comes from a turn towards God. Thinking of the Earth as longing for the fall certainly removes any sense of it as an inert backdrop to human dramas. It is caught up in the narrative of creation-fall-redemption which for Julian is a single event. Its existence and our performative interaction with it are indelibly part of the story.

The task is gardening, to which the servant is sent. The 'tru vnderstondyng' is realised not as a drama enacted with the Earth as a backdrop, but through and in the Earth. The ecological crisis on these terms can be met in part by the realisation that desecration of the Earth is a denial of the Incarnation, and in part by the realisation that bringing forth the fruits of the Earth is Christlike work, and it brings us into interactive encounter with Christ who is identified with the Earth. Christ dies and is reborn like the continuous rotting and reviving Earth. Out of the rotting comes new life.

Clothing and knitting provide a metaphor for the participative porosity of the servant as Adam and Christ, and of the participation of God with the Earth, so that as the servant is transformed through the fall, so is all the Earth. Julian recognises the body as being made of the 'slyme' of the Earth which includes all bodies, hence human materiality into which God is knitted involves all materiality. By this means the Earth may be re-enchanted, as Taylor would put it.

In culmination, the porous subjectivity of the Trinity and our sensual being, which is itself made of all the bodily matter of the Earth, suggests a cosmology that insists our attention to the Earth is also attention to God. God is worshipped by means of the Earth being gardened.

The ecological consciousness that emerges from Julian's response to the 14th revelation can be summed up as one which prays for understanding even as what it thinks it knows (for example that we are protected against the exigencies of the ecological crisis) is contradicted by what it sees (there are plenty who are not so protected, in ever-increasing numbers): a consciousness that realises its own blindness. This 14th revelation ecological consciousness sees the gifts of the Earth – breathable air, clean water, fertile soil – as the face of Christ expressing God's love. Gardening that same Earth is humanity's involvement in the salvific work of the Incarnation. Desecrating the Earth is a denial of the Incarnation. And if, as seems likely, there is to be a time of great ecological trial, then the Trinity is wholly involved and participatory as we pilot our way through Martin's canyon of stresses to, we pray, a reborn, newly compassionate world.

Note

1 Colledge and Walsh wonder if this is a scribal error (Colledge and Walsh 1978 p 532.208 fn), but both Paris and Sloane MSS are in agreement with what is here.

Conclusion
Julian's Porosity as a Basis for a New Ecological Niche

We have asked the question: can the Julian of Norwich texts be read today in such a way that they can help address the 21st-century ecological crisis, by transforming our 'buffered' subjectivity into the 'porous' subjectivity Julian brought to and learned from her revelations? We began by proposing that the ecological crisis is caused by humanity enslaved in a *Gestell* subjectivity that is buffered and adversarial, regarding nature as a utility in service of human ends, and its human self, too, as utilitarian. We suggested that the Julian of Norwich texts were able to address the *Gestell* cause of the ecological crisis, because the powerful language that Julian uses to describe her own porous encounter with her revelations can restore porosity in her readers, thus releasing us from captivity. We then developed a triadic hermeneutical approach, drawing heavily on Paul Ricoeur in particular, to reading the Julian texts that took account of their historical and manuscript challenges and foregrounded the text's transformative power to change the subjectivity of the reader. The triadic framework engaged with the text in a way that was, first, performative, recognising that making sense of the text requires active, responsive engagement; second, porous, recognising that the reader is already a relational self and that performative reading will make that evident and third, niche creating, recognising that reading creates new worlds from a changed subjectivity. Using this structure, we studied a number of themes and extracts from the Julian texts under the broad heading of 'wound', and the eighth and 14th revelations. At the close of each of these studies some initial expressions of an emerging porous ecological consciousness were offered. These began with the assertion that inasmuch as our reading had restored our porosity, the Julian texts had already contributed to a response to the ecological challenge.

This book has not solved the ecological crisis. Its argument is that the ecological crisis is caused by *Gestell* subjectivity; facing the crisis requires a transformation of that subjectivity to one that is porous, not *Gestell*; the Julian texts have the power to do this. I hope I have demonstrated that the texts can have this power, but I have not *proved* empirically that they do. With the help of enactive science, it might be possible to conduct an experiment that could empirically measure porous responses: in the same way as

DOI: 10.4324/9781032623948-7

Schilbach and colleagues conducted their face-to-face experiments, measuring responses in the brains of each of the participants, so they might be persuaded of the value of a study that measured the brain responses of a reader coming face-to-face with the Julian texts, and see if there was a similar stirring of 'dark matter' (Schilbach et al. 2013 p 394). That there would be such a stirring is the implication of Oliver Davies' argument in 'Learning Presence' (2017). But suppose we were to conduct such an experiment and found that it was indeed the case that people respond to the text as we know they respond to a face-to-face encounter with other humans? Would we have all of humanity reading the Julian texts as a way of solving the ecological crisis? This in itself is a proposal that comes straight out of a *Gestell* perspective: we have identified a solution, proved it works in a controlled environment, so now let us apply it universally (on the *Gestell* assumption that humans, like nature, can be ordered about), and the problem will be solved. (On this model, we could presumably simply make people look at each other.) This book is both more modest and more radical than that.

I have suggested, and I hope demonstrated, that the effect of the Julian texts on her readers can be to render us porous again. As she has enacted her porous, performative interaction with her revelations, so Julian has brought her readers with her, at no time claiming a special mystical status for herself but always ensuring her own subjectivity is as porous to her readers as it is to the Christ she meets in her revelations. Her invitation is to take up the text and read it as she 'read' her revelations; as Watson puts it, with 'slow, deliberative and prayerful' attention (1992 p 96). There is a Ricoeurian discipleship called for: we are summoned to the text, to be changed by it, and as Merold Westphal noticed, this hermeneutical turn acknowledges and underlines our fallibility and creatureliness (2009 p 273). The 'act of trust' (Williams 2000 p 72) could also be construed as a cry for help from a subjectivity bound to *Gestell* and unable to free itself, yet recognising its need to escape. This is to open oneself to the possibility of a restored porosity. If the book has succeeded in demonstrating the text can effect a transformed subjectivity under these conditions, then it has shown that the Julian texts have something important to offer our 21st-century selves that addresses the underlying need of the ecological crisis: that we must find again our deep relationality with each other and nature. This is my modest addition to the growing number of studies of the many ways of reading and learning from the Julian texts: I am *'in medias res'* (Ricoeur 1995 p 91), with neither the first nor the last word on Julian.

What is more radical is the suggestion that this transformation of self, which the Julian texts (but not only they) can bring about, is our *only* hope of continuing as inhabitants of Earth into and beyond this current century, in short, that the ecological crisis is calling humanity to a new way of being human.

If Julian is to be our guide, then the 'new way' is through porosity to God. And a number of the writers on whom I have drawn are themselves convinced that the creation or restoration of a right relationship between humanity and the planet requires first of all an acknowledgement that our subjectivity is attuned to the sacred. Taylor sees the porous self transformed into a buffered self as a result of humanity turning away from the sacred, as the medieval world view was replaced by that of the Enlightenment. Nature ceases to be 'enchanted'. Of this turn, Ricoeur writes that 'the retreat of the sacred' is a 'spreading desert' (1995 p 64), and Francis quotes his predecessor Pope Benedict: 'The external deserts in the world are growing, because the internal deserts have become so vast.' (2015 p 158). Francis calls for a 'profound interior conversion' (p 159) while Ricoeur asserts: 'humanity is simply not possible without the sacred' (1995 p 64). Both concur that the project of growth without limit is as a result, ironically, of humanity's inability to be satisfied with only material things. We are not, in fact, just consumers, even though we have claimed that nomenclature and predicated our economies on being such.

Choosing the Julian texts as our route out of enslavement generates or regenerates an acknowledgement of the sacred, because Julian's niche is infused with God. At the conclusion of each chapter that studied the text there were specific expressions of porosity from Julian that gave shape to a new ecological niche, which can be summarised as: wonder; contemplative looking; interdependence; identification with the Earth; gardening; humility and gratitude. For Julian, these categories come out of her sense of the divine: her wonder is evoked by the wound of her longing for God; her contemplative looking is reverent dread of God; her interdependence is borne of a deep understanding of the materiality of the Incarnation of God; her identification with the Earth comes about by means of her understanding that Christ's face is manifest in the Earth as an expression of God's love for every part of it and gardening is, for her, the work of Christ and humanity for God who wills the fruit of that labour; her humility and gratitude are evoked by God's greatness. In these concluding paragraphs, I shall explore porosity, the restoration of which is Julian's contribution to addressing the ecological crisis, through these categories and on Julian's theological terms.

Wounds, wonder and identity with the Earth

Julian asks for wounds: for her they are a gift, one to which she remains open throughout her account, by means of her continuous 'marvelling' or wonderment at what she is being shown, and also her reverent dread. The failure of the *Gestell* self to receive the natural world as a gift is a symptom of a world from which God has, in Taylor's terms, been 'top-sliced'. For some writers, the wounds of porosity to nature are made through a renewed wonderment at nature. Michael McCarthy writes of encounters with nature that evoke 'joy': for him there is no other word that can do justice to the feeling that is deeper than excitement or amazement, that touches him to the core. He first experienced it as a 15 year old boy, on the Dee estuary:

> I stopped, sat down on the embankment and listened, and another [redshank bird] call drifted to my ears, and it suddenly seemed to be pulling

everything together, this ethereal mournful fluting, all the beauty of the untouched estuary and the great skies and the distant mountains, all its richness of life, and I realised for the first time where it was coming from: the very heart of wildness [...] *it was wonderful.* I loved it with as intense a love as I had ever experienced, and there, sitting on the embankment, in the sunshine and the wind, with the wild calls drifting to my ears, I looked on the natural world, and I felt joy.

(McCarthy 2015 p 55, my italics)

'It was wonderful' evokes wounded Julian-porosity. McCarthy is not invoking God but his response to his encounter with nature, which became porous over the hour that he spent sitting on the banks of the Dee and remained porous thereafter, has the quality of a sacred connection to something greater that is discerned, not as distinct from the material, but within it.

Evelyn Underhill articulates an unfailing connection of the material to God in her advice on contemplative looking. 'From Alp to insect', it does not matter what material thing you gaze upon, what matters is your 'impassioned' attentiveness, which

soon transcends all consciousness of yourself, as separate from and attending to the thing seen [...] for all things in this world towards which you are stretching out are linked together, and one truly apprehended will be the gateway to the rest.

(Underhill 1915/2000 p 48)

Underhill, like Davies after her, calls this contemplation 'intimate communion' (p 49) and explicitly invokes Julian's hazelnut which was 'realised by her as the direct outbirth of, and the meek dependence upon, the Energy of Divine Love' (p 52). Understood in this way, contemplative, wonder-filled looking at nature is not pantheism but a new means to penetrate to God. It has the same quality as Ricoeur's summoned self, whose *cogito* subjectivity is undermined by the call of poetry, which is ultimately the call by and to the sacred. Julian's looking has this quality of porous penetration: she is not satisfied until she has reached to the heart of the matter, which for her is God's love: 'wytt it wele, loue was his menyng' (LT p 733.16). The challenging proposition from Julian's porosity is that, without God, there is no generative encounter: the Unmade cause of what is made is what energises. But Underhill, and McCarthy though perhaps not in those terms, would have us understand that contemplative seeing *will* kindle encounter with what is Unmade, wherever the seer starts from. We just have to be open to the possibility, be patient and persist. If the encounter does not penetrate through to what is Unmade, which is the shared, sacred origin of both, it remains a face-to-face meeting of two separate objects. But in fact this is not what happens (Schilbach et al. 2013). The face-to-face encounter does not remain buffered; and that itself is a sign of a shared origin. The sacred emerges.

The Julian texts are full of porous identities: that of Julian with her readers throughout; of Julian with Christ in the eighth revelation; of Adam with Christ in the character of the servant in the 14th revelation and of Christ with the Earth, also in the 14th revelation. The porosity is illustrated by Julian's metaphor of being enclothed and of enclothing, and of the weave of the cloth itself in 'knitting'. As porous, performative encounter with nature penetrates through, if it is allowed, to the common, sacred, Unmade origin, so the interdependence of all that is made is also felt: '[o]ld barriers will vanish' (Underhill 1915/2000 p 48). In his postscript, added in 1957 to his book *I and Thou*, Martin Buber states that the central revelation he had had and had sought to describe was the 'close connection between the relation to God and the relation to one's fellow men' (1923/2013 p 87).

As we recognise our identity with the 'slyme' (LT p 558.43) of the Earth so we can interpret Christ's 'family', in his observation that in serving the 'least of these who are members of my family' we serve him (Matthew 25.40ff), as meaning not just other human beings. Pope Francis agrees: 'when our hearts are authentically open to universal communion, this sense of fraternity excludes nothing and no one' (2015 p 67). He quotes the Brazilian bishops who wrote that 'God has joined us so closely to the world around us that we can feel the desertification of the soil almost as a physical ailment, and the extinction of a species as a painful disfigurement' (p 66). Porous identification makes possible an understanding of what is to be done, as Francis challenges us: we must 'dare to turn what is happening to the world into our own personal suffering and *thus* to discover what each of us can do about it' (p 15, my italics).

The porous identification of Christ with the Earth and with Adam's falling has a double meaning. First, the 'rotting and renewal' (Keller 2000 p 195) of the Earth in its seasonal round can be seen as a reflection of Christ's death and Resurrection, endlessly replayed as winter turns to spring and the promise of new life kindles a responsive awakening in the human heart that has not lost its connection by enslavement to *Gestell*. Michael McCarthy writes of the effect of hearing the cuckoo as the 'spring-bringer':

> In Europe, it is one of the fundamental sounds of our world, the supreme signal of the soft days coming again [... but] there is something more. The spring-bringers stir in us something deeper than delight when we encounter them; [...] it is not simply the fact of their arrival, and the marking of the seasonal changes [...] In coming back year after year, against all the odds that they face, the spring migrants are testaments to the earth's great cycle. They remind us that, although death is certain, renewal is eternal, that although all life ends, new life comes as well. Perhaps what they mean to us, really, is *hope*.
> (McCarthy 2010 pp 8f, my italics)

In a dialogue at Westminster Abbey Institute in November 2023, Charlie Burrell described the effect of rewilding on the Knepp estate: as they left the land alone, giving nature space and time, so, surprisingly quickly, 'life flooded in, and with life, came *hope*' (my italics).

Second, in Julian's terms, the identification of Christ with the Earth means the Earth is caught up in the falling of Adam and of Christ into Mary's womb and ultimately to death. The falling of the servant in the 14th revelation is into a hard and grievous place where he lies alone and unable to see the lord's unbroken loving gaze. I suggested an oblique reference to Christ's saying 'unless a grain of wheat falls into the earth and dies, it remains just a single grain, but if it dies, it bears much fruit' (John 12:24). The porous resonance of seasonal death and new life with the death and Resurrection of Christ can suggest an openness to a greater narrative for humanity, facing in this 21st-century EO Wilson's Eremezoic Era: the era of loneliness, where humanity will have to struggle to survive, bereft of the 'ecological services' we did not realise we needed before destroying them.

The fall of the servant into the grievous 'slade' is analogous to James Martin's canyon:

> Think of the twenty-first century as a deep river canyon with a narrow bottleneck at its centre. Think of humanity as river rafters heading downstream. As we head into the canyon, we'll have to cope with a rate of change that becomes much more intense – a white water raft trip with the currents becoming much faster and rougher – a time when technology will accelerate at a phenomenal rate. As the world's population grows, global tension and pollution will climb, and the danger of massive famines will increase [...] At the narrow part of the canyon, the world's population will be at its highest and the world's resources under their greatest stress.
>
> (Martin 2007 pp 7f)

Martin's vision is that it is possible to pilot our way through the canyon in such a way that the world into which we are 'reborn' on the other side is a compassionate world, but this is not assured. As in the eighth revelation, and the 14th lord and servant narrative, there is no guarantee of Resurrection or redemption. All the servant knows, as he lies alone and blinded to God's love, is his own pain. But the 14th revelation is a quest narrative, not an enemy narrative. The servant falls into his great pain only to emerge into restoration in the Trinity; and the lord knows this. Adam is not the enemy, to be blamed and condemned and scapegoated. He is to be redeemed. So in turn the 'fall' of humanity into ecological depredation might be read as a quest, not an enemy narrative, as George Marshall has urged (2014 p 231). Alex Evans draws on Margaret Barker's writing (2004) to propose the Old Testament temple story of atonement and restoration, which will fill the 'myth gap' he identifies in our failed attempts to make sense of the ecological crisis and how to respond to it (Evans 2017). Porosity of selfhood learned from Julian not only awakens us and makes us identify with the terrible suffering of the Earth, but also awakens us to the possibility of redemption, through the long journey that Ricoeur recognised of self transformation. Our response to the crisis is as described in the quest narratives: not to find someone to blame, but to look to our own transformation. This response should not be mistaken for a retreat into individual piety and away from the world stage where the crisis will have to be faced. It is, rather, a call to start the enactment of response to the crisis from a new subjectivity. Writers such as Evans and Marshall have long experience of the campaigns and actions that have been tried, and which have more or less failed, in addressing the ecological crisis. They are not proposing surrender, but a different story, which can start now. In seeking our own transformation into porosity, we are immediately also engaging with the world differently. Every encounter becomes an opportunity for transformation.

Gardening

In the 14th revelation, the servant is sent by the lord to garden. The prelapsarian command to Adam to 'till and keep' the Garden of Eden (Genesis 2.15) is retold here with added texture and meaning. As Adam is sent to garden and falls into the 'slade', so is Christ by the same command sent to garden, and fall, in his case to fall and dig so deep that he reaches and releases the 'grett root' (LT p 542.300f) of Adam out of hell. For our 21st-century ecological consciousness, porosity to the Earth is informed by this sacralising of our 'gardening' of the Earth as Adam's sacramental and Christ's redemptive work. Richard Sennett's craftsman attuned to 'wonder [...] enriched by the skills and dignified by the spirit of craftsmanship' (2008 pp 211, 286) might take his or her place in this reoriented way of 'making' that is in tune with the Earth. Olivier Clément also recognises the sacralising effect of attentive, prayerful working with one's hands (2000 p 122). 'Tilling and keeping' the Earth is being Christ's hands, but it is also tending and attending to Christ whose creatureliness is identified with the 'slyme'. Hence damage to the Earth is also damage to Christ. The harm that humanity is doing to the planet is an enactment of the Christian story. Christ is crucified again by our well-intended sin; his redemption of us could be, in this 21st-century iteration, a restoration of the Earth itself as humanity is renewed and reborn into a porous way of being with the Earth that is our refuge and home, as Christ is.

Humility

The learning from Julian's revelations is that this ecologically redemptive work cannot be done by humanity alone, lying in the 'slade', blinded to God's love. The helplessness of our generation in the face of mounting evidence of the harm we are doing to the planet attests to this. Captive to our lonely, buffered, *Gestell* subjectivity, we cannot see how to change who we are so that the niches we create for our habitation and flourishing are no longer so harmful. How do we feed ourselves without the forced productivity of the soil that demands chemical intervention and exhausting (for both human and soil), multiple cycles of harvest (eg Tudge 2004 p 198)? How do we keep ourselves warm or cool against the exigencies of climate without fossil fuels, and how can we transport ourselves and our products (eg Highfield 2017 p 36)? A complicated economy that has grown from a foundation of cheap, consistently available energy seems impossible to change.

The porous, Julian-taught response would be to pray. The 'drede of payne' that is an 'entre' to the one who is 'harde of slepe of synne' awakens contrition, making us porous enough to receive the 'soft comforte of the holy goste' (LT p 671.8). Our prayer is first of all penitent, without being able to point the finger of blame at anyone in particular, including ourselves. Rather our recognition is of the shared burden of harmful behaviour for which we are all, collectively, responsible, even as we know, like the servant in the 14th revelation, that we never intended harm. But the sorrow that arises from our porous identification with the harm and pain that has happened has a transformative power: not only does it increase our porosity to each other and the planet, it also creates porosity to God. A cry from the heart of our helplessness can have this effect. The beginning of our release from the captivity to *Gestell* is our realisation that we are unable to free ourselves. This is Julian's wound of contrition, the wound of those who really know their need. Only the contrite, humble self will be summoned to a restored porosity to God.

Gratitude

Julian's prayer also brings thankfulness. With the desacralising of nature by *Gestell* subjectivity came a loss of recognition of its gifts. We stopped seeing, and took for granted, the complex interwoven givenness of the Earth expressed in the spheres: the atmosphere which protects us and we did not make; the hydrosphere that hydrates and washes us and we did not make; the lithosphere that supports us and we did not make; the pedosphere which feeds us and we did not make and the biosphere which gives life and we did not make. Attempts to recognise the value of the spheres from a *Gestell* perspective miss the point as we try, with the best of intentions, to put a figure on what they give us, commodifying 'ecological services' (McCarthy 2015 pp 25ff) and making them even more redolent of the 'standing reserve' that was the mistaken view of them in the first place. A price cannot be put upon clean air: we cannot survive without it; it is a precious gift we have been given; it has to be outside any negotiation; we have to thank God for it, and fiercely protect it.

Julian retains her loyalty to holy church and in the context of a porous ecological consciousness for the 21st century we can interpret her loyalty as a new niche of recognition of the importance of collective penitence and gratitude that organised religion enables. Formal, ritualised acknowledgement of the dependence of humanity on the gifts of the Creator has always been a part of culture: where is it to be found in a *Gestell* world where humanity has claimed its role as *homo faber* and denied its dependence on anything greater than itself?

Our ecological consciousness born of porosity learned from Julian is fashioned by her experience of the Passion in the eighth revelation. Her porosity to the pain of Christ makes her porous also to the love which gives it birth and without which it will not come to pass. And having repented of her regret for asking for Christ's pains in her own body, having suffered them and the love which bears them, Julian clearly acknowledges that heaven is in the 'vernacle'-ugly, dying, bloody Christ on the Cross. In so doing, she travels with Christ from death into resurrected life: the same, bloody, dying Christ is the one who is suffused with joy. And so our porous ecological consciousness can learn from Julian that pain, love and joy are all to be found in one place, that our direction of travel is heavenwards, to what is Unmade, but it can only travel through what is made, it cannot deny, suppress, control or destroy materiality, but celebrate it and serve it, be thankful for it and love it, and therein find God, through whom all things came to be.

Appendix
Addressing the Historical and Manuscript Challenges of Julian of Norwich
A Case for My Methodological Approach

Introduction

We have received magnificent writings of a woman who tells of powerful, transformative visions she received in May 1373, writings which I hope I have shown are capable of transforming us today. But we know almost nothing of the woman who wrote them, and the extant manuscripts of the texts, one of which is a much shorter account of the same revelations, are late, at odds with each other, and not capable of being attested with any certainty to the historical Julian. I want to be candid about the difficulties. Julian's writings are many things to many people and we who read and love them are only too capable of seeing in her what we want to see. Medieval scholars are wary of those who make assertions about Julian without recognising the questionable historical and manuscript assumptions upon which they are based (eg Alexandra Barratt 2009). But identifying and fully acknowledging the difficulties has also served my purpose in this book, which is why I have included this Appendix, though much of what is here may be found elsewhere, particularly in the introductions to scholarly texts of Julian's writings. The uncertainty to which the difficulties give rise supports the hermeneutical approach I have taken, which does not depend upon detailed knowledge of the author, origin of text, or 21st-century readers being able to imagine themselves in the 14th century and to think in the same way as Julian or her original audience.

Evidence for the 14th-century Julian of Norwich

There is independent external evidence of an anchoress living in the cell abutting the church of St Julian in Norwich in the late 14th and early 15th centuries from legacies left to her, from the account of a visit by her contemporary Margery Kempe, and from the rubrics added by scribes to the extant manuscripts of Julian's revelations.

Evidence from legacies

There are four legacies bequested to Julian, recluse at Norwich. The first is from Roger Reed, rector of St Michael's, Coslany, in Norwich, who left two shillings to 'Julian anakorite' on 20 March 1393-4. The second is the will of Thomas Emund, a chantry priest of Ayslesham (which could be Aylesham) in Norfolk, which was proved in 1404, leaving a bequest of one shilling to 'Juliane anachorite apud st Juliane in Norwice'. The third is from John Plumpton, citizen of Norwich, who made his will on 24 November 1415, proved four days later, bequeathing 40 pence to 'le ankeres in ecclesia sancti Juliani de Conesford in Norwice' and 12 pence each to her serving-maid and to Alice, her former maid. Finally, Isabel Ufford, daughter of Thomas Beauchamp, Earl of Warwick, left bequests to the house of Augustinian canonesses she joined after her second husband died, to other religious houses, and to one recluse: item jeo devyse a Julian recluz a Norwich 20s' (Watson and Jenkins 2006 pp 5, 431ff). Isabel Ufford died in 1416 though her will may have been made earlier. She joined the religious house sometime during or after 1382.

The Julian who is the recipient of the bequests, if she is the Julian of the writings, would have been at least 74 before she died. Some scholars have suggested that 'Julian' was in fact a succession of Julians, each of whom took the name of the church to which they were anchored (eg Colledge and Walsh 1978 p 34). But other scholars have contested this, for example Barry Windeatt has shown there is little evidence for anchorites changing their names. Moreover, he notes, 'Julian' was a girl's name in the 14th century (2016 p xiv).

Evidence from her contemporary Margery Kempe

Margery Kempe writes of her 'holy spechys & dalyawns' (Meech and Allen 1940 p 42.12) with the anchoress Julian. Margery had been, she says, directed by Christ to go to Norwich to visit the 'Vykary' of St Stephen's, the Carmelite Friar 'Wyllyam Sowthfeld' and 'an ankres in the same cyte whych hyte Dame Ielyan' (pp 38.12ff). Margery writes that among other things she consulted Julian on the private vow of chastity she had made with her husband. This, she writes elsewhere, they had made on 'Mydsomyr Evyn' (23.9), and in a footnote to this line (p 269) Meech and Allen, extrapolating from the textual evidence, propose that the date was 23 June 1413. On this argument, Kempe's visit to Julian would have taken place at a time when 'our' Julian was living as an anchoress in Norwich. Kempe says she told Julian of her own revelations and asked if there was any deceit in them. Julian tells her to be obedient to the will of God and fulfil them with all her might, if to do so was not against the worship of God or profit of her 'evyn-cresten' (p 42.22). The term 'evyn-cristen' and the sentiment behind the advice are familiar in the text of Julian's writings.

Evidence from the scribal rubrics of the manuscripts

The Short Text rubric, a scribal introduction to the copy made, by its own account, in 1413, refers to Julian alive and living in Norwich as an anchoress ('recluse') at the time (Windeatt 2016 p xix), which substantiates the evidence of the Emund bequest, proved in 1404 and hence before 1413, but not Plumpton's proved in 1415. The rubric at the end of both complete manuscripts of the Long Text does not write of her being alive but does attest to the revelations being Julian's. The date of her revelations, 1373, is given within the Long Text itself, but at no point in either the Long or the Short Text does the narrator refer to herself as Julian, nor as an anchoress.

Although it is likely, it is not conclusive, then, that the anchoress whom we know lived in a cell abutting the church of St Julian in Norwich at the end of the 14th and the beginning of the 15th centuries was the author of the Short and Long Texts. As we have seen in our close reading, the Julian of the text would be delighted at the way in which she remains hidden.

Manuscript challenges

There are two extant texts, the Short Text and the Long Text. The Julian of the texts speaks of experiencing her revelations in May 1373 (LT p 285.3f) when she was 30 years old (LT p 289.2), aligning her chronologically with the historical Julian. But the manuscripts themselves are unstable: all of them are written later, and most of them much later, than when the historical Julian was alive, and they do not always agree with each other. This means that the manuscripts are also incapable of demonstrating conclusively that the Julian in the text is the Julian(s) of the legacies and the Margery Kempe visit. I will identify the challenges in relation to each manuscript in turn.

The provenance of the extant manuscripts

The earliest manuscript, referred to as 'A' by Colledge and Walsh and textual scholars thereafter, is a copy of the Short Text within a collection of other writings of the period including those of Richard Rolle, Jan van Ruysbroeck and Marguerite Poirete, held at the British Library (British Library MS Additional 37790, fols. 97–115 (formerly the Amherst MS)). Colledge and Walsh (1978), Watson and Jenkins (2006) and Windeatt (2016) all concur that it was probably written by one person in the mid-15th century, and annotated and corrected by various hands. The introductory rubric says it was written in 1413, and that Julian was still alive and living as an anchoress at the time:

> Here es a visionn, schewed be the goodenes of god to a deuoute womann, and hir name es Julyan, that is recluse atte Norwyche and y[1]itt ys onn lyfe, anno domini millesimo CCCCxiij, in the whilke visyonn er fulle many comfortabylle wordes and gretly styrrande to alle thaye that desires to be Crystes looverse.
>
> (ST p 201.1ff)

A, however, is a copy of a copy. If the Short Text is a basis for the manuscripts of the Long Text, it may be that A itself is not the one, but, in common with the fluid treatment of medieval manuscripts, passages may have been rewritten, phrases cut and it may even be the case that passages from the Long Text had been added 'back' into later copies of the Short Text, though if there were such cross-fertilisations 'it is hard to see how anyone copying [the Short Text] could have consulted '[the Long Text] without becoming swamped by its additions' (Watson and Jenkins 2006 pp 33f).

The Westminster text (Westminster Cathedral Treasury MS 4 fols. 72-112)[2] consists of a set of excerpts from the Long Text which are included in an anonymous compilation of religious works in Middle English. The date of the compilation, judging from the dialect, is early 15th century, placing it closer to Julian, though the manuscript in which it survives is c 1500 (Watson and Jenkins 2006 pp 417f); it is the only pre-Dissolution manuscript of the Long Text (Colledge and Walsh 1978 pp 8, 27). The manuscript runs continuously with no breaks or headings, recording passages of what would be read as teaching from the first, second, ninth, tenth and fourteenth revelations, with some 'plausible' readings unique to this manuscript (Windeatt 2016 p lvii).

Bibliothéque Nationale MS Fonds anglais 40, referred to (in the United Kingdom) as the Paris text, since it lives in the Bibliothéque Nationale in Paris, contains only the Long Text. The handwriting is much more clumsy and unskilled than that of A, and is thought to be an 'unconvincing imitation, each letter individually formed, of a hand of c. 1500' (Colledge and Walsh 1978 p 7). The manuscript itself is thought to be dated around 1650. Precisely because the hand is 'clumsy and inept', and a by rote imitation of an earlier hand, Colledge and Walsh decided to use this as the basis for their scholarly text of 1978, as it might be surmised that the scribe had no wish to change anything and certainly not to correct anything (Colledge and Walsh 1978 p 7). Their preference has been shared by other editors of scholarly texts: Denise Baker chose to use the Paris text as the basis for her Norton critical translation (Baker 2005) and it features as the main source of the hybrid text of Watson and Jenkins (2006). However Marion Glasscoe (1993) and the most recent critical edition by Windeatt (2016) use Sloane (see below). Windeatt's argument for not using Paris as his base text is that it or one of its ancestor manuscripts has been subject to a process of dialectal translation into East Midlands Standard English (Windeatt 2016 pp lviiff) and is therefore some distance from the language the historical Julian would have used.

There are two manuscripts of the Long Text known as the first (British Library MS Sloane 2499) and second (British Library MS Sloane 3705) Sloane texts, because Sir Hans Sloane acquired and preserved them. Both are in the British Library. The second is an 18th century copy of the first, and for that reason I have not referred to it. The first Sloane text, referred to as 'Sloane' in the book, contains only the Long Text and is, like Paris, dated around 1650. The 'sprawling and unattractive hand' (Colledge and Walsh 1978 p 8) is thought to resemble that of Mother Clementina Cary, daughter of Lady Blount, to whom Cressy (see below) dedicated his printed edition. Mother

Clementina, who died in 1671, founded the English Benedictine convent of Our Lady of Good Hope at Paris, the daughter house of Our Lady of Consolation at Cambrai. If it is not Mother Clementina's hand, then it is a hand of the same school. The quality of the paper is poor and the text is written on both sides, sometimes obscuring what is on the converse, particularly in the first eight folios, and the handwriting deteriorates as the text goes on. Marion Glasscoe justifies her use of this manuscript for her critical text of 1978, reissued in 1993, with the argument that it is more faithful to the historical Julian's original diction (Glasscoe 1993 p ix). It is not favoured by other scholars because of its clear intention to 'modernise' (Watson and Jenkins 2006 p 26), giving the lie to Glasscoe; however Windeatt agrees with Glasscoe, arguing that Sloane, in its northern form of East Anglian language, uses the dialect that the historical Julian would have used, and this, for him, is 'decisive', because it is 'more likely to preserve closeness to her ways and patterns of thought' (Windeatt 2016 p lxvii).

The Cressy printed Long Text (1670), kept in the British Library, entitles itself: 'XVI revelations of divine love, showed to a devout servant of our Lord, called Mother Juliana, an anchorete of Norwich: who lived in the days of King Edward III.[3] Published by RFS Cressy MDCLXX.' There are printer's flowers on the second and third leaves which are identical to ornaments in pamphlets by William Assheton and John Gadbury, both printed in England in 1670, indicating that the Cressy publication was also printed in England (Colledge and Walsh p 6). Cressy was a Catholic convert who was for a time priest and confessor to the exiled English Benedictine nuns at the convent of Our Lady of Consolation at Cambrai, and in 1651 to their daughter house, the convent of Our Lady of Good Hope, in Paris (Summit 2009 p 31f). Like other Catholics at the Restoration in 1670, Cressy was ready to come back to England. Here, then, we surmise, 'when Catholic publishing returned home' (Summit 2009 p 31), he published his edition of Julian of Norwich, based on the Paris and Sloane complete versions of the Long Text that had been used by the nuns in France. Cressy dedicated the edition to Lady Mary Blount of Sodington and urged her to allow Julian to cross the 300 years that stood between them and speak directly to Mary as she is revealed to Julian. Julian 'intended it for You' (Summit 2009 p 32). As Windeatt observes, the edition is of little value to scholars who have access to Paris and Sloane (2016 p lxiii); for me, however, Cressy's dedication points to the same power in Julian to cross the centuries and speak directly to the reader that I am calling upon today.

Austin Baker was priest to the nuns at Cambrai in the 17th century. He had asked Robert Cotton to send works of medieval devotion for the nuns 'their lives being contemplative the common books of the world are not for their purpose, and little or nothing is in these daies printed in Englaish that is proper for them' yet 'there were manie good English books in olde time' (Summit 2009 p 29). The ensuing anthology sent by Robert Cotton included extracts from the 13th revelation in the Long Text, copied from Cressy or

Paris (Windeatt 2016 p lxiv), and is known as the Upholland manuscript, as it was formerly kept at St Joseph's College, Upholland, Lancashire.

In summary, the rubric of the manuscript of the Short Text dates itself 1413, when a Julian of Norwich was alive, but is itself a copy made around 90 years later; the Westminster manuscript of excerpts from the Long Text was written around 100 years after the historical Julian(s) had died; and the Long Text manuscripts of Paris and Sloane around 150 years after that. Cressy and Upholland, also 17th century, offer no further evidence of original authorship. Thus, none of the extant manuscripts is contemporary with the anchoress Julian of the 14th and early 15th centuries, and none can demonstrate conclusively that they originated from her.

Dating the Short and Long Texts in relation to each other

It is not even possible to prove that the Short Text was written first and the Long Text later. The copies, all late, do not offer any external evidence for their chronological relationship. Internal evidence can be gathered but it is not conclusive. Although the Long Text refers to Julian's reflections over 20 years (LT p 520.86), and so can be surmised to have been written later in Julian's life, internally the Short Text has no reference to when it was written. A passage in the Short Text which seems to assert a special role for contemplatives is absent from the Long Text and could be relevant to the chronological relationship of the two texts. The men and women 'that desire [...] to lyeve contemplatyfelye' are contrasted with 'thaye that er occupied wilfullye in erthelye besines, and evermare sekes worldly wele' (ST p 215.41ff). The same point is made, not to be pre-occupied with worldly things, in the Long Text, but is addressed generally, not to a particular group. It simply encourages 'vs' to 'loue and haue god that is vnmade' (LT p 301.24ff). It might, then, be argued that the difference between the two texts on contemplatives confirms that the Short Text should be dated before the Long Text, since Julian clearly comes down on the side of all her 'evyn cristen', not exclusive contemplatives, and the change could indicate a development in her thinking. But she is already thinking this way in the Short Text, eg 'And in alle this I was mekylle styrrede in charyte to myne evynn cristene, that thaye myght *alle* see and knawe the same that I sawe' (ST p 224.8f, my italics). It could equally be argued that the passage was added for other reasons, for example, that self-styled contemplatives had sought Julian's advice and she added in a reference to them. It is also conceivable that in times of great fear of accusations of heresy, the Short Text was written after the Long Text, with the contemplatives added, but the 'difficult' sections omitted, as indeed they have been excluded from the Long Text extracts of the Westminster manuscript, for example, references to the motherhood of God and Christ and the revelation 'example' of the lord and the servant which attributes the fall not to disobedience or greed but to anxious and loving obedience.

This reverse dating is of course not proven, and there remains at least one difficult passage suggesting universal salvation in the Short Text that is omitted from the Long: 'for in mankynde that schalle be saffe is comprehende alle, that ys alle that ys made and the makere of alle, and he that loves thus, he is safe' (ST p 221.30ff). The reverse dating hypothesis is briefly surveyed by Alexandra Barratt (2009 p 18 and fn). Barry Windeatt points out that the Short Text was deemed important enough to have been composed or copied as late as 1413, after the Long Text would have been written (2015 p xxi), but argues that, on balance, autobiographical details such as that the curate arrived with a child (ST p 208.22ff) and that Julian's mother tried to close her eyes, thinking she was dead (ST p 234.29ff), omitted from the Long Text, are more likely to have been recorded in a testimony written nearer in time to the experience rather than to have been inserted into an abridged version later. The case made by Reynolds and Bolton Holloway (2001) that Westminster was written first, followed by the Long Text, with the Short Text being written in 1413 as an abridgement of both 'has not won general acceptance' (Windeatt 2016 p xix). Nicholas Watson disagrees with Windeatt's autobiographical argument, and handles differently the questions related to fear of controversy, using these to date both texts later than the consensus of mid-1370s for the Short Text and mid-1390s for the Long Text. He points out that while the dating of the Julian texts is uncertain, that of responses to Lollard heresies is not, and these, together with corresponding internal textual evidence, can be used to argue for a 'more prolonged and hesitant' composition of both texts (1993 p 641). Watson nevertheless supports the view that the Short Text was chronologically first and the Long Text second. For me, the not entirely implausible suggestion that the Short Text may have been second simply adds to the uncertainty about Julian and her writings. Internal evidence, which I accept, confesses that the Long Text at least was the product of many years of study, but where the Short Text sits in relation to that remains unclear.

Manuscript culture and the demise of the critical text

The plethora of late and conflicting manuscripts means that none can be claimed as the 'critical' text for Julian. A modern translation that does not do justice to the textual difficulties falls short, and should not be used to make claims about what the historical Julian said or meant. Barratt (2009) is particularly scathing about theologians presuming to comment on the historical Julian's theology on the basis of such manuscript uncertainty. She argues that we should have good critical editions of each of the manuscripts, rather than trying to conflate them or choose between them or use one as a base and interpose bits of others where it seems to make more sense to us. Otherwise we cannot avoid our own projections on to Julian's meaning. Watson and Jenkins discuss this in their introduction (p 27f) but still go on to produce a hybrid text based upon Paris interposed by Sloane, Westminster, Cressy and Upholland. An attempt has been made to provide such a comprehensive edition of each of the manuscripts by Reynolds and Bolton Holloway (2001), but these include what Watson and Jenkins regard as 'highly speculative' histories of the composition and origins of the different versions (Watson and Jenkins 2006 p 462).

The idea of a 'definitive form' for a medieval work is in any case foreign to that culture (Watson and Jenkins 2006 p 27). Attempts to create critical texts which try to reflect as far as possible the original author's intention are questionable (Johnston and Van Dussen 2015). From the moment transmission begins and words emerge on a page, changes take place to the text, depending on where the writing takes place, what the scribe's intentions are, what the readers' intentions are, and the life of the manuscript after it has left one pair of hands and reached others. Each manuscript has its own history, and should be treated as an artefact in its own right. As Stephen Nichols argues, modern (as distinct from medieval) philologists are used to the idea of a 'fixed text reflecting as far as possible its author's original intention' (2015 p 35). They have made the assumption that a printed text constructed from many manuscripts of a work purged of all the extraneous matter *is* the critical text, somehow closest to the original intention of the author. The modern philologist has not seen that this notion of a critical edition is a modern phenomenon, arguably as far away from any supposed original as it is possible to be. All that is regarded by the modern eye as extraneous, such as 'paintings, rubrics, commentaries, marginalia and decorations' (p 35), seen as detracting from the text, making it susceptible to scribal error, improvement and commentary, are intrinsic to the medieval manuscript and part of the creation of the text. The printed book that the earlier manuscript versions of a text have become does not reflect any originary state but only 'modern principles of textual scholarship' (p 35). It is as though we were claiming to understand a human being by confining our research to their 'production' from gestation to birth, as Johnston and Van Dussen suggest (2015 p 3). We know this would be to miss most of what a human being is: we should include cultural, social and environmental influences that take place continuously from birth to later life. Similarly, a text produced in manuscript form is never static but goes on to experience numerous changes, and should be studied as such. Moreover, there was a manuscript economy. Pascale Bourgain writes of the ways in which texts circulated that could well have been the story of the Julian texts: they would have been copied at different points of their creation, not necessarily after they had been finished, memorised, retold, spread by lending ('renting'), fleeing from persecution or war, travelling on pilgrimage, being bought and being sold (2015 p 147). Seth Lerer proposes the term 'premodern book', which should be understood as an individual object in its own time (2015 p 19). Medieval textual composition was collaborative, as Andrew Taylor explains, using Bonaventure's categories of those who simply copied; those who copied and compiled; those who copied and annotated for the purpose of clarifying; and those who copied and wrote their own material, but retained their own material as principle. Only the last of these might be called an author; the others are respectively scribe, compiler and commentator (2015 p 199). Although Bonaventure places the scribe and the author at either end of the spectrum, their work could not always be clearly distinguished. All of it required scribal labour. To demonstrate this point, Taylor describes the famous picture of Jean Miélot, secretary of Philip the Good of Burgundy, with the paraphernalia of the scribe: knife, ink, weights, paper, quills; but also a collection of books by him on his desk, at his feet, and on a stool in front of him, all in addition to the book from which he is copying (p 200).

Daniel Wakelin offers a nuanced argument about the implications of scribal corrections, avoiding the suggestion that medieval copyists felt they could do what they liked. Focusing on the content of the text rather than its appearance, he suggests that '[c]orrecting manuscripts nurtures intelligent responses to literary works and, in a knot that cannot be untied, is also nurtured by these responses' (2014 p 8). In exercising intelligence, scribes 'contribute to the long history of critical attention to English literature' (p 4). Combining both the visual aspects and content, Stephen Nichols presents an intriguing possibility: that reading a text and interpreting its visual signs are a 'dual literacy': they 'double the potential for that rupture between perception and consciousness [...] and thus offer a dual route of penetration to the underside of consciousness' (1990 p 8). There was certainly an experience of that as I read the Paris text in the manuscript reading room at the Bibliothèque Nationale. The text of this manuscript has little adornment (which is why it is popular with scholars seeking as 'pure' a version as possible) but even this copyist had picked out some passages in red (not just the rubrics) and I could not but be influenced by that, finding myself reading again the text in red to see what, for the scribe, might have been special about it and what additional meaning might be made from it. Meanwhile the deteriorating handwriting of the Sloane scribe, from careful lettering at the outset to little more than a scribble by the end, had a different effect, as I imagined her working perhaps under pressure of time, perhaps becoming bored by some of the theological ruminations, or just longing to finish her task, finding in turn my own interpretation of the text was again affected by the way the text was presented.

This historical approach to manuscript culture of course opens up immense possibilities for interpretation and understanding of periods in which the manuscripts were written: the ideas that generated the copies and the ways in which the copies were treated. As Bourgain (2015) suggests, the number of surviving copies is one way of measuring not only an author's renown but also the intellectual and cultural habits of the time. The story of the Julian manuscripts itself tells a fascinating tale, as Jennifer Summit describes in her essay 'From Anchorhold to Closet' (Summit 2009). Summit argues that we should treat Julian to a 17th century view, when the extant manuscripts appeared. Julian should be seen as an important author of the early modern period because that is when she was reproduced and, in particular, sent to the nuns in exile at Cambrai and printed for a Catholic noblewoman. Valid as this proposal is, it should not preclude scholars from mining the text itself for wisdom as I have chosen to do. We have to recognise that historical comments on the content are, in the case of the Julian texts, speculative at best.

Concluding summary and a case for my methodological approach

The modern concern to produce a critical edition is, by the foregoing observations, put in its own historical place, and any anxiety to find some original core of writing of the Julian texts, which as such perhaps never existed, is allayed. These observations also demonstrate a porosity between manuscript and reader or copier which supports the way I read the Julian texts. The arguments presented here remove the requirement to look behind the texts we have received for some shadowy author who probably did not exist in the way the modern author exists. For my purposes, it clears the ground made unstable by the lateness of the manuscripts and their minor but numerous internal disagreements. I cannot turn to the manuscripts that we have in order to learn about their historical author(s), but neither need I look only at the anatomy of the manuscripts. As medievalists are released from the burden of seeking an author and divesting the manuscript of its 'additions' as they study it, so I am released from the burden of trying to work out whether the historical Julian really 'wrote' what I am reading. I can concentrate on the content of the text as it is presented. I recognise Barrett's argument against concocting the historical Julian's theology on shaky manuscript evidence, and I recognise the value of treating manuscripts as artefacts with their own histories rather than as pointers to what their original author(s) intended. My hermeneutical approach is consistent with these scholars' concerns in not making any claim at all about the 'original' or historical Julian, but only about the Julian to be found in the text. The person of Julian is important to my reading, but in considering who she is from the internal evidence, I have done so in order to find the Julian of the text only. The Julian to whom I have referred, then, is to be understood as the Julian of the text, not the Julian of history. The references to medieval thought are there only insofar as they help our reading; they are not load-bearing.

Notes

1 Colledge and Walsh use the character yogh here and elsewhere. For the sake of clarity, I replace it with 'gh' or 'y'.
2 Kept by Westminster Abbey on behalf of Westminster Cathedral.
3 Edward III reigned from 1327 to 1377.

Bibliography

Arendt, Hannah. (1954/2006). *Between past and future: Eight exercises in political thought*. New York: Penguin.

Arendt, Hannah. (1958/1998). *The human condition*. Chicago: University of Chicago Press.

Badiou, Alain. (2003). *Saint Paul: The foundation of universalism*. Translated by Brassier, R. Stanford: Stanford University Press.

Bahr, Arthur. (2015). Miscellaneity and variance in the medieval book. In Johnston, M. and Van Dussen, M. (Eds.), *The medieval manuscript book: Cultural approaches*. Cambridge: Cambridge University Press, pp. 181–198.

Baker, Denise (Ed.). (2005). *The showings of Julian of Norwich*. New York: WW Norton and Co.

Barratt, Alexandra. (2009). Julian of Norwich and her children today: Editions, translations, and versions of her revelations. In Salih, S. and Baker, D.N. (Eds.), *Julian of Norwich's legacy: Medieval mysticism and post-medieval reception*. New York: Palgrave Macmillan, pp. 13–27.

Barker, Margaret. (2004). *Temple theology: An introduction*. London: SPCK.

Bentham, Jeremy. (1789/1962). An introduction to the principles of morals and legislation. In Warnock, M. (Ed.), *Utilitarianism*. Glasgow: William Collins Sons and Co, pp. 33–77.

Blitz, Mark. (2014). Understanding Heidegger on technology. *The New Atlantis*, **Winter**: 62–80.

Bourgain, Pascale. (2015). The circulation of texts in a manuscript culture. In Johnston, M. and Van Dussen, M. (Eds.), *The medieval manuscript book: Cultural approaches*. Cambridge: Cambridge University Press, pp. 140–159.

Bourquin, Guy. (1982). The dynamics of the Signans in the spiritual quest. In Glasscoe, M. (Ed.), *The medieval mystical tradition in England*. Exeter: Exeter University Press, pp. 182–198.

Bradley, Ritamary. (1982). Christ, the teacher, in Julian's showings: The biblical and patristic traditions. In Glasscoe, M. (Ed.), *The medieval mystical tradition in England*. Exeter: Exeter University Press, pp. 127–142.

Bragg, R. and Atkins, G. (2016). *A review of nature-based interventions for mental health care*. Natural England Commissioned Reports Number 204.

Breton, Stanislas. (2011). *A radical philosophy of Saint Paul*. Translated by Ballan, J.N. New York: Columbia University Press.

Brincker, Maria. (2015). Navigating beyond "here & now" affordances—On sensorimotor maturation and "false belief" performance. In Di Paolo, E. and De Jaegher, H.

Bibliography

(Eds.), *Towards an embodied science of intersubjectivity: Widening the scope of social understanding research*. Lausanne: Frontiers Media, pp. 105–109.

Brodie, Edmund. (2005). Caution: Niche construction ahead. *Evolution*, 59(1), 249–251.

Buber, Martin. (1923/2013). *I and thou*. Translated by Gregor Smith, R. London: Bloomsbury Academic.

Caputo, John. D. and Scanlon, Michael. J. (1999). *God, The gift and postmodernism*. Bloomington: Indiana University Press.

Carlisle, Clare. (2014). *On habit*. London: Routledge.

Clark, Andy, and Chalmers, David. (1998). The extended mind. In *Supersizing the mind: Embodiment, action and cognitive extension*. New York: Oxford University Press, pp. 220–232.

Clark, Andy. (2011). *Supersizing the mind: Embodiment, action and cognitive extension*. New York: Oxford University Press.

Clément, Olivier. (2000). *On human being: A spiritual anthropology*. Translated by Hummerstone, J. London: New City.

Colledge, Edmund and Walsh, James (Eds.). (1978). *A book of showings to the Anchoress Julian of Norwich*. Toronto: Pontifical Institute of Medieval Studies.

Copeland, Shawn M. (2010). *Enfleshing freedom: Body, race, and being*. Minneapolis: Fortress Press.

Cressy, Serenus (Ed.). (1670). *XVI revelations of divine love, shewed to a devout servant of our lord, called mother Juliana, an Anchorete of Norwich: Who lived in the Dayes of King Edward the Third*. London: Cressy.

Cummins, Fred. (2015). Voice, (inter-)subjectivity, and real time recurrent interaction. In Di Paolo, E. and De Jaegher, H. (Eds.), *Towards an embodied science of intersubjectivity: Widening the scope of social understanding research*. Lausanne: Frontiers Media, pp. 328–337.

Darwin, Charles. (1887/1958). *The autobiography of Charles Darwin 1809–1882*. London: Collins.

Davies, Oliver. (1992). Transformational processes in the work of Julian of Norwich and Mechtild of Magdeburg. In Glasscoe, M. (Ed.), *The medieval mystical tradition in England*. Exeter: Exeter University Press, pp. 39–52.

Davies, Oliver. (2015). Reading theologically. *Rebecca Hussey Lecture*, Lambeth Palace.

Davies, Oliver. (2016). Niche construction, social cognition, and language: Hypothesizing the human as the production of place. *Culture and Brain*, 4(2), 87–112.

Davies, Oliver. (2017). Learning presence: The mystical text as intimate hypercommunication across time. In Lewin, D., Podmore, S. and Williams, D. (Eds.), *Mystical theology and continental philosophy*. London: Routledge, pp. 13–31.

Descartes, René. (1637/1970). Discourse on the method of rightly conducting the reason and seeking for truth in the sciences. In Translated by Haldane, E.S. and Ross, G.R.T. *The philosophical works of Descartes*. Cambridge: Cambridge University Press, pp. 79–130.

Dickens, T.E and Rahman, Q. (2012). The extended evolutionary synthesis and the role of soft inheritance in evolution. *Proceedings: Biological Sciences*, 279(1740), 2913–2921.

Di Paolo, Ezequiel and De Jaegher, Hanne. (2015). *Towards an embodied science of intersubjectivity: Widening the scope of social understanding research*. Lausanne: Frontiers Media.

Elias, John. Z. and Tylen, Kristian. (2015). Instituting interaction: Normative transformations in human communicative practices. In Di Paolo, E. and De Jaegher, H. (Eds.), *Towards an embodied science of intersubjectivity: Widening the scope of social understanding research*. Lausanne: Frontiers Media, pp. 377–388.

Evans, Alex. (2017). *The myth gap: What happens when evidence and arguments aren't enough?* London: Transworld Publishers.

Fantasia, Valentina, De Jaegher, Hanne and Fasulo, Alessandra. (2015). We can work it out: An enactive look at cooperation. In Di Paolo, E. and De Jaegher, H. (Eds.), *Towards an embodied science of intersubjectivity: Widening the scope of social understanding research*. Lausanne: Frontiers Media, pp. 110–120.

Fiddes, Paul S. (2013). *Seeing the world and knowing God: Hebrew wisdom and Christian doctrine in a late-modern context*. Oxford: Oxford University Press.

Flannery, Tim. (2007). *The weather makers: Our changing climate and what it means for life on earth*. London: Penguin.

Flannery, Tim. (2015). *Atmosphere of Hope: Solutions to the climate crisis*. London: Penguin.

Francis, Pope. (2015). *Laudato Si'*. Vatican: Vatican Press.

Fuentes, Agustin. (2015). Integrative anthropology and the human niche: Toward a contemporary approach to human evolution. *American Anthropologist*, 117(2), 302–315.

Gadamer, Hans Georg. (1966/1976). The universality of the hermeneutical problem. In Translated by Linge, D.E. *Philosophical hermeneutics*. Berkeley: University of California Press, pp. 3–17.

Gadamer, Hans Georg. (1967/1976). On the scope and function of hermeneutical reflection. In *Philosophical hermeneutics*. Translated by Hess, G.B. and Palmer, R.E. Berkeley: University of California Press, pp. 18–43.

Gadamer, Hans Georg. (1975). *Truth and method*. Translated by Bardon, G. and Cummings, J. New York: Seabury.

Gallagher, Sean. (2015). The cruel and unusual phenomenology of solitary confinement. In Di Paolo, E. and De Jaegher, H. (Eds.), *Towards an embodied science of intersubjectivity: Widening the scope of social understanding research*. Lausanne: Frontiers Media, pp. 406–413.

Gillespie, Vincent. (2011). Vernacular theology. In Strohm, P. (Ed.), *Middle English*. Oxford: Oxford University Press, pp. 401–420.

Glasscoe, Marion (Ed.). (1993). *Julian of Norwich revelations of love, Sloane text*. Exeter: Exeter University Press.

Heidegger, Martin (1927/1962). *Being and time*. Translated by MacQuarrie, J. and Robinson, E.S. London: SCM Press.

Heidegger, Martin. (1949/1977). *The question concerning technology and other essays*. Translated by Lovitt, W. London: Harper and Row.

Heidegger, Martin. (1949/2012). *Bremen and Freiburg lectures: Insight into that which is and basic principles of thinking*. Translated by Mitchell, A. and Raffoul, F. Bloomington: Indiana University Press.

Highfield, Roger. (2017). Global energy futures: Can Oxford save the world? *Oxford Today*, 29(2), 36–41.

Hodgson, Phyllis (Ed.). (1982a). *The book of privy counselling*. Salzburg: Institut fur Anglistik und Amerikanistik, Universitat Salzburg.

Hodgson, Phyllis (Ed.). (1982b). *The cloud of unknowing*. Salzburg: Institut fur Anglistik und Amerikanistik, Universitat Salzburg.

Hughes, Graham. (2003). *Worship as meaning: A liturgical theology for late modernity*. Cambridge: Cambridge University Press.
Huxley, Julian. (1942). *Evolution: The modern synthesis*. London: Allen and Unwin.
IPCC. (2014). *Climate change 2014 synthesis report: Summary for policymakers*. Geneva: Intergovernmental Panel on Climate Change.
IPCC. (2022). *Sixth assessment report: Climate change 2022: Impacts, adaptation and vulnerability: Summary for policy makers*. Geneva: Intergovernmental Panel on Climate Change.
Janz, Paul. D. (2009). *The command of grace: A new theological apologetics*. London: T&T Clark.
Jeanrond, Werner. G. (1991). *Theological hermeneutics: Development and significance*. London: MacMillan.
Jenkins, Jacqueline. (2009). Playing Julian: The cell as theater in contemporary culture. In Salih, S. and Baker, D. N. (Eds.), *Julian of Norwich's legacy: Medieval mysticism and post-medieval reception*. New York: Palgrave Macmillan, pp. 113–129.
Johnson, Elizabeth A. (1992). *She who is: The mystery of God in a feminist Theological discourse*. New York: Crossroad.
Johnson, Elizabeth A. (2007). *The quest for the living God: Mapping frontiers in the theology of God*. London: Bloomsbury.
Johnston, Michael and Van Dussen, Michael (Eds.). (2015). *The medieval manuscript book: Cultural approaches*. Cambridge: Cambridge University Press.
Keller, Catherine. (2000). No more sea: The lost chaos of The eschaton. In Hessel, D. and Radford-Ruether, R. (Eds.), *Christianity and ecology*. Harvard: Harvard University Press, pp. 183–198.
Konvalinka, Ivana, Xygalatas, Dimitris and Bulbulia, Joseph, et al. (2011). Synchronized arousal between performers and related spectators in a fire-walking ritual. *Proceedings of the National Academy of Sciences of the United States of America*, **108**(20): 8514–8519.
Koubova, Alice. (2015). Invisible excess of sense in social interaction. In Di Paolo, E. and De Jaegher, H. (Eds.), *Towards an embodied science of intersubjectivity: Widening the scope of social understanding research*. Lausanne: Frontiers Media, pp. 60–70.
Kristeva, Julia. (1984). *Revolution in poetic language*. New York: Columbia University Press.
Kyselo, Miriam. (2015). The body social: An enactive approach to the self. In Di Paolo, E. and De Jaegher, H. (Eds.), *Towards an embodied science of intersubjectivity: Widening the scope of social understanding research*. Lausanne: Frontiers Media, pp. 78–93.
Laland, Kevin N., Uller, T. and Feldman, M.W. et al. (2015). The extended evolutionary synthesis: Its structure, assumptions and predictions. *Proceedings of the Royal Society B*, **282**(20151019): 1–14.
Laland, Kevin N. and Sterelny, Kim. (2006). Perspective: Seven reasons (not) to neglect niche construction. *Evolution*, 60(9), 1751–1762.
Laroche, Julien, Berardi, Anna, Maria and Brangier, Eric. (2015). Embodiment of intersubjective time: Relational dynamics as attractors in the temporal coordination of interpersonal behaviors and experiences. In Di Paolo, E. and De Jaegher, H. (Eds.), *Towards an embodied science of intersubjectivity: Widening the scope of social understanding research*. Lausanne: Frontiers Media, pp. 40–56.

Lerer, Seth. (2015). Bibliographical theory and the textuality of the codex: Toward a history of the premodern book. In Johnston, M. and Van Dussen, M. (Eds.), *The medieval manuscript book: Cultural approaches*. Cambridge: Cambridge University Press, pp. 17–33.

Levinas, Emmanuel. (1984/1989). Ethics as first philosophy. In Translated by Hand, S. and Temple, M. *The Levinas reader*. Oxford: Blackwell Publishers, pp. 75–87.

London, British Library MS Additional 37790, fols. 97–115. A (formerly Amherst).

London, British Library MS Sloane 2499. The Sloane text.

London, Westminster Cathedral Treasury MS 4 fols. 72–112. The Westminster text.

Lorenzo, Bernadette. (1982). The mystical experience of Julian of Norwich, with reference to the epistle to the Hebrews (ch 9), semiotic and psychoanalytic analysis. In Glasscoe, M. (Ed.), *The medieval mystical tradition in England*. Exeter: Exeter University Press, pp. 161–181.

Lovelock, James. (1988). *The ages of Gaia: A biography of our living earth*. Oxford: Oxford University Press.

Lovelock, James. (2001). *Homage to Gaia: The life of an independent scientist*. Oxford: Oxford University Press.

Lovelock, James. (2006). *The revenge of Gaia: Why the earth is fighting back and how we can still save humanity*. London: Penguin.

Lovelock, James. (2014). *A rough ride to the future*. London: Penguin.

Magill, Kevin J. (2006). *Julian of Norwich: Mystic or visionary?* London: Routledge.

Maitland, Sara. (2012). Overblown and Unloved: Wind farms at the edge of beauty. www.Aeon.co/essays.

Marshall, George. (2014). *Don't even think about it: Why our brains are wired to ignore climate change*. New York: Bloomsbury.

Martin, James. (2007). *The meaning of the 21st century: A vital blueprint for ensuring our future*. London: Random House.

Mayr, E. (1982). *The growth of biological thought*. Cambridge: Harvard University Press.

McCarthy, Michael. (2010). *Say goodbye to the cuckoo*. London: John Murray Publishers.

McCarthy, Michael. (2015). *The moth snowstorm: Nature and joy*. London: John Murray Publishers.

McGann, Marek. (2015). Enacting a social ecology: Radically embodied intersubjectivity. In Di Paolo, E. and De Jaegher, H. (Eds.), *Towards an embodied science of intersubjectivity: Widening the scope of social understanding research*. Lausanne: Frontiers Media, pp. 19–28.

McGilchrist, Iain. (2009). *The master and his emissary: The divided brain and The making of The Western world*. New Haven: Yale University Press.

McGraw, John J., Wallot, Sebastian, Mitkidis, Panagiotis and Roepstorff, Andreas. (2015). Culture's building blocks: Investigating cultural evolution in a LEGO construction task. In Di Paolo, E. and De Jaegher, H. (Eds.), *Towards an embodied science of intersubjectivity: Widening the scope of social understanding research*. Lausanne: Frontiers Media, pp. 365–376.

McNeill, J.R. (2000). *Something new under the sun: An environmental history of the twentieth-century world*. London: Penguin.

Meech, S.B. and Allen, H.E. (Eds.). (1940). *The book of Margery Kempe*. London: Early English Text Society OS 212.

Merleau-Ponty, Maurice. (1964). The philosopher and his shadow. In *Signs*. Translated by McLeary, R.C. Evanston: Northwestern University Press, pp. 159–181.
Merleau-Ponty, Maurice. (1968). *The visible and the invisible*. Translated by Lingis, A. Evanston: Northwestern University Press.
Murray, Robert. (1992). *The cosmic covenant*. London: Sheed & Ward.
Naess, Arne. (2016). *Ecology of wisdom*. London: Penguin Classics.
Nichols, Stephen G. (1990). Introduction: Philology in a manuscript culture. *Speculum*, 65(1), 1–10.
Nichols, Stephen G. (2015). What is a manuscript culture? Technologies of the manuscript matrix. In Johnston, M. and Van Dussen, M. (Eds.), *The medieval manuscript book: Cultural approaches*. Cambridge: Cambridge University Press, pp. 34–59.
Paris, Bibliotéque Nationale MS Fonds anglais 40. The Paris text.
Pigliucci, M. and Müller, G.B. (2010). *Evolution: The extended synthesis*. Cambridge: Harvard University Press.
Popova, Yanne B. (2015). Narrativity and enaction: The social nature of literary narrative understanding. In Di Paolo, E. and De Jaegher, H. (Eds.), *Towards an embodied science of intersubjectivity: Widening the scope of social understanding research*. Lausanne: Frontiers Media, pp. 314–327.
Popper, K.R. (1959). *The logic of scientific discovery*. London: Routledge and Kegan Paul.
Quash, Ben. (2013). *Found theology: History, imagination and the holy spirit*. London: Bloomsbury.
Raczaszek-Leonardi, Joanna, Debska, Agnieszka and Sochanowicz, Adam. (2015). Pooling the ground: Understanding and coordination in collective sense-making. In Di Paolo, E. and De Jaegher, H. (Eds.), *Towards an embodied science of intersubjectivity: Widening the scope of social understanding research*. Lausanne: Frontiers Media, pp. 352–364.
Reynolds, Anna Maria and Bolton Holloway, Julia (Eds.). (2001). *Julian of Norwich: Showing of love*. Florence: Sismel, Edizioni del Galluzzo.
Reynolds, Fiona. (2016). *The fight for beauty: Our path to a better future*. London: Oneworld Publications.
Ricoeur, Paul. (1975). Phenomenology and hermeneutics. Translated by Bradley DeFord, R. *Nous*, 9(1), 85–102.
Ricoeur, Paul. (1977). Toward a hermeneutic of the idea of revelation. Translated by Pellauer, D. *The Harvard Theological Review*, 70(1/2), 1–37.
Ricoeur, Paul. (1990). *Oneself as another*. Translated by Blarney, K. Chicago: Chicago University Press.
Ricoeur, Paul. (1991). Narrative identity. Translated by Muldoon, M.S. *Philosophy Today*, 35(1), 73–81.
Ricoeur, Paul. (1995). *Figuring the sacred: Religion, narrative and imagination*. Translated by Pellauer, D. Minneapolis: Fort Press.
Rubenstein, Mary-Jane. (2008). *Strange wonder: The closure of metaphysics and The opening of awe*. New York: Columbia University Press.
Schilbach, Leonard, Timmermans, Bert and Reddy, Vasudevi, et al. (2013). Towards a second-person neuroscience. *Behavioural and Brain Sciences*, 36: 393–462.
Schumacher, E.F. (1975). *Small is beautiful: A study of economics as if people mattered*. London: Sphere Books, Ltd.
Scott, Michael W. (2013). The anthropology of ontology (religious science?). *The Journal of the Royal Anthropological Institute*, 19(4), 859–872.

Scott, Michael W. (2014). To be a wonder: Anthropology, cosmology and alterity. In Abramson, A. and Holbraad, M. (Eds.), *Framing cosmologies: The anthropology of worlds*. Manchester: Manchester University Press, pp. 31–54.
Sen, Amartya. (2010). *The idea of justice*. London: Penguin.
Sennett, Richard. (2008). *The craftsman*. London: Penguin.
Sheldrake, Philip. (2016). *Befriending our desires*. Collegeville: Liturgical Press.
Sterelny, Kim. (2012). *The evolved apprentice: How evolution made humans unique*. Cambridge: MIT Press.
Straus, Erwin. (1952/1966). *Phenomenological psychology: Selected papers of Erwin W. Straus*. Translated by Eng, E. New York: Basic Books.
Summit, Jennifer. (2009). From anchorhold to closet: Julian of Norwich in 1670 and the immanence of the past. In Salih, S. and Baker, D.N. (Eds.), *Julian of Norwich's legacy: Medieval mysticism and post-medieval reception*. New York: Palgrave Macmillan, pp. 29–47.
Taylor, Andrew. (2015). Vernacular authorship and the control of manuscript production. In Johnston, M. and Van Dussen, M. (Eds.), *The medieval manuscript book: Cultural approaches*. Cambridge: Cambridge University Press, pp. 199–214.
Taylor, Charles. (2007). *A secular age*. Cambridge: Harvard University Press.
Tudge, Colin. (2004). *So shall we reap: What's gone wrong with the world's food—And how to fix it*. London: Penguin.
Turner, Denys. (2004). *Faith, reason, and the existence of God*. New York: Cambridge University Press.
Turner, Denys. (2011). *Julian of Norwich, theologian*. New Haven: Yale University Press.
Underhill, Evelyn. (1915/2000). *Practical mysticism: A book for normal people*. Toronto: General Publishing Company.
UNEP. (2002). *GEO-3: Past, present and future perspectives*. London: Earthscan Publications Ltd.
UNEP. (2012). *GEO-5: Environment for the future we want*. Malta: United Nations Environment Programme.
Vandermeer, John. (2004). The importance of a constructivist view. *Science*, 303(5657), 472–474.
Wakelin, Daniel. (2014). *Scribal correction and literary craft: English manuscripts 1375–1510*. Cambridge: Cambridge University Press.
Ward, Benedicta. (1995). Julian the solitary. In *Julian reconsidered*. Oxford: SLG Press, pp. 11–29.
Watson, Nicholas. (1992). The trinitarian hermeneutic in Julian of Norwich's revelation of love. In Glasscoe, M. (Ed.), *Medieval mystical tradition in England*. Exeter: Exeter University Press, pp. 79–100.
Watson, Nicholas. (1993). The composition of Julian of Norwich's revelation of love. *Speculum*, 68(3), 637–683.
Watson, Nicholas and Jenkins, Jacqueline (Eds.). (2006). *The writings of Julian of Norwich: A vision showed to a devout woman and a revelation of love*. Pennsylvania: Pennsylvania State University Press.
Webster, John. (2013). "Love is also a lover of life": Creatio ex nihilo and creaturely goodness. *Modern Theology*, 29(2), 156–171.
Weil, Simone. (1951/2001). *Waiting for God*. Translated by Craufurd, E. New York: Perennial Classics.

Westphal, Merold. (2009). Hermeneutics and holiness. In Crisp, O. D. and Rea, M. C. (Eds.), *Analytic theology: New essays in the philosophy of theology*. Oxford: Oxford University Press, pp. 265–279.
Williams, Rowan. (2000). *On Christian theology*. Oxford: Blackwell Publishers.
Williams, Rowan. (2014). *The edge of words: God And the habits of language*. London: Bloomsbury.
Wilson, E.O. (2001). *The diversity of life*. London: Penguin.
Wilson, E.O. (2006). *Creation: An appeal to save life on earth*. New York: WW Norton and Company.
Windeatt, Barry. (2015). *Julian of Norwich: Revelations of divine love*. Oxford: Oxford University Press.
Windeatt, Barry. (2016). *Julian of Norwich: Revelations of divine love*. Oxford: Oxford University Press.
WWF. (2014). *Living planet report 2014*. Gland: WWF International.

Index

affordances 53–54, 69; in niche construction 54, 87; Passion and revolution in 103–104; porous interaction between Julian and Christ 114
Allen, H.E. 162
animal laborans 13
Anselm of Canterbury 67
Anthropocene era 11
Arendt, Hanna 2, 13–14, 23
Arosi people 60
atmosphere: defined 17; gases in 17; harm to 2; heating of 18
Augustinian canonesses 162

back-stage self 40
Badiou, Alain 36
Barker, Margaret 157
Barratt, Alexandra 167
Benedicite Dominus 66
benefit-cost ratio 24
Bentham, Jeremy 24
beseeching 6
beseking 6
Bibliothèque Nationale 169
Bibliothèque Nationale MS Fonds anglais 40 3
biophilia 23
biosphere 2, 21
biota 21
Blanton, Ward 103
Blitz, Martin 9, 16
blyndnes 129
blyssydfulle godhede 62
bodely lycknesse 130
Bonaventure 169
Book of Privy Counselling, The 80
Bourgain, Pascale 168–169

Bourquin, Guy 84
Bradley, Ritamary 65
Breton, Stanislas 104–106
Brodie, Edmund 53
Buber, Martin 2, 14
buffered subjectivity 1

carbon dioxide 20; emissions reduction 17, 25
Carlisle, Clare 57–58, 68
Carpaccio 31
Cartesian *cogito* 29
Christ: 'blessydfulle chere 122; body 100; body in the Passion 118; death 96–104, 116–119; humanity 110; Incarnation 140; Julian's subjectivity 49; manhood 138; Passion 76, 100, 102, 107, 111, 118, 126; Resurrection 120; sensory being of 116; subjectivity 110, 141; suffering 116–119; as teacher 65; *see also* Christ's wounds; crucifixion
Christ's wounds 62–63; hermeneutical framework 63; Motherhood and woundedness 63; performative interaction between Christ and his beloved 63
Churchill, Winston 12
Clark, Andy 23, 47, 56
Clément, Olivier 14
climate change 16–18
Cloud of Unknowing, The 80, 85
cogito self (Descartes) 3, 5, 15, 33
cogito subjectivity 33
Colledge, Edmund 66–67, 100, 125, 163
commercial fisheries 19
compassion 5
contra 114

contricion (contrition) 5; and 'holy church' 68–72; and 'reuerente drede' 72–75
Copeland, Shawn 36
cosmic covenant 111
Covid-19 pandemic 26
Criste Jhesu' 66
crucifixion 76, 96–104, 107, 112
Cummins, Fred 48

Darwin, Charles 49–50, 53, 131
Darwin's subjectivity 50
Davies, Oliver 3, 36–37, 46, 60, 67
'deep ecology' movement 45
Descartes, René 3, 15
Drede of payne 72, 159
dwellid contynually 50
Dyonisi of France 67

Eagleton, Terry 27
Earl of Warwick 162
ecological consciousness 6
ecological crisis 1–2, 91; failure of approaches to solve 22–26
ecological damage, Heidegger's *Gestell* subjectivity 15–16; atmosphere 17–18; biosphere 21; fail to save 22; hydrosphere 18–19; lithosphere 20; pedosphere 20
eighth revelation 96. 67; Christ's death 98–104; Christ's final, suffering 116–119; Cross 111–116; ecological consciousness 124–126; Julian's mother tries to close her eyes 107–108; Julian's own experience of the pains of Christ 105–107; Julian's pains become Mary's pains 108–109; pain spreads to whole cosmos 109–111; Philippians quotation 104–105; transition from death into life on the Cross 120–122; twenty disconcerting alternations 96–98; *see also* fourteenth revelation
eighth revelation and ecological consciousness 124–126
Emund, Thomas 162
evyn cristen 83

fabrication 13
farming 20
Fiddes, Paul 103
finitude 33
Flannery, Tim 11, 17
fMRI scanning 45–46

fossil fuels 21
fourteenth revelation 71, 87, 128; culmination and transformation 147–151; first layer of seeing 132–135; Julian-inspired ecological consciousness 128; Julian longs for seeing and knowing to become one 129–130; Julian's longing 130–132; servant character 135–139; servant's subjectivity 139–147; sin, nature of 128; *see also* eighth revelation
Francis, Pope 2
'From Anchorhold to Closet' (Summit) 169
Fuentes, Agustin 10, 54

Gadamer, Hans-Georg 33
Gaia hypothesis 17
Galileo 13
Gallagher, Sean 47
gardening 158
generative poetics 32
genotext 36
Gestell 1–2, 8, 33, 41, 45, 58–59, 91–92, 126; enslavement 5; habit of objectification 45; salvation from 3, 26–28; self 31; subjectivity 2, 8–11, 15, 58, 159
Gillespie, Vincent 66
Glasscoe, Marion 80, 85
global warming 18
God: dome 69; louely lokyng 137; love 72; pryve kepyng 110; wrath 120; *see also* Christ
Golden Legend, The 67
Golding, William 17
Gospel of Nicodemus 67
gratitude 159–160
greenhouse gases 2, 21

habit of holiness 69–70
harmony with nature 10–11
Hebrew Scriptures 32
Heidegger, Martin 1–3, 8, 11, 14, 16, 26–27, 29, 32, 37, 54
Heidegger's *Gestell* subjectivity: ecological damage 15–26; enslave to 8–11; porous self 26–28; presences 12; standing reserve 11–15
hermeneutical approach 1, 29
hermeneutics (Ricoeur) 29, 48
Holloway, Bolton 167–168
holy church 5, 68–69, 71, 136; intersubjective interactivity 71

'holy spechys & dalyawns' (Kempe) 162
homo faber 13
Hughes, Graham 44
human destruction of habitat 1
human-dominated biosphere 21
human-life-supporting capsule 23
human subjectivity 8
humility 158–159
Husserl 37
Huxley, Julian 53
hydrogen bombs 16
hydrosphere 2, 18–19
hygh vnperceyvable prayer 90

'in all his truth' 92
inappropriate farming 20
Incarnation as Christ 'falls' into Mary's womb 6
Industrialisation 11
integrative perceptual 85
intersubjective interactivity of holy church 71
ipse 34
ipse0 34

Janz, Paul 36, 86
Jeanrond, Werner 33
Jeffries, Margot 11
Jenkins, Jacqueline 103, 168
John 19:28 101
Johnston, M. 168
Julian-consciousness 37
Julian-effected porosity 1
Julian of Norwich: 8th revelation (*see* eighth revelation); 14th revelation (*see* fourteenth revelation); anakorite 162; approach of transformative, performative encounter 38; constancy 40; eighth revelation 111; encounter with Christ 28; 'evyn cristen' 82; habit of contrition 71; pain-that-is-love 108; performative engagement 40, 42; seeing-as-God-sees is a mixture 137; self in 50; self-negation 80; 'sense-making' of her revelations 54; sickroom companions 93; subjectivity 79–81, 97, 106; subjectivity as everyman 93
Julian of Norwich, historical and manuscript challenges: contemporary Margery Kempe 162; dating the short and long texts 166–167; evidence for 14th-century 161–163; evidence from legacies 161–163; handwriting deteriorates 165; historical and manuscript challenges of 161–163; Long Text 161–163, 165–166; manuscript culture and the demise of the critical text 167–170; medieval textual composition 168; provenance of the extant manuscripts 163–166; Short Text 164, 166; writing 161
Julian of Norwich's porosity 60, 75, 78; Christ's wounds 62–63; contrition and 'holy chyrch' 68–72; contrition and 'reuerente drede' 72–75; 'intimate communication' of her writing 60; Julian's subjectivity is '*evyn cristen*' 79–84; mysticism 65; praying 87–91; subjectivity of contrition 65–67; text's wounds 63–64; wound of compassion 75–79; wound of 'contricion' (contrition) 64–65; wounds 60–62
Julian's wound of compassion 61–62, 75, 79; ecological consciousness 91–94; *evyn cristen* 79–83; exploration of 75–79; post-Ricoeurian hermeneutical approach 5; texts 32

Kathmandu 93
Keller, Catherine 125
Kempe, Margery 3, 113, 162
King Edward III 165
Koubova, Alice 38, 49, 85
Koubova performance 129–131
Koubova's experiment 41, 56, 76, 133
Koubova students 134
Koubovian audience 80
Kristeva, Julia 65
Kristeva's genotext 38
Kyselo, Miriam 47

Lake Baikal in Siberia 18
Lake Victoria treatment 19
Laroche, Julien 69, 98
lectio divina 60, 136
Levinas, Emmanuel 106
life-giving blood 102
lithosphere 2, 20
'lokyth vppon 132
longing to God 5
Long Text 59
Lorenzo, Bernadette 63, 85
lothfullnesse 117
love God 134
Lovelock, James 11, 16–17

Index

Magil, Kevin 85
Magill, Kevin 63, 65
Maitland, Sara 22
Marion, Jean-Luc 65
Marshall, George 25–26, 157
Mary 60, 108, 110; womb 6, 139, 143, 157
mass deforestation 20
materiality 89
Mayr, E. 53
McCarthy, Michael 23
McGann, Marek 54, 57, 69, 98, 122
McGilchrist, Iain 2, 14
McGraw, John 56
McNeill, JR 10–13, 16, 21, 27
Meech, S.B. 162
mental health care 23
Merleau-Ponty 44
Merleau-Ponty, Maurice 37–38, 79
Michael McCarthy 92
Miélot, Jean 169
mightie desyre 61
modern synthesis 53
Mother Juliana 165
Mydsomyr Evyn 162

Naess, Arne 13, 25, 45, 92
neural activity 46
Newcomen, Thomas 11
New Testament 67
niche construction 51–53; forms habitat and thus habit 57–58; learning and teaching 55
Nichols, Stephen 169
Nile perch 19
nitrogen 17
non-*Gestell* self 31

Our Lady of Consolation 165
Our Lady of Good Hope 165
ovyr passynge 83
Owen Falls Dam 19
oxygen 17–19

Paris 3
paroxysmic homology 32
participative porousness 61
Passion of Christ 39–40, 69, 140
Passion revelation 119
pedosphere 20; harm to 2
performative aspect of our existence 38
performative interaction 59
Phenomenology and Hermeneutics (essay) (Ricoeur) 33
phenotext 36
Philippians quotation 104–105
phusis 67, 74, 103–105
Plumpton, John 162
poetic texts 32
Poetry 32
polyphonic complexity 66
Popova, Yanne 42, 48
Popper, Karl 49
porosity: defined 5; of encounter 4; of Julian to Christ 6; reuerente drede 5
Porosity of selfhood 157
porosity of subjectivity 110
porous subjectivity 1–2, 6, 14, 27, 75, 118; Christ's 6; Trinity's 6; *see also* Julian of Norwich's porosity
post-Ricoeurian hermeneutical approach 29
post-Ricoeurian terms 138
post-Ricoeurian triad 74
premodern book 168
psalms 30
Pylate 67

Quash, Ben 4, 31
'The Question Concerning Technology' (Heidegger) 8

Raczaszek-Leonardi, Joanna 48, 56
rapidification 15
reading self 33–34
Reed, Roger 161
Reformation 15
renewable sources of energy 22
Resurrection of Christ 6, 36, 49; *see also* Christ
reuelation 31
reuerente drede 72, 93
Revelation of Love 80
reverent dread 74
Reynolds, Fiona 23, 167–168
Ricoeur, Paul 3–4, 8, 13–14, 29–30, 49, 104
Ricoeur development 32; affordances in niche construction 54; habitat and habit 57–58; hermeneutical approach 53–58; niche construction 52–53; performative and porous encounter 55–57; porosity 48–49; reading 51–52; ricoeurian foundation 43; self 43–48; social niche construction 54–55; text restores the porosity of reader 49–51

Ricoeurian foundations 4, 29, 43, 51–52, 58–59; enactive insights in performative encounter 38–41; independence of text 30–31; introduction 34–35; in medias res 31–32; performative encounter as enactive 'conversation' 42–43; performative philosophy and theology 35–36; poetic text 32–33; reading self 33–34; turning to enactivists 36–43
Roman Catholicism 56
Rubenstein, Mary-Jane 44, 60

Sally-Anne task 45
Schilbach, Leonard 45
Scott, Michael 44–45, 60, 92
scribal rubrics of manuscripts 162
secularism 15
self, priori relational 43–48
self-effulgent crucifix 56
semantic clash 131
Sen, Amartya 24
Sennett, Richard 13
Shakespeare's plays 31
Short Text 59
Short Text rubric 162
Smith, Chris Llewelyn 22
social lives 37
social niche construction 54
social selves 45
soft inheritance 53
sovereyne gostely lykynge 97
standing reserve 11–16
St Cecilia's three wounds 61
steam engine 11
St Paul's *phusis* 65

subjectivity 8
'subjectivity' of geology 49
subjectivity of servant emerges from the fall 140
subject-object divide 33
Summit, Jennifer 169
suspicion 33
syngell Adam 137

Taylor, Charles 2, 5, 14–15, 27, 31–32, 134, 169
technological paradigm 15
technology, danger of 9
the Cross 112; transition from death into life on 120–122
transformative materiality 85
triadic hermeneutical approach 138
Trinity 66, 137–138
Turner, Denys 65

Van Dussen, M. 168
verie contricion, wound of 64–65

Wakelin, Daniel 169
Walsh, James 66–67, 100, 120, 163
water 18–19
Watson, Nicholas 42, 63–64, 66, 103, 167–168
Westminster text 164
Westphal, Merold 33
wildlife habitats, damage on 22
Wilson, EO 10–11, 22–23
Windeatt, Barry 42, 64, 66, 99, 114, 116, 143, 162, 167
windmills 16
woundedness 60

x-rays 45

Printed in the United States
by Baker & Taylor Publisher Services